Second Edition

Technical Theater

for Nontechnical People

D REW C AMPBELL

Illustrations by Kis Knekt

**ALLWORTH
PRESS**
NEW YORK

08 07 06 05 04   5 4 3 2 1

Illustrations © 1998, 2004 Kis Knekt

Published by Allworth Press
An imprint of Allworth Communications, Inc.
10 East 23rd Street, New York, NY 10010

Cover design by Derek Bacchus
Cover photo: stage image/comstock.com
Page composition/typography by Sharp Des!gns, Lansing, MI

ISBN: 1-58115-344-9

LIBRARY OF CONGRESS CATALOGING-IN-PUBLICATION DATA
Campbell, Drew.
Technical theater for nontechnical people / Drew Campbell ; illustrations by Kis Knekt.—Rev. ed.
p. cm.
Includes bibliographical references and index.
1. Theaters—Stage-setting and scenery. 2. Stage management.
I. Title.
PN2091.S8C28 2004
792.02'5—dc22
2004000851

Printed in Canada

Contents

Acknowledgments

As I say several times in this book, theater is a collaborative process and there is no such thing as a one-man show. My deepest thanks to all who helped me through the years of birthing this book.

Thanks to all the people who read my work and gave generously of their ideas and reactions: Ann Marie, Denise Martel, Sheila McNerney, Jolene Obertin, Wendy Austin, Reid Edelman, Diane Frohman, Harry Magalong, Robin Morris and Kathleen Cunneen.

Thanks to my teachers: John Lucas, David Schrader, Richard Isaacs, Craig Anderton, James Berton Harris, Dean Markosian, Dave Loftin, Bernie Works, Ron Beebe, and many others.

Thanks to all of my students for teaching the teacher and keeping the excitement alive, especially: Kita Grinberg, Anita Pederson-Arbona, Chris Wong, and all the members of the Lick-Wilmerding High School Stage Crew.

Thanks to my family: my mother, Phyllis Campbell, a theater expert herself; my father, David Campbell, who gave countless writing tips; my brothers Jim and Charles, who are the finest I could ever hope for; and Heather Radley, for learning to cope with Campbell men.

In preparing the revised edition, I am eternally grateful to lighting designer Clay Alexander, show control experts Bryan Hinkley, Drew Dalzell, and John Huntington (who, literally, wrote the book on the subject) and costume designers Kate Crowley, Catherine Forester, and Tara Maginnis (whose Costumes.org site should be on everybody's bookmark list).

Why This Book

When I left graduate school in the eighties, I headed to the Pacific Northwest, to Seattle, which at the time was considered a hotbed of theatrical innovation. I had received my degree in "theatrical technology" and I was a hotshot—as those who suffered through me can tell you. I was ready to practice my craft with the best theater artists I could find, indulging in a feast of high-tech theater. After a brief stint at the Seattle Repertory Theater, however, I found myself working for a theatrical lighting and sound company that supplied rental equipment for anybody who was doing anything, well, "theatrical"—not only plays, but also weddings, bar mitzvahs, conventions, press conferences, whatever. We even lit a nighttime bike race and a thoroughbred horse show.

One of my jobs was to organize rental equipment for pickup, a task that put me in the vicinity of the front counter. As I was setting up a package to go out one day, a thirtysomething, office-dressed woman came in the door. Glancing around the shop, she edged over to the counter and smiled at me, clearly uncomfortable. She was in a wilderness, surrounded by racks of unfamiliar equipment, and she had evidently decided to "go for it."

"Hi," she said nervously, "I'd like to rent some sound."

I looked down at the two-inch-thick catalog of sound equipment sitting on the counter and considered my options. Educate—or embarrass? I was not in a particularly good mood, as I recall, so I went for the latter—a genuine cheap shot.

"Excuse me, could you be less specific?" I said, and immediately regretted it.

"I'm sorry," she said, smiling with relief as she realized what she had forgotten to say at first. "It's for a big party." She settled back, now satisfied that I had all the information I needed.

That's when I decided that both of us needed this book.

As human beings, we are constantly showing ourselves to each other. Much of the time, it is just a private, personal act between individuals. But every now and then, we decide to go public and make some sort of hoopla about it. We present plays, throw parties, hold conventions, play concerts, introduce new products, meet the press, get married, sing opera, and dance the story of the tadpole. We create "shows" of infinite variety. Some of us do it professionally. Some of us do it at Sunday services or the company kegger. Some of us would rather not do it at all; but whether we are showing off, showing skin, showing gratitude, or just showing up, it's all the same thing. It's a "show." And it does not take long before that show grows beyond our own technical knowledge, especially for that substantial portion of the population whose VCRs are still flashing "12:00." I cannot count the number of times someone has said to me, "Oh, don't worry, it's a simple show, we just need a few lights," or "No, no, we don't need anything special, just a microphone."

That's fine, I thought. So, why do you need *me?*

Why do you need a technician? Because there are a lot of people in the world who have no desire to be technicians, no desire to go through the years of training, mistakes, and experience that are necessary to bond with things mechanical, electric, or electronic. These same people, however, still need the technology in everyday living, particularly when it comes time to do the "show." They don't want to master the technology; they want to use it. They want to stand in the right place onstage. They want to communicate with a designer or a technician. They want to walk into a rental company and know what to ask for. They just want to survive backstage.

So here was this well-meaning and otherwise competent woman, standing next to my counter, biting her lip and casting her eyes around the shop, looking for something familiar so she could point to it and say, "There! I'll take one of those!" unaware that a few magic words like "mixer" and "microphone" would go a long way toward getting what she needed. She was not stupid. She was not prejudiced. She just didn't have the vocabulary to communicate in a foreign language. Actually, after talking for a while and sounding out more information, I discovered that she was short on facts because she wasn't even in charge of the event. She had been sent by her boss, who did not have any idea what was required either. Hey, people get busy sometimes.

But I digress.

If you want to be a technician for a career, and learn all the ins and outs of everything that was ever plugged into a wall, more power to you and the pun is intended. Enjoy your life! The world will depend on you more and more. But put this book back on the shelf. There are some really thick, detailed ones that will serve you better.

If, however, you have something else to pursue in your life—whether you are a dancer, drama teacher, playwright, actor, fashion show coordinator, meeting planner, minister, publicity person, or anyone else who needs to go public—read on. This book is for you. We are going into a jungle, but have courage. By the time we are through, the trees will be the right size, the animals will howl on cue, the sunlight will filter mysteriously through the leaves, and all those scary technical tigers will be rugs in front of your fireplace.

General Notes

A Note about Gender

One of the as-yet-unsolved problems in the English language is the absence of a gender-neutral, third-person singular pronoun. Unlike the French, who have the glorious use of the pronoun "on," we must struggle along with only "he" and "she" and all their related forms (his, hers, himself, herself, etc.). The closest approximation—"one"—has a cold, businesslike quality to it, and, personally, I find using "his or her" a bit awkward. Therefore, I have decided to simply alternate between the masculine and feminine forms. While you are reading, you may encounter generic technicians or designers who have assumed one sex or the other. Please do not interpret this to mean that any job is limited to only half of our population. I am often heartened that jobs in the theater business tend to be less gender-specific than those in other industries. The word "actor" seems to have become a neutral word for both sexes, however, so I will stick to that rather than alternating with "actress."

Highlighted Words

As you are reading, you will notice that many terms appear in **boldface type**. This will indicate a term you should know. All terms in boldface appear in the glossary at the end of the book.

CHAPTER 1

Breaking It Down: Who Does What

Theater is collaborative. We never do it alone. There's no such thing as a one-man show. Being backstage means being surrounded by people—people who assume a wide variety of titles and responsibilities. As a show person, you do not need to know how to do all their jobs. You do not have time to do all their jobs. You need to know who to talk to when the carpet is coming up behind the podium, or the work light backstage is burned out, or the Frosty the Snowman costume is ripping open. Scenic designers, prop coordinators, stage managers, tech directors, first hands, flymen—they surround you at every turn, and, if they are any good, they are there to help you. So who are all these people? And who can help you staple down that carpet?

Not an easy question. There are constant overlaps between areas of responsibility, and many things must be worked out case-by-case. Sometimes a simple task requires input from several departments. Consider this example:

The script calls for a lamp to be sitting on a table. The **scenic designer** talks to the **director** and decides what the lamp should look like. Then the designer shows the design to the **propmaster**, who either buys the item, pulls it from stock, or builds it. The finished lamp is brought to the stage, where the **electrician** wires it up. The **lighting designer** decides how big a bulb to put in it and when it should be on (with more input from the director). The lighting designer then communicates that information to the **dimmerboard operator** who, under the direction of the **stage manager**, operates the light during the show. If the light has to move during a scene change, that task is the responsibility of the **stage crew chief**. One object—eight people. Hard to believe we get anything done at all.

Fig. 1. Who's in charge of the lamp?

Talking to the wrong person, however, can really gum up the works. Consider poor, hapless director Steve, who tells the dimmerboard operator to turn the lamp on later than he did last night, thereby circumventing normal procedure and causing the following headset conversation:

Stage Manager: Light Cue 49, Go.

Dimmerboard Operator: No, not yet.

SM: What?

DBO: Not yet. He said he wants it later.

SM: Who?

DBO: Steve.

SM: What? When?

DBO: Before the show.

SM: No, I mean when does he want it? He didn't tell me. Are you sure?

DBO: Are you saying I don't know my job? Hey, I'm just doing what I'm told here.

SM: Well, I want to be sure. Where is he?

Assistant SM (from backstage): I think he's in the bathroom.

SM: Well, um . . .

DBO: All I want is for somebody to tell me what to do.

Lighting Designer (suddenly coming onto the headset): Hey, what planet are you people on? Cue 49 is late and you've missed two more. Let's go!

SM: Well, he said he wants it later.

LD: Who did?

SM: Steve.

LD: What? When?

SM: Before the show!

LD: No, I mean, when does he want it? And why the heck haven't you called Cue 50?

SM: I should call it now?

LD: YES!! Go now! GO, GO, GO!!

Follow Spot Operator: Is that Go for us?

SM: Yes, I mean NO! Who said that?

DBO: Well, I think we should Go.

SM: Fine, Go! Everybody Go!

Stage Crew Chief: OK, main curtain coming in!

Meanwhile, Steve, the well-meaning director, returns from his trip to the bathroom to find follow spots crisscrossing the auditorium, the main curtain bouncing up and down, and a gaggle of actors standing bewildered on the stage, trying to improvise themselves into the wings because the scene-ending blackout never happened.

If we are to work together, then, it must be with predetermined areas of responsibility and lines of communication. Most things fit pretty neatly into one of the following six categories: costumes, props, lighting, sound, stage management, and scenery.

Costumes

Any kind of clothing, or anything at all worn by a performer, including masks and jewelry, is considered a costume. Makeup and wigs are sometimes handled by separate departments, but they are usually treated as a subset of the costume shop. This area is designed by the **costume designer**, and is managed by the **costume shop manager**, who is assisted by a **first hand**, as well as **cutters**, **stitchers**, and **drapers**. During the run of the show, costumes are handled by the **dressers**.

Props

Anything that is carried by an actor, or *could* be carried by an actor within the context of the play, is a **prop**. Pictures on the wall, for example, are props, because an actor, while portraying a character, could move them. A kitchen countertop, however, is scenery because the character he is playing would not rip up and move a real countertop, even though the actor himself might be able to do so. It is a tenuous definition. The distinction between props and scenery gets muddy at times, and clear assignments should always be made at the start of the building process. Props are designed by the **prop designer** (or the set designer if there is no prop designer), and managed by the **propmaster**. Props are built by **prop carpenters** and **craftspeople**, and handled during the run by the **props crew**, a subset of the **stage crew**.

Lighting

Anything electrical that is not sound equipment is the responsibility of the lighting department. There are two exceptions to this: the "running" lights, which are the small (generally blue) lights that allow people to see in the darkened backstage areas, and the "ghost" light, the naked bulb on the tall stand that gets set out on the stage when the theater is empty. Both these lights are usually set up by stage managers. In a theater with union stage crews, the ghost light is the only light on the stage that does not have to be turned on by a union electrician. The arrival of the ghost light center stage means the work call is over, and the union workers must clock out. Whether you are union or not, the ghost light keeps people from killing themselves in a dark theater. Lighting is designed by the **lighting designer** and managed by the **master electrician**, with the assistance of the **electrics crew**. The lights are operated during the run by the **dimmerboard operator** and, if spots are used, the **follow spot operators**.

The **lighting cues** (instructions that tell the lighting operators what to do and when to do it) are handled by three different people. The lighting designer creates the *content* of a cue (what lights are on and how bright) as well as its *time* (how fast the lights change from one "look" to another). During the performance, however, it is the **stage manager** who tells the operator when to perform the cue and the dimmerboard operator who actually pushes the buttons and pulls the levers. In technical terms, we say that the stage manager "calls" the cue and the operator "runs" it. So, if you would like a cue to occur in a different place in the script, tell the stage manager. If you want it to look different, talk to the designer. Talking directly to the dimmerboard operator is rarely a good idea. For one thing, the operator may not have the big picture and he may screw something else up by making changes on his own. For another thing, the designer's name is going on the show, so it is only decent that he supervise the changes himself. Finally, if you go straight to the operator, you will screw with everybody's recordkeeping and the possibilities for mistakes will multiply.

Sound

Microphones, sound effects, and the playback of recorded sound are all part of the sound department. Sound people should also handle headsets for backstage communication. The **sound designer** is in charge of this area. Sound is often a one-person operation, but if the sound designer doesn't run the show, there will be a separate **sound engineer**. If you have a large live band onstage, there also might be a second engineer running a separate mixer called a **monitor mixer** that feeds the **monitor speakers** the band uses to listen to themselves. When the sound system is first installed, there may be additional sound crew people in the theater.

Stage Management

The **stage manager** (SM) handles rehearsal schedules, runs the rehearsal itself, provides assistance to the director, and, during the run, is in charge backstage. The SM is also responsible for being a clearinghouse of information about the entire production process. *When in doubt, ask the stage manager,* particularly if the question has to do with schedule.

Almost all stage managers have at least one assistant, the ever-useful **ASM**.

The ASM is the gofer, the essential yet thankless job of getting done whatever needs to get done. It is impossible to predict when you will need an errand run, when you will need a prop handed to an actor, why you will need a curtain pulled back, a phone answered, or an animal fed, but one thing is for sure: It will be the job of the ASM. Besides being an everything-to-everybody position, it is also a primary training position, the entry-level job in the backstage world.

The **company manager** makes all travel, lodging, and food arrangements for the cast and crew.

Finally, many companies have a **production stage manager** (PSM) who oversees the entire production process. The PSM is responsible for coordinating the entire process. In the Broadway theater world, the PSM works for the producer and moves from show to show, releasing day-to-day control of each show to the stage manager when it opens. In regional or repertory theater, the PSM is in charge of the entire season while each show has its own stage manager. In one-shot productions, the PSM is often the stage manager as well.

You should not forget the position of PSM just because your theater is nonprofessional. It is mighty useful to have someone overseeing the entire process—especially if she does not have to worry about the moment-to-moment rehearsal process, as the stage manager does. A good PSM makes everybody's process smoother and more creative.

Scenery

Anything that I have not already mentioned is scenery. Not surprisingly, scenery is designed by the **scenic designer**, and is managed by the **technical director** (TD). *Technical director* is a very loose job description, one of the loosest in the business, but usually he is in charge of deciding how the set will be built. Sometimes, he also oversees the properties and lighting crews, particularly in small theaters. His oversight, however, is always limited to practical matters, such as money, equipment, and staff. He is *not* a designer, and should never be put into the position of making design decisions.

The TD is the voice of reason in the technical process, which, unfortunately, often makes him the bearer of bad news. The TD is the one who must tell you that the effect you want is too expensive, too time-consuming, or simply not possible. His opinion may bring you down occasionally, but it's better to know your idea won't work ahead of time, instead of on opening night.

The scenery is built in the **scene shop.** This shop often has a **scene-shop manager** or **master carpenter** (or both) who is in charge of carpenters and welders. In the **paint shop**, **scenic artists** do the painting and decorating under the supervision of the **charge artist**. During the run, the scenery is handled by the **stage crew** and their chief. Flying scenery is operated by the **flyman**.

The point I made about lighting (that is, if you have a problem, it is best to talk to the area head instead of to the crew) holds true for scenery as well. If the problem involves a change in how things look from the front, tell the designer. If it only involves a change in how things operate mechanically, out of sight of the audience, tell the head of the crew. If you are not sure, tell the designer.

---

*Remember, if you have any doubt about who to ask, go to the **stage manager**. The stage manager is always the best port in a storm.*

You might be saying to yourself at this point, "But we don't have all those people!" Don't worry. Lots of theaters combine some or all of these jobs. Your technical director might also be designing the lighting, your stage manager might also be running sound, and your master electrician might also be operating the dimmerboard. All of the above jobs are still done. People just do more than one.

Of course, every theater is unique, and exceptions exist for every rule that I have given here. Talk to the people you work with. Take some time to learn who does what. What you are really "breaking down" are the walls of miscommunication.

CHAPTER 2

Touring a New Space:
What to Look For

So you're going to do a show. Well, assuming your uncle doesn't have a barn (and take it from me, barns aren't the greatest theaters in the world), you've searched around and found somewhere to put on the performance. Or, you are still searching and you need to evaluate several different spaces to determine their usefulness.

Theater can be done anywhere, as generations of street performers have shown us. Besides "real" theaters, I have done shows in and on basements, boats, rooftops, breweries, swimming pools, cafes, backyards, more hotel ballrooms than I'd like to remember, and, yes, barns. Every space has its peculiarities and its unique problems. Strange architecture, no easy access, low ceilings, moody lighting, and never, ever enough room. But don't despair. Enjoy! It's these peculiarities that make a theater what it is. You think you've got problems? The Trinity Square Theater in Providence, Rhode Island (a first-class repertory house), has a brick pillar right in the middle of the stage. There's no taking it out. It holds up the roof. Every designer who does a show in that theater must find a way to incorporate a brick pillar into the set. And these people win Tony awards.

So the first thing to do when entering a new space is relax. You can do your show here. The question is: Do you want to? And if you do want to, how will your show have to adapt to fit this space?

When visiting a new space, these are the things you should bring with you:

- *A notebook and a pen* to take notes and write down measurements.
- *A fifty-foot tape measure.* Twenty-five feet is often not enough.

- *A flashlight* for lighting up those creepy spaces above and beneath the stage.
- *A camera* for documenting the details of the space. Having a Polaroid makes it easy, but in these days of one-hour photo developing, a regular one is okay. Make sure you have a flash. And film.

Ready to go? Let's walk.

Is This the Right Space for You?

Before you get into any of the details, you should make a general determination if the space you are looking at is even in the ballpark for your show. A few quick questions can eliminate a lot of miss-fits.

- *Is it big enough?* Do you have enough stage space? Look at the chart in "How to Do a Show in a Hotel" (page 235) to see how much space you need for various kinds of shows. Is there enough space to store scenery that is not onstage? Is the audience area big enough for the number of people you are expecting?
- *What does it sound like?* Different kinds of shows need different kinds of acoustics. Spoken-word theater needs a space with no distracting noises (like traffic or air-conditioning), where an actor speaking onstage can be clearly heard. There should be very little echo in the space, so that speech is not garbled. Look for carpets, low ceilings, draperies, and quiet neighborhoods. Acoustical music and singing call for a space with *lots* of echo—it fills out the music. Look for hard surfaces, like marble, tile, and paneled walls. Electrified music (dance bands, rock bands, etc.) should never, ever be put in a space that is mostly hard surfaces. No matter how softly the band plays, the noise will be deafening.
- *Can the space be scheduled appropriately?* Remember to give your tech people the time they need to set up. If you want to do a large party with a big lighting rig and a dance band, don't choose a space where a wedding will be winding down two hours earlier.

Space for Stuff

Do you have enough room? Don't estimate. *Measure.* Measure the **playing space**, the amount of the stage that will be visible to the audience. Measure it both horizontally (how wide and how deep) and vertically (how high). The vertical measurement will determine how tall your scenery can be and how much room there is for lighting.

Now take a look at the **wing space**, the part of the stage the audience cannot see. Remember, whatever scenery is not onstage will have to be stored here, and any part of the wing that is visible to the audience is not usable as storage. Is there room for **prop tables**, **changing booths**, and actors waiting to go onstage? Check out surrounding hallways as well. Are you allowed to use them for storage during the performance?

I did a production of *Good News* some years ago that contained a full-size automobile, a 1920s roadster (it didn't work, unfortunately, but it looked *great*). When it came offstage, it took up so much room in the wings that we finally had to attach cables and a motor to it and hoist it up in the air. In the end, that still didn't save us any space, because the sight of a car hanging overhead was too spooky and nobody would stand underneath it.

What about access? Think about how the scenery will be brought into the space. What is the smallest door the scenery will have to pass through? Measure its height, width, and, for good measure, the distance diagonally across it. Will the scenery have to turn any sharp corners? With a friend, stretch out the tape measure and pretend it is solid, like a board. Try to figure out the longest board that could still turn the corner.

Are there stairs? How many? Stairs mean that scenery cannot roll—a serious obstacle, in some cases. Is there an elevator? How big is it? How much weight can it handle? Is there a **loading dock** where a truck can back up and park?

Space for People

How many performers are in your show? Look at the **dressing rooms**. Will there be space enough for the actors to dress, put on makeup, and warm up? Is there space to store the costumes, and is there space for the costume crew to work? Do you need separate rooms for principal performers? The conductor? Do you have **fast changes** in your show that require a changing booth to be set up in the wings?

Are there bathrooms? Can the toilets be flushed during the show without being heard in the theater?

Is there a stage door? A **green room** where actors can wait for their cue to go onstage? It's a very bad idea to have actors milling around in the wings waiting to go on. They will invariably make noise and distract the performers onstage.

One extremely important actor space that is frequently overlooked is the **crossover**. The crossover is the path that actors use to get from one side of the stage to the other without being seen by the audience. It also refers to the movement itself, as in "Do you have time to make that crossover?" The easiest crossover space is right behind the set, on the stage, but there may not always be enough room between the set and the back wall to get a person comfortably through. In some theaters, there is a hallway outside the stage space that is used as a crossover. Others go beneath the stage. Watch out for the theater where you have to go outside the building to cross over. There's always a chance that it might be raining, and backstage doors have a funny way of being locked when you least expect it. (In this situation, I generally tape over the locks during the performance.) You may be required to re-stage a scene so a performer exits and later enters on the same side of the stage. Know your show. Is there a time when you need a way for the performer to get quickly from one side to the other?

The crossover seems to be a particular problem with dance companies, since they often have little or no scenery to hide a crossover and the dance space sometimes extends all the way to the upstage wall. Dance also creates more problems because dancers often exit and re-enter several times during a piece with little time to spare. Again, in extreme cases, be prepared to re-choreograph.

A good crossover can allow for some tricks as well. In *Desert Song* (a delightfully sappy 1920s Sigmund Rombard operetta), the show opens with the rebel forces onstage, planning their next raid. Suddenly, the alarm is sounded offstage and the rebels have to flee stage *right*, running from the French Army. Two French officers run on from stage *left* and have a brief conversation, giving the actors playing the rebels enough time to make the crossover and a quick costume change. Moments later, the troupe enters stage *left*, now dressed as French soldiers, seemingly chasing the departing rebels but, in fact, chasing themselves. Good, clean fun, and impossible without a fast crossover.

The Rigging System

Look up. Look at the rigging system over the stage. Is there one? If the space is not traditionally used for performances, you are probably looking at an ordinary ceiling. In this case, you will probably have to bring in **light trees** to put the lights on, and all your scenery will have to be freestanding. This usually means fewer lights can be used, unless you have a reasonable sum of money to invest in a **truss**. A truss is a long piece of gridwork supported by towers on each end. Trusses allow you to hang more lights (and hang them directly over the stage, instead of out to the sides), but they are considerably more expensive than trees, both in rental of equipment and in labor costs. For more about trees and trusses, see chapter 13, "Corporate Theater: How to Do a Show in a Hotel."

If there is some kind of rigging system over the stage, then you are probably looking at rows of pipes that run parallel to the front of the stage. These pipes are called **battens** and, if they are there, it's time to ask some questions. Are the battens rigged to fly, or are they **dead-hung?** In other words, is there some kind of system installed where the battens can be raised and lowered (rigged to fly), or are they just hung in one spot, unable to be moved (dead-hung). If the battens are dead-hung, forget about any piece of scenery bigger than a Draculean bat moving during the show. You can still install scenery or lighting on these pipes, but they cannot move during the show.

If the pipes are rigged to fly, then the tech people handling your show are going to want to know the answers to these questions:

- *How many line sets are there?* Go to the wings. On one side of the stage or the other, there should be some ropes that come down from the **grid,** loop around a big pulley on the floor, and then go back up out of sight. These are the **purchase lines** that you use to operate the rigging system. Each one of them is attached to a metal cage, an **arbor,** full of metal weights, or **counterweights,** that offset the weight of whatever you are trying to fly. The arbor, in turn, is attached to a set of cables that pull a pipe (a batten), up and down. The batten is where you attach the thing you are flying. The whole enchilada—purchase line, arbor, cables, and batten—is called a **line set.** In general, each thing that you want to fly requires its own line set. The lighting people will also want some of the battens for lights.

- *Are any of the battens permanently wired for lights?* Any pipe that is being used for lighting is called an electric, and a pipe that is *permanently* furnished with lighting circuits is called a hard-wired electric. You can still put lights on a pipe that isn't hard-wired, but using hard-wired electrics can save the lighting crew a lot of time. More than likely, your lighting designer will use the hard-wired electrics and then add a few temporarily wired electrics of her own. Often, the first electric, the one closest to the proscenium, is hard-wired, while the rest are not. This is because the first electric generally has more lighting instruments on it than any other electric. Furthermore, most lighting designers can agree on where the first electric should go. It's all the other ones that change from show to show and designer to designer.

- *What else is hanging?* What hanging things are permanently assigned to battens, and cannot be moved? Many battens will be taken up with permanent lighting equipment (including work lights), draperies, and other equipment. Acoustical shells, those huge, curving walls that sit behind choirs and orchestras, are notorious for being stored in the air

and eating up a lot of space. Look for them.
- *How high is the grid?* This is a critical piece of information. If you have a twenty-foot-high piece of scenery that flies, you will need another twenty feet above it in order to fly it up out of the audience's view. In practice, you will usually need a grid at least three times the height of your proscenium in order to pull scenery far enough out of sight.

Masking

Stand in the auditorium, or wherever the audience will be sitting. Walk from one side of the seating area to the other, looking at the backstage area. Pay attention to how much of the backstage area you can see. What kind of draperies does your space have? Are there **legs** on the sides to hide the wings? Are there **borders** overhead to hide the lights? Is there a **grand drape** to close at the beginning and the end of your show? If you are working in a very temporary space, like a hotel ballroom, you will have to rent draperies, in the form of **pipe-and-drape.**

The Lighting System

Your master electrician and lighting designer will want to ask some questions as well:

- *Where are the lighting positions?* You've probably got part of the answer from the rigging section. If the electrics aren't hard-wired, then the lighting and set designers have to sit down and decide who gets which battens. If, however, the electrics *are* hard-wired, then lighting will go on those and scenery on the rest, unless the lighting designer has special requests for more battens. There are also lighting positions out over the audience. These are called **front-of-house** positions, often abbreviated *FOH*. The horizontal ones are called **beams**; the vertical ones are called **booms**. Is there a follow spot booth?
- *What is the lighting inventory?* The lighting people will want to know how many instruments are available and what type they are. The **lighting inventory** is a list of all the instruments and should include how many of each type there are, what wattage they are, and what accessories the theater owns for them. If not enough instruments are available, then you will have to either borrow them, rent them, or do without. If you are in a hotel, remember that track lights are rarely powerful enough to light a performance, so you should not count them in an inventory.

- *What kind of power is available?* Is there a circuit plot? A **circuit plot** shows where you can plug in all the lighting instruments. You usually cannot plug lighting instruments into standard wall sockets. A dedicated stage lighting system needs far more power than those little electrical outlets can provide. The only time that those outlets are useful for stage lighting is when you only have a few small lights. Read chapter 13 to find out what kind of power you need for temporary setups.
- *What kind of a control console is it?* How many **dimmers** are there? Is the **control console** a computer-controlled board or a manual one? If it is a computer board, get the name of it. The designer will want to know which kind he is facing ahead of time. Ask how many dimmers are available. This may determine how many lighting instruments you can use.
- *What kind of plugs does the lighting system use?* There are, at present, two kinds of plugs used for stage lighting: the **stage plug** and the **twist-lock**. These two plugs are incompatible. If you bring lighting equipment with stage plugs into a theater with twist-lock circuits, that equipment will be useless unless you change the plugs, a time-consuming process. Household plugs like the one on your reading lamp (known as **Edison plugs**) are rarely used onstage.

The Sound System

Make a list of everything you need the sound system to do. Do you need to amplify a single person speaking? Multiple people speaking? Do you need to play a tape or a CD? Do you need to have wireless mics? Do you have a band that needs to be amplified?

Once you've determined the sound needs of your show, ask whoever takes care of sound equipment in the space if the system can handle it. If you are talking to the right person, you may be able to stop there. If you don't have a knowledgeable person who knows the space, at least try to get answers to the following questions:

- *What is the inventory of sound equipment?* As in lighting, it's extremely useful to have some sort of list that shows everything that the theater is equipped with. This will help your sound person come up with a plan of attack.
- *If there is a mixer, how many channels does it have?* Every piece of sound equipment has to be plugged in to the mixer, and each piece of equipment get its own **channel** in the mixer. Tape decks and CD players are generally in stereo, with a plug for left and right, so they each need *two* channels.

Monitors and Headsets

The people in your show will need to hear what's happening onstage when they are waiting for entrances. That is the purpose of a **monitor system**. A monitor system has a microphone hanging over the stage that feeds sound into speakers located backstage. When touring a new space, ask these questions about the monitor:

- *Which rooms can hear the monitor?* You will want to warn the actors if, for example, they will not be able to hear their cues in the bathrooms.
- *Where is the microphone that's picking up the sound from the stage?* This is useful not only because you should keep the lighting and scenery from hitting it, but also because you should know where to stand if you don't want your catty conversation being carried to the dressing rooms.
- *Is there a paging system?* Can the stage manager make announcements over the monitor system?
- *Can the dressing rooms "talk back" to the paging system?* Some snazzy systems allow the people in the dressing rooms to answer back when they are paged. This is a good thing, because the performers can let the stage manager know that they heard her.

A **headset system** is the system that the crew uses to talk to each other. It is just like a phone system where, if you plug your phone into the wall, you can join in on the party line. A headset system has four parts: a **base station**, **belt packs**, **headsets**, and a whole lot of **cable**. The base station provides power to the system and makes the whole thing work. You can't get by without one. It is often built into the wall somewhere. Each person has a belt pack that picks up the voices in the system and feeds them into a headset. The headset is the part that goes on your head and makes you look like a telephone operator. The cables plug everything together. Here are the questions you should ask about the headset system:

- *Is the system permanently built in, and, if so, where are the plugs?* In a theater with a built-in headset system, there should be plugs all over the place where you can plug your belt packs in.
- *How many headsets and belt packs do they own?* You will need one belt pack and one headset for everybody you want to have on the system.
- *Do you have more than one channel?* Some headset systems have more than one channel, so two different conversations can be going on at once without disturbing each other.
- *Are the headset and monitor systems connected?* This allows the sounds

from the stage to be broadcast into the headsets as well as allowing the stage manager to page the backstage area through her own headset. It can also allow the dressing rooms to hear the conversations on the headset, which prevents those conversations from straying into unprofessional territory.

Answering the above questions may help you to decide if you want to do your show in a given space. If your space passes the test, then you are ready to start planning your show there. Let's go on!

CHAPTER 3

Scenic Design: Space, Texture, and the "Big Statement"

Why build scenery? Good question.

Why take wonderful scripts, cast them with brilliant, lively actors, entrust them to spirited, creative directors, and then encase them in piles of expensive, distracting, noisy, heavy, monolithic scenery?

Like I said, good question.

When I was in graduate school, my brilliant scene design teacher, Richard Isackes, took all the tech theater students down to the stage and made us stand, one at a time, on a three-foot-high platform stuck out on the edge of the apron. From this uncomfortable position, we peered out through the blinding stage lights into the audience where he sat, hidden in the darkness. As we stood there, unaccustomed to being in the glare of the spotlights, he called out commands to us, sounding slightly annoyed if we did not respond to his liking.

"State your name, please!"

"Count to ten!"

"Do it backwards!"

"Speak up!"

"Is there a problem?"

I have never forgotten that feeling of psychological nakedness, that sensation of being scrutinized and rebuked for the smallest mistake. When he was done harassing us from the darkness, Richard came down to the stage.

"That's what an actor does every day," he said. "Let's never forget that."

People come to the theater to see actors perform! So why do we persist in thinking that we have to have a truckload of scenery onstage? Just because a play takes place in Versailles does not mean we have to have the Hall of Mirrors, complete with cascading cherubim, just to get the idea across. Somebody once told me that a set designer has five seconds to get his point across, "because that's how long the audience will look at the scenery." Granted, I have heard some gasps come out of the audience when the curtain went up, but if the performances did not carry the show, the audience was just as bored as if the scenery were made of cardboard. We all love to watch the chandelier crash down on the stage in *Phantom of the Opera,* but we don't walk home humming the scenery—we remember the actors and their performances. We must have a gene kicking around in our collective pool that keeps telling us, "You're doing a show. You must build scenery." That has been the normal thought pattern for most of this century, after all, and even with the development of other design areas, we all have a tendency to fall back on scenery.

When modern theatrical design really began around the turn of the twentieth century, the entire playing field belonged to the scenic designers. Lighting was in its infancy, costumes were still being handled by the actors themselves, and sound had not been invented yet. This situation persisted until after World War II, when the costume designers began to gain prominence, showing their talents in the immense musicals of the period, such as *Camelot* and *My Fair Lady.* Later, in the sixties, lighting began to come into its own when the position of lighting designer was created as a separate entity from the stage electrician. In fact, with the advent of the rock-and-roll musicals (*Hair, Jesus Christ Superstar*), much of the design emphasis moved to lighting. In the eighties, with an audience that had become accustomed to movies, the sound designer became increasingly important. Audiences demanded a more complete sound environment and actors had to be clearly audible, even when speaking naturally. These days, actors use microphones more than ever before, and more shows make use of "ambient" sound—a constant stream of background sounds. Some people say that the growth of amplification has gone hand in hand with the decrease in good vocal training, but in my view, the growth of sound design—an abstract, emotionally evocative medium—is a positive trend, bringing us back to what is truly important in the theater: the imagination and the performer.

When dealing with scenery, the first and most important question you should ask yourself is this: *What is the show about?* Then, ask yourself: What do we need, what do we *really* need to get that point across to the audience? Often, the answer might not even be scenic. A voice announcing departures can suggest "airport," the shadows from sunlight through a window can say "drawing room," a uniform can indicate "police station." Even if the answer is scenic, constant attention to that question—*What is the show about?*—can help you approach scenery in an intelligent way that won't end up stressing your technicians, your budget, or, most important, your show. After all, this is not *Field of Dreams*. Even if you build it, they may not come.

Having said all that: The purpose of this chapter is not to turn you into a scenic designer. Rather, the purpose of this chapter is to help you see a script in a new, more visual way, as well as to help you understand why stage designers make the choices that they do. Scenic design can be thought of as the art of addressing three issues: space, texture, and the "statement." Space and texture are the practical, real-world ways that we create an environment onstage. However, without grounding these practical pieces in a solid artistic concept, you may be stuck with a grandiose pile of junk, totally inappropriate for your play. Let's start, therefore, with the Big Picture and afterwards we'll talk about how to create it. Along the way, I will also help you understand the most fundamental theatrical drawings—floorplans, elevations, and renderings.

The Big Picture: The Statement

A designer I worked with in college always began a new production by finding one defining object for that show in the real world. A few days after he started work on *A Streetcar Named Desire,* we were walking down a street in Providence, Rhode Island. It was winter, and the red brick colonials around us were frosted with snow. Most of the houses had little neoclassical façades over their front entrances and severe-looking paned windows with storm shutters. In short, it was about as far as you could get from the steamy New Orleans inner city of Stanley Kowalski and Blanche DuBois. Suddenly, he grabbed my arm and pointed. "Oh my god, *Streetcar!*" he gasped. Following his arm, I looked for what had gotten him so worked up, and sure enough, there was *Streetcar*. It was a tall, wrought-iron gate that closed in front of a set of brick stairs. The iron was ornately, even grotesquely, wound around the gate, giving a sense of great wealth, with a hint of new money gone bad. Each vertical bar was capped with a little brass ball, and the handles were two languid curlicues. Best of all, the whole thing was completely rusted.

The next day we came back with the Polaroid and, for the entire design period, we covered the walls of the studio with photos of that gate. Time and time again, it pulled us back to what we really wanted to say about the play: the faded glory, the grotesque sensuality, the decay. We did not always use these "inspiration pieces" on the sets that they inspired, but this time, it was too good to pass up. We built a perfect replica of that gate on one side of the set, complete with the red-brick stairs, and it gave us immense pleasure to see Blanche pause in front of it every night to give her now-clichéd closing benediction: "I have always depended on the kindness of strangers." That gate said more about her condition than two tons of scenery could have.

The Statement is the ultimate answer to the "What is the play about?" question. It is the rallying point for all the designers. The Statement may be a visual (like the *Streetcar* gate), audible (like a piece of music, or Chekhov's "plucked bow string" at the end of *The Cherry Orchard*), written (a word, a speech), abstract or concrete, simple or complex, in the show or out of it. The Statement may be a painting, a piece of junk, a pop reference, or a newspaper article. Whatever it is, it gives the designers a place to start, and a place to return to when they need inspiration.

This is not to say that any production can be boiled down in its entirety to one sentence or object or thought.

The Statement is the talisman that the director gives to his flock. Discovering it, expressing it, and sharing it are all things that the director must do to get the ball rolling and keep it on the move.

How to Read a Script Like a Set Designer

The first time you read a script, forget about designers. Just read it! Enjoy. Visualize only if you want to. Follow the story and savor the characters. Read the script like an audience member.

Once you have finished being an audience member, however, take that hat off and put it away for a while. Now put on your designer hat and read the script again.

The most important thing that the set designer is looking for in the script is the number and kind of spaces that the show requires. The purpose of the scenic design is to service the actors and the script. Don't start out trying to make something that is visually impressive. Start by answering the question "What kind of space do I need?"

As you read through the script with your set designer hat on, start making lists. Make lists of locations. Is there more than one? Where are they? Are they interior spaces or exteriors? Do they require doors or windows? What kinds of specific physical objects do they require? Does the action require more than one of them to be visible at once? What is mentioned specifically? What is only suggested?

Sets break down into three rough groups and by the time you finish your read-through, you should have a pretty good idea which one fits your show best. It is worth noting that each of these groups has its own set of difficulties and none of them should be seen as "easier" to design or build than any other.

The One-Set Show

This is a show that takes place in one location, like a bedroom, an office, or a backyard. The set does not change, although furniture and props may be moved around within it. These shows are generally more realistic, and have a fair amount of detail on the set. One-set interiors—particularly those where the walls are built to surround all three sides of the set—are often referred to as **box sets**.

The Multi-Set Show

Shows that move from location to location sometimes require fully realized sets for each location. Large musicals such as *Guys and Dolls* are multi-set shows. Often, the designer creates a surrounding "frame" of scenery, while inserting different sets within the frame. For example, since *Anything Goes* takes place on a ship, a designer might create a shiplike atmosphere with decks, railings, and portholes, while changing walls around to create different rooms.

Multi-set shows aren't restricted to musicals, however. The nonmusical play *The Crucible* takes place in four different locations. Again, these locations have a common element: They are all rooms in wood-frame buildings in Salem, Massachusetts. The successful designer will tie them all together with common elements, reducing the number of pieces that have to be changed for each scene. The amount of detail on each set is usually less than for a one-set show.

Multi-set shows also require time during the play to change scenery. Hence, they are often written with the scene changes happening during intermissions. In the case of musicals, there are often short scenes between the long ones. These scenes, called **in-ones**, are made to be played in front of a downstage curtain in order to allow time for the scenery to be changed upstage. The name comes from the term used to describe the scenic drop that flies in behind them. This is called an "in-one drop" because it falls just behind the first set of drapery legs, the "in-one" legs. (The second set of legs is called "in-two," the third set is called "in-three," and so on.) Multi-set shows are often the most expensive way to do scenery.

Sometimes, multi-set shows will have more than one of the locations onstage and visible to the audience throughout the show. This is necessary if the play changes quickly from location to location, as is sometimes the case when the playwright actually wrote a movie script but is trying to make it work on stage.

The Unit Set

Another solution to scripts with multiple locations—the **unit set**—does not require full-blown sets for each scene. Rather, the designer creates a space that will accommodate lots of different scenes. Then, smaller pieces are added and subtracted to communicate specific locations. Major scenic elements, like the walls, do not change, while smaller elements—furniture, banners, window frames, coffins, ship's wheels, and so forth—are added and subtracted. The plays of Shakespeare are often done this way, particularly since Shakespearean stage directions are rarely specific about locations: "A ship." "A grove." "Rome."

Unit sets have different areas on them that are used for different scenes. If there are small, intimate scenes, then the designer must create some small, intimate places, and the lighting designer must turn off the lights on all the other areas. If there are crowd scenes, then there must be large, open spaces. The space should be designed to be subdivided in as many ways as necessary. Unit sets may tax the creativity of the design team, but they are often the most rewarding solution, offering simplicity and low cost while maintaining the atmosphere of the show.

Whether a show really needs full sets, as in the true multi-set approach, or would be better served by a "unit" approach, is a stylistic decision as well as a budgetary one. The flow of the show is critical: If you cannot create a multi-set show without getting bogged down in lengthy scene changes, try a unit approach instead.

The Backstage Survival Guide to Reading a Floorplan

I would not even do Thanksgiving dinner for my family without a floorplan. It is the single most important drawing in the theater, and every single person on a theatrical team should know and understand the floorplan. A floorplan is how people talk to each other about space.

Find the Theater

No, don't get up. I don't mean find the actual space. Locate it on the drawing. Find the permanent part of the theater—the part that is always there, even when the set is gone. Look for thick, dark shapes, possibly with crosshatching inside them. In a proscenium theater, find the proscenium. In a thrust or arena space, find the audience or another landmark. In a hotel ballroom or other "nontheatrical" space, look for the walls and doorways. Get yourself oriented to the space as a whole before you try to understand where the scenery is.

A floorplan can be understood as a bird's eye view of the stage after someone came along with a gigantic chainsaw and sliced the roof off the theater. Actually, the slice is usually taken about head high, that is, about five to six feet off the stage floor. Any object that falls underneath the slice is shown as

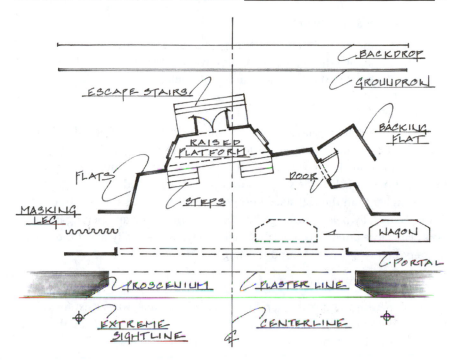

Fig. 2. Sample floorplan

a solid line. Anything above it is shown as a dashed line. Anything that the chainsaw would actually cut through, like a wall, is shown as a heavier line with the interior of any shape filled in with crosshatching. (This is why the proscenium arch is drawn this way—the chainsaw would cut through it.)

Find the Center Line

The **center line** is the beginning of all measurements in a theater space. Look for a line that alternates between short and long dashes and ends at the bottom of the drawing with a symbol that looks like this: ℄. The center line, not surprisingly, runs down the center of the set, from upstage to downstage. The plaster line runs across the set, connecting the two proscenium arches. Technicians installing a set in a theater use the plaster line and the center line to get the set in the right place, and you should always find these first on any floorplan. Of course, there is no law that says these two lines have to be on a drawing, but they should be there if you are in a "real" theater and if the designer is theatrically trained. If these lines are not present, you will have to move on to the next step to get your bearings.

Find the Major Scenic Elements

Locate the principal walls and **platforms.** Remember, if they are "above the slice," that is, above the actor's head, they will be drawn as dashed lines. Anything "below the slice" is drawn as a solid object.

Find the Heights

Heights on a set are usually measured from the "real" stage floor, that is, the permanent floor, not whatever platforming is in the set itself. Heights are usually shown in circles, with a "+" or a "–" to show how much that platform is above or below the stage floor. A platform marked "+8" is eight inches higher than the real stage floor, or one step up. A surface marked "–1'6" is actually below the stage floor, so there must be an opening in the floor. Pay close attention to heights, since they will radically affect the performers' ability to move around the stage.

Look for Traffic Patterns

How will performers move around the stage? What alleyways exist for the performers to move through? Are there places for long crosses? Are there reasons to go to different parts of the stage? Is there a crossover?

Look for Doors and Windows

The floorplan should indicate which way they open, or if they open at all.

Pay Attention to Masking

Has the designer created enough walls or drapes so the audience won't be able to see backstage? A good floorplan will have a little "+" sign in each bottom corner showing the **extreme sightline.** This is the "worst" seat, the seat that, through the combination of being way out to the side and close to the stage, has the best view of the backstage area. There will be one on either side of the auditorium. If you design the masking so these two people cannot see backstage, then you probably have prevented everybody else from seeing backstage as well.

Look for Moving Scenery

Any piece of rolling scenery should have more than one position marked, usually an onstage position and an offstage one. Flying scenery will only have one location marked (the onstage one), but it should be marked as a flying piece.

Look for "Weird Stuff"

This basically means anything that we have not covered so far. Every set is different, so there might be anything. *Make sure you understand what every single line on the drawing means, unless you are prepared for some tech-week surprises.*

Note! Even with a good floorplan, it may be necessary to ask the designer to make a three-dimensional model. It is very difficult to imagine how a floorplan will translate into real objects. A model is the only way to really see how things will play together onstage. Even if you have a model, however, you must know and understand the floorplan. For one thing, in some situations, you may never *get* the model, no matter how much you want it. In addition, a floorplan is far more precise than a model, it contains real measurements, and it can be folded up and put in your pocket. Gotta love that.

Texture and Color: Giving the Show a "Look"

As you are reading the script, it is useful to try to imagine what kinds of materials would be appropriate. It is this choice of materials that gives the show its "look." Will you rely on painted muslin, or will you utilize three-dimensional sculptures carved out of foam? What about scaffolding and chain-link fencing? How about neon, vinyl, brick, or bales of hay? The list is endless. It helps to come up with a list of adjectives that describe the feeling you would like the set to convey to the audience. Make the adjectives as colorful and descriptive as you can. "Comfortable" might describe a room, but it may not tell the designer much. How about "academic," or "lived-in," or "like a rabbit burrow"?

The texture of the set is derived from the mood and atmosphere of the script and characters. One thing to keep in mind about texture is how much it disappears over distance. Most of the audience will be a long way away from the scenery. If you put something textural on the stage and then step back ten feet to admire it, you are not seeing what the audience sees. Step back into the middle of the house and see how much of the texture actually shows. You will quickly see that what looked rough and coarse at ten feet looks like a Formica countertop from row M.

Color is another way of expressing texture, and all the same thoughts apply. Color brings out emotional responses and, as such, can be discussed with emotional adjectives. Again, stay away from "bright" and "dark." Try "belching" or "pasty" or "aggressive."

Coordinating Texture in Scenery and Lighting

Different textures call for different lighting treatments, so be sure to keep the lighting designer informed about how the scenery is going to look.

The direction of the lighting can reveal or destroy texture. Light coming from straight ahead will wipe it out. Light coming from the sides, above, or below will emphasize it.

Shiny textures and light colors may create problems for lighting, namely, **glare** and **bounce**. A textured surface will tend to "eat" light and not allow it to go anywhere else. Slick, smooth surfaces, especially floors, send the light on its way toward surfaces that should not be lit. Glare is produced when a light shining from upstage toward downstage—known as a **back light**—is reflected into the audience's eyes by a shiny floor. It can be extremely distracting to the audience. Bounce is the opposite: Light coming from downstage bounces off the floor and splashes onto the walls upstage. If you are doing *One Flew Over the Cuckoo's Nest,* for example, try not to give in to the temptation to build the hospital ward set completely out of shiny institutional white. If you do, the bouncing, glaring light beams will splash up onto the walls and into the audience and prevent you from getting the isolated pool of light that you will need when Chief strangles . . . oops, almost gave it away.

To control bounce, you must tone down the *color* of the floor. To control glare, you must tone down its *shine.*

The point is, shiny, light-colored sets make it difficult to isolate lighting. You may not think that isolating lighting is an issue for your show, but it almost certainly is. Isolation is how you steer the audience's eyes around the stage. With a bright, shiny set, you will constantly end up with light where you don't want it. Also, a shiny white stage will not go to blackout as easily as a dark-colored one. You would be amazed at how much light a set can pick up from an EXIT sign.

Be aware of the color wheel. Poor color combinations can be disastrous. As you will read later on, color filters change light in lighting instruments by *subtracting* colors, not by adding them. A light that has been colored red has had all the other colors removed. If that red light hits a green surface, that surface will turn black. There is no green in the light to reveal the green on the surface. I lit a punked-out production of *Titus Andronicus* once and the director asked for one battle scene to be lit entirely in red. Unfortunately, neither he nor I had talked to the costume designer. Turns out that all the actors in that scene had hair dyed green. Oops! Black hair everywhere.

Particularly offensive color combinations include red and green, blue and amber, and yellow and lavender. In these mismatched situations, it is usually the lighting that has to change—it is easier to change a color filter than to dye a costume. Remember, though, that the colors have to be strong and pure to be a problem. I solved the punk hair situation by just mixing in a little green light around the edges.

Coordinating Texture in Scenery and Costumes

Scenery and costumes are also closely related. It is even more important to coordinate them, since it is more difficult and time-consuming to make changes.

Some things to think about:

It is important that the set and the costumes have similar palettes. This means that the set and costumes are using related sets of colors and textures. Notice that I did not say the *same* colors, just related ones. It can lead to visual confusion if the set designer uses neon colors while the costume designer is exploring earth tones. Of course, visual confusion may be just what your show is about, but at least make the choice consciously. It often helps if the set and costume designers can agree on a painting or two from which they can extract a palette.

It is equally important that the set and costumes do not use the *same* colors. While the designers should agree on a palette, they should use different parts of it so the actors will not appear to fade away into the set. *Most of the time, this means the set should be darker than the costumes.* The set is not moving, the actor is. Therefore, the actors should get the brighter colors to allow the audience to track them more easily. Above all, avoid putting the exact same color on a wall and on a costume that stands in front of it.

CHAPTER 4

The Tools of Scenery: Surface, Texture, and Tricks

In the previous chapter, we discussed how scenery can establish mood, underscore themes, and reveal and support the characters on stage. This is the design perspective. From a more pragmatic standpoint, however, scenery basically does five things. First, it gives the actors a place to stand. Second, it gives the audience a physical surface to look at behind the actor. Third, it provides "real" physical elements, such as doors and windows. Fourth, it helps the play to move from one location to the next, through the use of multiple settings. Finally, it occasionally tricks the audience into believing something happened that really did not.

A Place to Stand: Platforms, Stairs, and Ramps

The most basic job of scenery is to provide a place for a performer to stand, feel comfortable and be seen by the audience. Molière once said that a platform and a chair was *all* you needed.

Platforms

Scenic platforms are made out of a variety of materials, but they all consist of a frame covered by some kind of top (or **skin**), all of which is held up by **legs**. Regular platforms tend to come in 4-by-8-foot sizes (usually abbreviated as 4 × 8), mostly because platforms use plywood for the top and 4 × 8 is the standard size for plywood sheets from the lumberyard. When you look at the **stock scenery** that most theaters have, you will see a lot of 4 × 8s. A platform can be built in any size and shape, of course, but, like mobile homes, it

Fig. 3. Decks are made of platforms

is easier and cheaper to build rectangles. If you are renting platforming, it will probably only be available in a few sizes, one of which will most certainly be 4 × 8. Other common rental sizes are 4 × 4 and 4 × 6.

Platforms are combined to build a **deck**. Stock platforms will sometimes have **coffin locks**—latches that lock the platforms together—built in. Otherwise, the platforms are bolted together.

Sometimes, for visual effect, a designer will decide to have the deck slant toward the audience. This is called a **raked stage**, or simply, a **rake**. There are lots of reasons to use a rake. It makes the performers easier to see, for one thing. A raked stage can also make the upstage area feel closer to the audience and it is a good device to improve the intimacy of the audience-actor relationship. It is best used in theaters where the audience seating area is raked very little, or not at all. A rake can also be used to increase the effect of **perspective**, the scenic trick used to increase the apparent size of the stage. If the tops of the walls slant downward as they go upstage, the combination of the top of the wall coming down and the raked floor coming up will make the stage appear larger, sort of like that railroad-tracks-coming-together-in-the-distance trick you learned in fifth-grade art class. Using this effect to fool the audience is called **false perspective**.

The raked stage is firmly rooted in theatrical history. When scenic design was being invented in Renaissance Italy, false perspective was all the rage, and all the stages were raked. The trend continued into Shakespeare's day and actors had to get used to playing on a shallow hill. Since the actors were literally climbing up the hill as they walked away from the audience, the term **upstage** was created for this area. Conversely, **downstage** meant closer to the audience. As you know, these terms are used today on any stage, raked or not.

If you are considering a raked stage, you should know that actors adapt remarkably well to a slanted playing surface, as long as it is not too steep. Rakes are measured in "inches per foot." A one-inch-to-the-foot rake, for example, rises one inch in altitude for every foot you walk upstage. A one-inch rake is quite shallow, almost unnoticeable to the audience and easy to walk on, while a two-inch-to-the-foot rake feels quite steep, and requires some practice. Good rakes fall somewhere between one inch and two inches to the foot. For obvious reasons, dancers are not wild about working on rakes. Opera singers are less picky (they sing more and move around less). Surprisingly, runway fashion models seem to be able to work on anything short of a cliff.

Steps

The human body is remarkably rigid in its requirements for steps. If the steps rise too slowly, you constantly feel as though you are stumbling too quickly, and they exhaust you. Furthermore, the ratio of how high you have to lift your foot each time (the **rise**) to how far forward you move with each step (the **run**) is very important. Architects use a rather complicated formula to determine these measurements, but for our purposes, we can use the "eighteen-inch rule." Simply stated, this rule says that *the rise plus the run should be about eighteen inches.* One of the most commonly used ratios is an eight-inch

Fig. 4. Different staircases for different users

rise for a ten-inch run. This yields a staircase that is comfortable to climb, but rises fairly quickly. A six-inch rise and a twelve-inch run gives a more ceremonial look, suitable for a ballroom scene, an awards ceremony, or any scene where women will be wearing long dresses. Anything shallower than six-by-twelve, though, and the stairs start to get awkward. Performers may find themselves lurching up it, constantly trying to decide whether to put one foot or two on each step. Designers of large public plazas seem to get this one wrong fairly frequently, a good example of function being a slave to form. I live in San Francisco, and I always marvel at the awkwardness of the steps leading up to City Hall. Beautiful building. Lousy steps.

If you need a steeper, more utilitarian-looking stair (a scene in a base-ment, for example, or aboard a ship), or you just don't have as much space, you can use a nine-by-nine-inch stair, but any steeper and it begins to look and feel like a ladder. As it is, women in long period dresses or heels may need help getting up and down a nine-by-nine. One common use of this steeper stair is for getting actors off high platforms out of sight of the audi-ence. Any staircase with this purpose is called an **escape stair**.

Another way in which the human body is very choosy is in each stair's height relative to the others. Put simply: *It is imperative that all the risers in a staircase are the same size.* As you climb a staircase, you tend to lift your foot only a fraction of an inch higher than necessary to clear each step. Whether this is because of human laziness or just a physiological obsession with efficiency is anybody's guess, but the result is that, if you make one or more of the steps higher than the rest, you will have created what technicians affectionately refer to as an **actor trap**, that is, a piece of scenery that lays in wait for preoccupied actors, causing them to trip, stumble, and forget their lines.

When I was in school at Brown University, we used to take our coffee breaks on the patio outside the theater, just above the post office. (It has since been moved.) We would watch the students come up the single flight of hundred-year-old steps from the basement and marvel at how often people would trip on the top step, spilling coffee and books all over the sidewalk. It literally happened every ten minutes. One day we took a tape measure to the step and, as we suspected, found that it was higher than the rest. How much higher? Less than half an inch. Ever since that experience, I have been impressed by how quickly and firmly the human body adapts to its surroundings. After climbing just a few steps, people's bodies were cutting the heights so close that a half-inch discrepancy was causing them to trip. I was no exception. Even after I knew the higher step was there, I still lost a cup of coffee to it now and then.

If you really need to have an uneven step in your staircase (if you are using a stock staircase, for example, and it falls a little short), put the odd step at the bottom. There are two reasons for this: First, people tend to pay more attention to the steps at the bottom of a staircase, and second, if they do trip, they don't have as far to fall. You laugh, you laugh. . . .

While we're on the subject of safety, any escape stair with more than two steps should have a handrail (called an "Equity rail" after the actor's union that requires it) on at least one side. Any stair bigger than four steps should have it on both sides. Finally, make sure that you have a strip of white tape along the front of each step so people can see where they are stepping. Don't use phosphorescent "glow tape," though. It will never "charge up" in the backstage gloom and thus will not be visible.

Since the risers on your stairs are going to be six, eight, or (rarely) nine inches, it follows that the platforms that they lead to will also be multiples of six, eight, or nine inches in height. Because the eight-inch riser is such a common and comfortable step, stage platforms are often raised to multiples of eight: sixteen inches, twenty-four inches, thirty-two inches, and so on. The rental platform world is usually sized for six-inch-high steps (more platforms are rented for graduations than for Shakespeare), so their platforming tends to be in six-inch increments, that is, twelve inches, eighteen inches, twenty-four inches and so on.

A Surface to Look At: Walls, Drapes, Paint, and Fabric

In the theater, walls are called **flats**. Even if they're not flat. It's just one of those things.

Like platforms, flats can be built in any shape or size, but most theaters carry stock sizes in two-foot increments, such as 4 × 8, 2 × 10, and 2 × 8. When the size of a flat is listed, the width is first, followed by the height. A 4 × 8, for example, is four feet wide and eight feet high. People have been known to violate this rule, however, so if you're renting, be sure to check which is which.

Unfortunately, few rental houses carry flats of any size, although they might build them for you if you want to buy them. These companies make most of their money off corporate clients, and those clients generally prefer soft draperies.

Flats must be supported to stand upright. The best thing to use is other flats. Set the flats at angles to each other and then nail them together. If that doesn't do it, you can add braces on the back. Whatever you do, don't try to suspend the flats from the ceiling with wire or rope. This always sounds like a good idea, but it won't keep the flats from swinging in the breeze. Attach the flats to the *floor*.

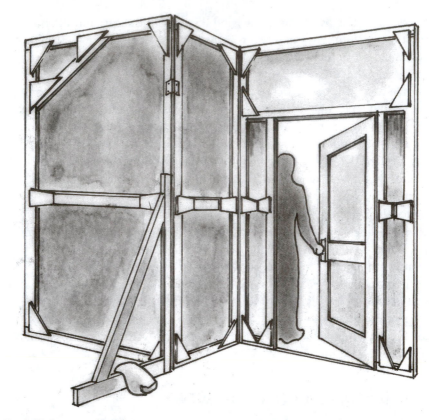

Fig. 5. Walls are made of flats

If you want to add some quick and easy texture to your walls, try covering them with a decorative fabric or with Styrofoam™.

Styrofoam comes in many different shapes and sizes, but the two most common are polyurethane foam, commonly known as **beadboard** (because it is made up of tiny white beads), and polystyrene foam, commonly known as **blueboard** (because it is blue). Beadboard is cheaper and less dense. It comes in big sheets, like plywood, weighs next to nothing, and makes marvelous-looking rocks if you gouge it out with whatever tools of destruction (screwdrivers, files, car keys) you have lying around. For best effect, dilute some ordinary white glue (one part water to two parts glue), get some cotton cheesecloth (*not* polyester cheesecloth), dip it in the glue, and lay it over the mutilated Styrofoam, pushing it into all the nooks and crannies with a paintbrush. The cheesecloth helps the Styrofoam take paint better, plus it will keep it from cracking and breaking when people rub up against it.

Blueboard is much more dense and can be cut with a fair amount of detail using standard woodworking tools. One good blueboard trick is to paint it with a little acetone. Acetone is a solvent that eats away at the Styrofoam, leaving behind a lovely, craggy surface that looks for all the world like stone. SAFETY ALERT! *The acetone trick produces dangerous fumes, so do it outside where there is a breeze blowing.* Like beadboard, blueboard also should be covered with cheesecloth before painting. The thing to remember about any kind of foam is that it will not take any weight at all, so do not use it anyplace where people are going to sit or walk. It has no structural strength; it is purely decorative. Incidentally, if you don't need a huge amount of foam, try prowling around lumber yards, contractor supply houses, or construction sites. They often have scrap pieces left over that are useful to you but not to them. Considering Styrofoam's well-deserved reputation as an environmental nightmare, why not put this scrap to use instead of buying new sheets?

Drapes

What says "show" more than draperies? From Fellini films to Las Vegas revues, the image of a grand drape slowly parting to reveal a spectacle behind it is a piece of cultural imagery that we can never escape. By the way, did you know that the Romans *dropped* the front curtain at the beginning of the show instead of raising it? It fell to the ground and was dragged away by slaves. The idea of raising the curtain up out of sight was invented during the Italian Renaissance, when many of the stage crew were former sailors and sailboat rigging was brought to the theater. To this day, many of the rigging terms we use backstage are actually sailing terms. It is also how the superstition about not whistling backstage got started. The sailors climbing around over the stage communicated by whistling. If you were standing around below them whistling "I Left My Heart in Verona," people could get confused overhead and you were likely to end up with a sandbag on your noggin. I suspect that this whole don't-walk-under-a-ladder thing got started the same way. Today a safety rule, tomorrow a superstition.

Like the raked stage, draperies are an old tradition in the theater and, like anything else that is ancient, the terminology is extensive and rather particular. The fact that each variety of drape has its own name may seem excessive, but it is worth taking the time to learn them since this kind of terminology can make it easier to communicate with technicians, and isn't that why we're here?

Okay, let's start downstage (closer to the audience, remember?). The first drape is the **grand drape**, also called the main drape, the grand curtain, or the main rag. It is the one that has to open for the show to start. It often has a decorative **valence**, a little short drape made of the same material, that

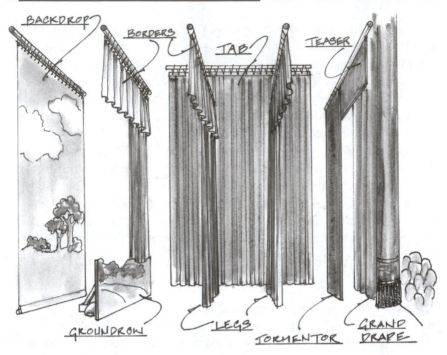

Fig. 6. Names of draperies

runs all the way across the top and does not move. Sometimes a designer will design a main curtain with a logo for a particular show. This is called a **show drop**, and it is used in place of the normal grand drape. In Britain, the law states that the asbestos **fire curtain** must be down when the audience enters the theater (to calm their fears, I gather), so many theaters have beautifully painted ones.

When the grand drape goes up, you usually see a small drape running across the top of the stage behind the valence, hiding the first row of lights. Unlike the valence, this drape is dark (usually black) and is not meant to draw attention. This is called a **teaser** (I suppose because it "teases" the audience by barely covering the lighting equipment). The sadistic theme continues with the two vertical drapes hanging down from the ends of the teaser. These are called **tormentors**, or often, torms. Off in the wings, many theaters have another set of drapes that hang perpendicular to the proscenium, and help mask the wings. These are called **tabs**.

Moving upstage, we see several more sets of drapes hanging parallel to the arch—each set with one drape running across the top like a teaser and one hanging down from each end like tormentors. The one above is a **border**, the ends are **legs**. Hold it, you say. What's the difference between the teaser/

torms and the border/legs? And the answer is, nothing really, except that the most downstage set of borders and legs is generally referred to as the teaser and the torms. Actually, sometimes the teaser and torms are framed draperies, like soft-cover flats, and they form a **portal**. What's more, the teaser and torms are sometimes painted in a design that matches the show and put out in front of the grand drape. In this case, they are called a **false proscenium**. Confused? Check out figure 6.

Enough terms? *I know, it is difficult, but language is important when we seek clarity, and clarity can keep you alive backstage.*

For those of you who are working in the convention and meeting world, your drapes come as **pipe-and-drape**. This is a lightweight fabric panel that is pre-sewn with a pocket running along the top. The installers then slip a long pole into this pocket and suspend the whole thing between two vertical pipes on stands. These drapes usually come in ten-foot lengths, stand about eight feet tall, and are very high and sound-transparent. So you have to be quiet backstage. Sorry.

When hanging drapes, you should consider how thick the pleats in the fabric should be. This is called the **fullness**. A drape that is hanging in "zero fullness" is perfectly flat—no pleats whatsoever. A drape hanging in "100 percent fullness" is pleated, accordion-style, so that it takes up exactly half as much width as it would if it were not pleated at all. In other words, a drapery that is thirty feet wide when stretched out will be fifteen feet wide when hung with 100 percent fullness. Drapes may be hung with more or less fullness, as is appropriate. The more fullness, the grander and more regal they look. Drapes, especially grand drapes, are sometimes manufactured with **sewn-in fullness**, which means that the pleats are sewn in permanently. This makes them nice and crisp and all the same size, but does not allow you to ever spread the drape out flat. This is a nice feature for a front curtain, but you should consider carefully before committing yourself to this option for any other drape.

Drops

What's the difference between a drape and a **drop**? Purpose, mostly. Drapes are considered part of the **masking**, that is, the things that you use to keep the audience from seeing what you don't want them to see. Drapes generally aren't meant to draw attention to themselves. Rather, they are the part of the stage that says: Don't look here. (Remember *The Wizard of Oz*? "Pay no

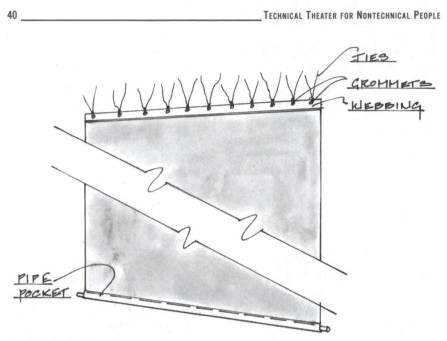

Fig. 7. Parts of a drop

attention to that man behind the masking!") Drops, on the other hand, are part of the scenery, and are meant to be looked at.

A standard stage drop is made from **muslin**. It has a strip of very heavy fabric, called **webbing**, across the top, which is studded with **grommets**– little brass rings embedded in the fabric. Small pieces of **tie line** are fed through grommets and then tied to the batten, the pipe above the stage that will hold the drop. The drop should also have a **chain pocket** running along the bottom, which holds a pipe or chain. The weight of the pipe or chain pulls the drop flat.

Sometimes, a designer will elect to cut out part of a drop (a "cut drop"), leaving an opening, if, for example, she wants the drop to look like leaves hanging down. Sometimes, when a drop comes up one side, across the top, and down the other side, it is called a **portal**.

There are also some special-use drops on stage that have names of their own: A **scrim** is a commonly used piece of stage magic. When lit from the front, a scrim appears opaque. When the front light is turned off, however, and objects behind the scrim are lit, the fabric appears translucent. This effect, called bleeding through, is most effective when the lights on the front of the scrim are rather bright. When the effect happens, all the light should be taken off the scrim and those on the objects or people behind should be brought up as high as possible. You can use a scrim whenever you want this effect. The national tour of *Les Misérables* used a scrim as a show curtain, so they could start each act by bleeding through to reveal the actors going about their business upstage. Then the show drape was raised, the front lights came on, and the show started. Bleeding through is also a good effect for magic appearances (the talking mirror in *Snow White* is a classic), or for when an actor is onstage thinking (or, more often, singing) about somebody who is not present and that other person needs to be seen. If you're planning on doing *Brigadoon,* for example, you'd better start scrim-shopping for the moment when Tommy Albright sits drinking in a New York City barroom, singing about his mythical mistress in the Scottish Highlands.

For a truly clean effect, a scrim should have a black curtain, called a **blackout drop**, hanging right behind it until just before the effect happens. Then, at the last possible moment, the blackout curtain "flies out" (gets pulled up out of the way) and the lighting effect happens.

It's best not to play a very long scene behind a scrim. The fabric is never truly transparent, and looking through it for a long time can tire out an audience.

Another type of specialty drop is one that goes all the way across the back of the stage and is used to impersonate the sky—a **cyclorama**, or, a **cyc** (pronounced like "psych"). Cycs are often curved to increase the illusion. They also make use of scrims. In fact, a cyc is sometimes a combination of drops—a scrim hanging in front of a muslin drop. Light is then thrown on the muslin drop, while the downstage scrim "confuses" the audience's eyes, making it difficult to tell exactly how far away the muslin drop really is, or, in fact, if it is there at all. The whole effect, if done skillfully, can be quite convincing. For situations where the cyc is being used as a background for modern dance, many designers will add a black scrim in front of it. That way, they just turn off the cyc lights and they have an instant black background for the piece about old age and death. There's always a piece about old age and death.

In both dance and drama, cycs are often lit from below with a set of footlights. This might necessitate a **ground row**, a short wall of flats running across the bottom of the cyc to hide the lights. The ground row can be plain black (common in the dance world), or it can be designed as part of the scenery, looking like a distant hill, some shrubbery, a fence, or whatever.

If you are considering projections, you should know that there are drops specially designed for use as **projection screens**. These highly reflective drops come in two main varieties—front and rear. **Rear-projection screens** can generally be projected on from either side, while **front-projection screens** are really only good for what their name suggests (for one thing, they often have seams holding together the panels of fabric, and those seams will show when a projector comes on from behind). A rear-projection screen can also make an excellent sky; try colored light coming from the front and clouds projected from the rear. You can front-project onto a plain muslin drop painted white if need be, but nothing compares with the sharpness and brilliance of a rear-projection screen. Rear-projecting onto muslin doesn't work; you can see the "hot spot" of the lamp behind the screen.

Fabric

As a fabric for draperies, *velour* is both traditional and unparalleled. It has a deep pile that looks luxurious under stage lights; it drapes in deep, thick folds; and it moves majestically when pulled aside. It is also quite dense and will not allow light to pass through from backstage, something very few fabrics can claim. Finally, a black velour curtain positively *eats* unwanted spill light, making it the cleanest, sharpest masking drape available. It is no accident that velour has been the fabric of choice for stage draperies for decades. All of this wonderfulness comes at a price, however. Velour is one of the most expensive fabrics available for stage drapes, and one of the heaviest. A properly sewn velour grand drape can weigh hundreds of pounds and is not something you want to put up and take down on a regular basis.

Duvateen is another commonly used drapery fabric, but it is only really good for temporary uses. Although it is cheaper and lighter than velour, it is not very durable and doesn't hang in folds as well. The **nap** side is a pretty good light-eater though, so it is often used to cover openings in the scenery where a full drape is unnecessary or unavailable, say, behind a door where the audience can just catch a glimpse of the backstage area. Keep a roll of duvateen around to tear pieces off when you need a little bit of fabric to solve a masking problem.

There are literally hundreds of other fabrics that can be used for draperies. Velour and duvateen mark the rough boundaries of the choices, both in beauty and price. Anything more expensive than velour is too expensive for the stage. Anything cheaper than duvateen probably will not hold up. Other fabrics will be a trade-off between price on the one hand and thickness, durability, and attractiveness on the other. Talk to your theatrical dealer and look at samples. Make sure you hold the samples up in front of a lamp. You shouldn't be able to see any light through them.

Besides draperies, there are lots of other uses for fabric on stage. Covering a flat with a decorative fabric is an easy solution if you don't want to paint it. Many fabrics also add three-dimensional texture to walls, something a two-dimensional paint job can't always do.

Erosion cloth, which landscapers use to cover newly seeded areas, is a loosely woven mesh of twinelike threads. It is usually light tan, and looks sort of raglike and medieval on stage. You can use it for backdrops, ground texture, or anything else that you want to look beaten-up and lowlife-like. One hint: After you pick it up from the landscape supplier, hang it up outside and beat it with a stick to get some of the dust and dirt off before you bring it inside.

Felt is a cheap way to make a wall look snazzy. Felt comes in lots of colors and in several widths. **Industrial felt**, by the way, is a heavier weight of felt that can be used to make props and hats.

A good theatrical supplier will also carry a line of **designer fabrics**, many of which are put out by our friends at Rosco Labs. They range from the glamorous to the cheesy and are worth taking a look at, especially if your show tends toward the Vegas look. These fabrics also tend toward the expensive side, so consider combining them with something less pricey, like duvateen or felt.

Paint

Scenic artists are not housepainters, at least not by profession. Painting your house is a completely different task than painting a mystical Shanghai sunrise or a dark Parisian cathedral or an Oklahoma prairie with corn as high as an elephant's eye. Consequently, scenic painters don't use house paint; they use **scenic paint.** First of all, the paint at the hardware store doesn't come in the vibrant colors that scenic painters need. Eggshell blue doesn't cut it for Ariel's undersea grotto. You need rich, mysterious, forty-fathoms-down blue. Not many people want their living room that color, though, so Home Depot doesn't stock it.

Household paint also doesn't dilute well. This is important because sometimes scenic artists need thin washes of paint that will tint, but not obscure, the surface underneath. In some cases, they actually need the painted surface to be translucent, like a scrim or a backlit wall. Scenic paint also needs to be completely "flat," that is, without any shine or sheen, which can be distracting to the audience.

Finally, hardware-store paint doesn't stay supple when it is painted on a soft surface, like a drop or a drape. Want an exercise in frustration? Paint a drop with household paint, let it dry, then fold it up and stick it in storage for a year. When you pull it out, prepare yourself for an avalanche of paint chips that have worked loose from the fabric. Scenic paint is designed to be flexible, even after it dries.

Scenic paint falls into three general categories: **analine dye** (which isn't actually paint), **"saturated" paint**, and **casein paint.**

Analine dyes don't get much use in scene shops these days, for reasons that I'll explain in a minute, but they are such a part of theatrical tradition that I can't resist a quick once-over. Besides, you might still run into them.

The difference between a dye and a paint is in how the liquid interacts with the fabric. Paint will bind itself to the threads of fabric, but still remain on the surface, while dye will actually invade the threads themselves and change their color. Paints can be washed out (with varying degrees of difficulty, depending on the type), but dye is forever. The big advantage of dyes is transparency. Because dyes color the threads themselves, rather than filling up all the space between them, you can use them on translucent or transparent drops. If you use full-strength paint on a scrim, it will become opaque.

Why don't we use analine dyes anymore? They are messy and toxic and expensive, for one thing. The other thing is the appearance of highly dilutable paints, like Rosco's Supersaturated paint, that are so rich with pigment you can dilute them with water up to twenty to one, making them thin enough to use on a translucent drop. Saturated paint is cheaper than dye, easier to work with, and washes out with water, so there you are.

Dyes are still heavily used in the costume world, however, where even scenic paint will flake off fabrics when they are worn or washed.

Saturated paints are based on a binding agent, like acrylic polymer or polymer resin, that is "saturated" with a large amount of powdered artist's pigment. Because there is so much pigment in the paint, you can add a lot of water and still have strong colors. These paints are more expensive than hardware-store paint, but keep in mind that diluting a gallon of saturated paint with a gallon of water has almost no effect on the color. Thus you can extend one gallon into two and cut the price in half without even breathing hard.

The third kind of paint, casein paint (pronounced kay-SEEN), is known in the art world as "fresco" paint, because it has to be used when it is fresh. Casein paint is based on a soy protein binder, which will actually go bad, just like the tofu in your refrigerator. An unopened can will last one to two years, depending on the brand, while an opened one will spoil in one to four months depending on the temperature. Once it spoils, fuhgeddaboudit, it's dead. Even though casein is an expensive paint, people still bother with it because, when it comes to rich color and supple flexibility, nothing else can touch it.

If you do get in a pinch and have to go to the hardware store, go armed with a sample of the color you want. Show the clerk and tell her you want the cheapest "flat latex" that they have. "Flat" means it won't reflect light. This is very important on stage. "Latex" means you can wash out your brushes with water. "Cheap" means it won't last five years, but so what?

Painting is not just about color, however. Sometimes painting is about adding texture to a surface, or protecting it from harm, or making it shiny, or making it not slippery. Paint treatments can do all of these things when applied properly.

Adding Texture to a Surface

This is usually done by adding some sort of material directly to the paint and then rolling it on. Sawdust works pretty well and you can't beat the price, but the best stuff is *stucco patching powder* (get it at the hardware store). This powder is used by commercial painters to patch stucco walls that have been plastered over and need to have their texture restored. It comes in three levels of coarseness, depending on how much texture you want. It is hard to get too much texture on stage, so go for the coarsest one. Stir it into the paint (follow the directions for amounts!) and roller it onto your flats. You will need two or three times as much paint to cover the same area so get extra. Get the really thick roller pads for this job (two-inch-thick nap).

Protecting a surface (such as a painted stage floor) is best done with clear acrylic glaze (a theatrical supplier will have it) or urethane. Urethane is a good deal tougher, but as for washing up the rollers afterwards . . . you might as well throw them out. It also takes longer to dry. Acrylic will take several coats over several days to really be strong and scuff-proof. Both acrylic and urethane come in gloss, semigloss, or flat. Get the flat, unless you want the floor to shine and reflect light. Talk to the lighting designer before you create a glossy floor. He will have to make changes in how he lights it, so the audience won't go blind from the glare.

For a truly Fred-Astaire, get-out-your-top-hat floor, use glossy urethane, which should be rolled onto the floor just like you would paint the walls in your home. There are lots of different varieties, so talk to the folks at the paint store. I used one kind that was marketed as "gym floor urethane," which produced the most incredible gloss I have ever seen. Get the opinion of the folks who sell the stuff before buying. As stated previously, if you use urethane, plan on throwing the rollers out, unless you want to spend the evening up to your elbows in paint thinner. Trust me, you would rather be watching Letterman.

Getting rid of slippery surfaces. Plywood, masonite, and other common floor coverings are often slippery when first installed, so try to get them painted before you rehearse on them. This can be a problem, especially if you are in a situation where the technicians are building the set during the day and you are coming in for rehearsal in the evening. One night you will come in and the floor will look beautiful—wonderfully smooth and shiny with a brand new layer of raw masonite on it. Watch it! That stuff is very slippery and dangerous. Anyone in stocking feet or ballet slippers *will* fall. Try to find out ahead of time when the new covering will be put on the stage and then do everything possible to see that it gets a coat of paint before you rehearse on it. This is a sticky logistical problem for everybody, since the floor will need several hours to dry. It may mean rehearsing somewhere else that night. After all, paint crews are famous for coming to work in the middle of the night, but they're not famous for liking it.

Real Things: Doors, Windows, and So On

Okay, time for an exercise. Get your tape measure (you do have one by now, right?), take this book, and get up from wherever you are. Spend a few minutes walking around your house (your office, your friend's house, your cave, wherever you are right now) looking at each door that you pass. What's it made of? How big is it? Are there windows in it? Is there a doorsill across the bottom or is it smooth? Where is the knob? How many hinges are there? Which side are they on? Does the door swing into the room or out? Or is it a sliding door? A rolling door? A folding one? What do the locks look like? What other kind of hardware does it have? A peephole? A mail slot?

Take some time to get familiar with the doors that you encounter. Go through the questions above to remind yourself what you are looking for. Remember to *measure* each one. It is going to become increasingly important for you to become sensitive to how big things are, because technicians are going to constantly ask you, "How big do you want that to be?" and it will just impress the doggies out of them if you have a precise answer.

Once you have looked at the doors in your home, broaden your research. You don't have to go to the library, or buy a lot of copies of *Architectural Digest*. As you go through your day, just try to become aware of what kind of doors you go through.

And what about windows? They have just as much variety. They push up like sashes, swing out like casements, and slide open like French doors. Some of them are even round, for God's sake. Take your tape measure to a few, just to get an idea.

What's the point? The point is, if you are going to put replicas of real things on stage, you better take some time and start looking at what real things *look like*. Nothing is more valuable in the theater than the ability to keenly perceive the world in all its aspects: mentally, emotionally, and physically. There are people in the world who can help you with the first two. I'm here to help with the third one. And although it may seem like an inconsequential thing to you, a little awareness of the infinite variety of everyday items like doors and windows can go a long way toward creating something beautiful on stage.

Designing and building doors and windows is a complicated process for two reasons: First, as I said, doors come in almost infinite varieties and finding the right one takes some effort, and second, because they are **practical**, that is, they have to really work. "Practical" is a general term for anything, from a faucet to a window, that is actually operated by a performer. Building something that has to work is a great deal different (and more expensive) than building something that is only decorative.

When you tell a technician that you want a door or a window, here's what he will want to know:

- *Is it "practical"?* Does it have to open and close or is it only decorative? A window that is built "nonpractical" is completely different than a practical one. A practical one is much more complex and expensive, so designating a window as nonpractical can save a lot of time and money. Unfortunately, once the window is built nonpractical, it cannot be changed without rebuilding the entire piece so, if you are in doubt, have them built practical. The worst thing that can happen is that the practical windows sit there unused during the run, a fact that won't make the guys in the shop happy, but they'll get over it. Of course, if you waste their efforts fairly frequently, they may stop asking you and start nailing the windows shut, so try and do your homework and give them the right information to start with.

Fig. 8. Different ways to hang a door

- *What kind of door is it?* As I said, there are lots of choices here: swinging, double, rolling, sliding, folding, screen, French, barn-style, Cross and Bible, the list goes on and on. This is where you really benefit from your research. You don't have to know them all (there are thousands), but the more you know, the more the tech people can help you. When working with a set designer, try looking through some architectural books and magazines for doors and windows that fit your ideas for the show.

- *How big is it?* Standard household doors are about two-feet-six-inches wide by six-feet-eight-inches high (have you measured yours yet?), but there is a great deal of variety out there. Doors were smaller in older houses, but that was partly because the people were smaller, so you may not wish to duplicate them exactly. You may also want to consider wider doors to accommodate period dresses, men with swords, actors in soap bubble costumes, whatever.

- *If it is a swinging door, which side are the hinges on, and which way does it swing?* This is a really important question for everybody. A general rule is that *doors open up and off.* This means that the hinges are on the upstage side, and the door opens toward offstage. A door hinged on the upstage side will cover the sight lines better, and a door that opens offstage will not block an actor entering. Of course, you may decide to break this rule for some reason—a murder scene where an unidentified arm reaches out from behind the door with a pistol, that sort of thing— but as a general rule it holds. Which way the door swings also determines whether the door has to be "finished," that is, painted and decorated, on one side or both sides.

- *What does it look like?* This is where the designer really comes in, but as I said, the more you know . . . Does it have a window in it? What kind of doorknobs? Plain or ornate? You get the idea.

- *What kind of abuse will it get?* Any carpenter worth her tool belt can build a stage door that can be closed good and hard, but I know a lot of carpenters who have seen their hard work slammed to smithereens because they weren't warned ahead of time that the door would have to put up with that kind of abuse. Actors can get very physical on stage and technicians can certainly accommodate them, but the shop needs to be told ahead of time what is expected. Saying, "By the way, Nora is really going to slam that door hard at the end," can save a lot of tech-week grumbling.

Moving Stuff Around: Gripping, Rolling, and Flying

Some of the time, your scenery will have to move during the play. In general, don't move something unless you have to but, if you have to, make sure that you take the time to decide which moving technique is most appropriate. No matter how beautiful your scenery is, if the audience has time to read the entire program between scenes, the effect of the show will be lost. A slick, well-choreographed scene change, however, can add life and vitality to a show, keeping the pace and emotion alive from scene to scene. When you think about moving scenery, keep asking yourself this question: "What is the fastest, smoothest way to get from this scene to that scene?"

Fast and smooth doesn't always mean elaborate or expensive. In fact, it often means just the obvious. In a world of motors, hydraulics, flying hardware, and automation, remember the scenic adage: *There's no tech like low tech.*

As suggested by the title of this section, scenery-moving techniques fall into three categories: **rolling** (moving horizontally on wheels), **flying** (moving vertically on cables), and **gripping** (moving in any direction in the hands of a technician). Before we discuss the specifics of each technique, let's decide which one we need. Here are some questions to help you decide which way to go:

- *Do you mind seeing technicians?* This is a stylistic question, and must be answered by the director. We depend on the audience's willingness to suspend their disbelief, and that willingness can be taxed by the sight of a technician gripping something offstage, even during a darkened scene change. On the other hand, let's not sell the audience short. The audience knows that they are sitting in a theater and they know that there are technicians backstage, so seeing one is not going to explode anybody's myth about what's really going on. Stylistically, however, during emotionally intense shows, it may be better not to force the audience to disconnect from the story. A visible technician may have that effect.

  Sometimes, the scene change can be choreographed into the show and the crew can be given costumes (be sure to warn your costume designer early on). This is particularly effective in big musicals, large-scale period pieces such as the Shakespearean plays, and musical revues. If you want the scene change to be truly "magic," however, and you don't want to see the crew, then you will almost certainly need rolling and flying scenery that is operated from offstage.
- *What kind of a theater do you have?* It doesn't make sense to spend a lot of time talking about lifting scenery up when you don't have a flying

system or a fly space. Or storing it backstage when you don't have any wing space. Go take a look at the theater and talk to the technicians. Go through chapter 2 and answer as many of the questions about touring a new space as you can. Pay particular attention to what kind of machinery is hanging overhead, and how much wing space is available.

- *How big is the scenery?* There is a limit to how big a piece you can fly. Flying systems are generally set up with lots of pipes, or **battens**, hanging parallel to the proscenium arch, which means that they are very good at picking up scenery that is also hanging parallel to the arch, like drops. There have been a lot of attempts over the years to design more flexible flying systems, but all of their cleverness and flexibility has faded before a tough reality of show business: There is rarely enough time to make an entirely different setup for every production. In order to survive the pressures of money, time, and space, we live by standardization, and standardization means that battens are parallel to the proscenium. What you can fly also depends on how much space you have available above the stage.

  Remember, you have to have storage space overhead for anything that flies out. If you have a thirty-foot-high drop, you must have thirty feet available to put it in when it flies out. There are tricks that technicians use for folding, or **tripping**, scenery as it flies out, but those tricks can be complicated and time-consuming.

- *How fast does the scenery have to move?* Flying is hands-down the fastest way to move scenery, so if speed is the greatest concern, think about taking the scenery up in the air.

- *How heavy is it?* There is a limit to the weight that a flying system can handle. There is also a limit to what a technician can move by gripping so, if your scenery is very heavy, consider rolling. Once in my life, I supervised the flying of an actual covered wagon, and I will never, *ever* try it again. Flying scenery should be *light*.

- *What's the big picture?* All of your decisions about moving scenery will be affected by other, larger concerns. How is the show designed as a whole? What other pieces are moving and how? Is this show part of a rotating repertory, where sets for other shows must be stored and played on in the same theater?

Gripping

Gripping scenery means just what it sounds like: Somebody walks out onstage, grips the scenery in her own hands and moves it. We spend a lot of time in the design process devising magic movements of scenery, trying to

Fig. 9. Walking up a flat

impress the audience with our cleverness, but it is not always necessary. Human beings are remarkably adaptable, capable creatures and they should be used whenever possible. I have spent countless hours devising effects, only to see the machinery get replaced with a stagehand walking out and picking up the scenery. Once again, *There's no tech like low tech.*

Of course, gripping scenery is not without pitfalls. If you follow these simple rules, however, you can enjoy years of trouble-free gripping.

Walking up a flat (lifting it up to a vertical position) is a basic skill that every show person should know. First, tip the flat up onto its long side. Then, one person **foots** the flat by pushing his foot against the bottom corner, while the other person lifts the other end of the flat and walks toward the first person, lifting the flat higher and higher as she walks. The first person's foot keeps the flat from skittering away, and before you know it, the flat is upright.

Carrying a flat is just as simple but it has a critical rule, known among my friends as "Bernie's rule," since we all learned it from Bernie Works, the all-knowing teacher of technical theater at the University of Illinois, Urbana-Champaign. Professor Works is legendary the world over for his constant invocation of the phrase: "One hand high, one hand low! That's what makes the scenery go!" Each person should reach up as high as possible with one hand and as low as possible with the other. Furthermore, you and your partner should mirror one another. If you have your left hand high, then your partner should reach up with his right. If you both reach as high and as low as you can, and you mirror one another, you can move surprisingly tall flats with little trouble.

Beyond these simple rules, gripping scenery is a matter of common sense, but since we all know that common sense is not so common, here are some things to remember:

- Lift with your legs, not with your back.
- When you have to change direction, turn your whole body. *Don't twist.*

- Get enough people. Don't be a hero. Heroes sit around discussing old wars when they get old because they don't have the muscles left to do anything else. Stay young, stay mobile, get someone to help you.

Rolling

What if your scenery is too big or too heavy to grip? Answer: Consider using mankind's second oldest tool (after the flashlight): the wheel.

First, let's get our terms straight. A rolling scenic unit is called a **wagon** and the rolling thing you attach to make the wagon move is called a **castor**, not a wheel. A castor contains a wheel as one of its parts, but the whole piece of equipment is called a castor.

Castors come in lots of shapes and sizes, from the small furniture castors on a rolling desk chair to the giant ones underneath your garbage dumpster, but there are two distinct groups of them: **swivel** (also called rotating), and **straight-run** (also called fixed). The difference is just what it sounds like: The swivel ones are free to rotate and turn in any direction, while the straight ones are locked down and will not rotate. Stage techs often refer to swivel castors as "smart" castors (I guess because they can head off in any direction they choose), while straight castors are called "stupid" castors (because they can only move forward and backward).

Wagons can use straight-run (fixed, "stupid") castors if they only have to move forward and backward. This is called, not surprisingly, a **straight-run wagon**, and it is the easiest type of wagon to use because it addresses both of the two major problems with using wagons onstage: getting them to go where you want them to go, and getting them to stay there. Straight-run wagons, since they are relatively incapable of moving from side to side, are the easiest to steer into place. They roll out, they roll back. End of story. They are also easier to keep in one place, since you only have to keep them from moving in two directions: forward and back. Straight-run wagons some-times have a metal blade, called a **knife**, which sticks down into a groove in the floor to keep the wagon on track.

Next time you go to a professionally produced, Broadway-style musical, take a look at the floor. Unless you're seeing *The Fantastiks* (the simplest musical ever produced), the floor will probably be crisscrossed with slots. These are the tracks that the wagons will be following. Try predicting where the wagons will end up. Amaze your friends.

Unlike straight-run castors, swivel castors can move in any direction you want. The bad news is, they can move in any direction *they* want. They are more difficult to drive and more difficult to keep in one place, but they offer you more flexibility.

You can also consider using both types of castors on the wagon, swivel

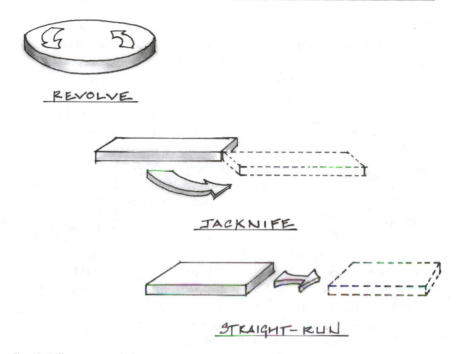

Fig. 10. Different ways platforms move

castors on one end, and straight-run on the other. This produces a wagon that is only steerable on one end, like your car. Wagons sometimes have this combination for the same reason that your car does: It is easier to steer a platform that only has rotating castors on one end. Unlike your car, though, a wagon should have the rotating castors on the rear, not on the front. This makes the platform easier to steer when being pushed from the back, particularly when maneuvering in tight spaces.

There are other kinds of rolling wagons that show up from time to time. Some shows switch back and forth quickly between scenes, and each of those scenes requires a full-stage set. For this situation, one rather expensive solution is the turntable, or **revolve**. Revolves require a major scenic commitment: Difficult and expensive to construct, they are notorious for bogging down tech rehearsals and breaking down at key moments. Nevertheless, there is a time and a place for them, so long as you have the money and, most important, the knowledgeable staff to handle them.

Of course, revolves don't have to take up the whole stage. They don't even have to be a full circle. One special kind of revolve pivots around one end: a **jackknife platform**. Some sadistic designers even put revolves in the middle of other revolves, but now we're getting out of hand.

Flying

As I said earlier, flying scenery goes back to the sailors who were brought in to rig the Italian Renaissance theaters in the 1500s. Actually, it goes back even further than that: right back to the Greek theater a thousand years before Christ. Some Greek plays ended with the entrance of a god who appeared to magically untangle whatever knots the mortals had tied themselves up in. These gods often entered in a large scenic machine, called a *machina*. Basically, they were lifted over the back of the scenery in giant hand-operated cranes, an effect called the **deus ex machina** (literally, a "god from a machine"). The phrase survives today as a term describing any late-entering character who comes with near-divine powers to punish injustice and repeal injury.

The actual machinery that we use today, however, is descended from the Renaissance. The sailors designed a system, known today as a **hemp flying system**, which was extremely flexible and survived well into this century. In fact, it is still used today in a few theaters. The hemp system consisted of hemp rope lines running from the scenery up over pulleys, which are sitting on a grid high above the stage. The lines traveled across the grid, went over more pulleys, and then dropped down to the stage level where they were attached to sandbags and tied off to the **pin rail**. The sandbags provided weight to counterbalance the scenery so that it could be pulled up and down without difficulty. The hemp system was so flexible because the pulleys could easily be moved around and ropes could be dropped just about anywhere. Once all the ropes for a given piece of scenery were brought up to the grid and down to the pin rail, they were all tied together and attached to sandbags. The sandbags provided counterbalancing weight, allowing the stagehands to pull up very heavy scenery with less effort.

The problems with hemp systems were twofold. First, all that hemp rope had a tendency to stretch out, so things had to be readjusted all the time. If the theater was dark for a couple of days, all the lines had to be carefully tied off to prevent slippage. (Theater trivia note: All of this tying-off led to the creation of a special knot called a "Sunday," used to tie off the lines after the Sunday show, the theater being dark on Monday night. The term persists today—if a stage tech wants you to tie off a line temporarily, he will ask you to "put a Sunday" on it.)

The second problem with the hemp system was that it required highly skilled operators. Even with the best technicians, accidents still happened. (How many murder mysteries have you seen where the tenor is offed by a sandbag?) The problem was knots. A hemp system required the constant tying and untying of many different kinds of knots. Knot tying was a life-or-death skill to Renaissance sailors and they knew what they were doing. In the modern theater, however, a properly tied bowline knot is as rare as a clean-shaven poet. In the absence of this skill, hemp becomes a dangerous, accident-prone system. Furthermore, even well-treated rope degrades over time, becoming brittle and weak.

The first thing that had to happen, therefore, was a switch from rope to a stronger, more durable material: **aircraft cable**, so called because that was the main use for it before theater came along. This switch, however, meant rethinking and redesigning the entire system. After all, cable couldn't be tied and untied all the time; it had to be permanently attached. And what about all those sandbags? How could weight be attached to the system without endangering anyone? It took some time, but, in the end, the thinkers and designers came up with what most theaters in this country use today: the **counterweight flying system**.

Conceptually, the counterweight system is built on the same idea as the hemp system: Tie a line to the scenery, send it up over a pulley, across the grid, over another pulley, and down to an operator who attaches some sort of counterbalancing weight to it. How all of that is accomplished, however, is substantially different.

First of all, the scenery is attached to a **batten**. This batten is lifted up by a group of cables called the **pickup lines**. Okay, get it out of your system: You always thought that a theatrical pickup line was something like, "Is this a dagger I see before my hand, or are you just happy to see me?" Small theaters may have only three pickup lines, a larger one as many as seven. All these lines go up to the grid where, as in the hemp system, they go over pulleys, travel across the grid, and then turn downward. Instead of sandbags, however, the lines attach to an **arbor**, a metal cage that travels up and down on a track. Rather than tying off sandbags to the lines, the technicians just pile **counterweights** (also known as **bricks**) into the arbor to counterbalance the weight. The battens and the pulleys that go with them are installed in permanent locations, and the arbor slides up and down a permanently installed track. No knots to tie and no rope to stretch.

There are two places, called **rails**, where the technicians go to operate a counterweight flying system. In a hemp system, the ropes were tied off at a **pin rail** off to the side of the stage. When the piece was first rigged, the call of "Meat to the Rail" went out, and everybody hauled out the piece. When the scenery was in the air, the sandbags were attached at ground level.

As the cables and arbors of the counterweight system were appearing, so was another innovation: the **loading rail**. Rather than bring the arbor to the technicians, the technicians now go to the arbor, climbing up to the grid while the batten is still on the floor.

Safety Alert! While loading bricks into an arbor is less dangerous than using a hemp system, even the best technician gets sweaty hands now and then. When weights are being loaded above, keep everybody out from underneath the loading rail! Before loading weights, the technician above should shout, "Clear the rail!" Once everyone is safely out of the way, the technician in charge underneath should shout, "Rail clear!" Only then should loading begin. The rail should remain clear until the technician above yells, "Loading complete!" Stay alert! A forty-pound counterweight dropped from the grid will go through you, the floor, and anything else between it and bedrock.

Once the weights have been loaded, the lines are actually operated from the pin rail, now renamed the **lock rail** because it holds the locks that keep the scenery from moving at the wrong time.

While cable has replaced rope on all the weight-bearing lines in a counterweight system, it is not much fun to grab onto. So, hemp rope is still found in one place: on the **purchase line**. "Purchase" is a strange word in the theater—it shows up all over the place. Besides the meaning everybody is used

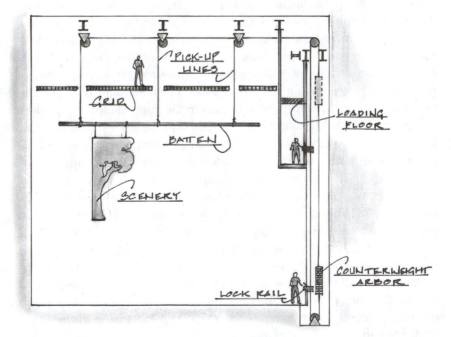

Fig. 11. A counterweight system

Dear Old Dad

Shift Plot

SHIFT A	FROM OFFICE TO PARK
Tim (fly rail)	1. (after Dean latches door) fly out wall #1
	2. (after platform C clears) fly in trees #1
Denise (fly rail)	1. fly out wall #2
	2. (after platform B clears) fly in trees #2
Valerie (stage right)	1. remove table unit stage right
	2. remove two dining room chairs stage right
	3. remove wing chair (with Craig)
Kirsten (stage left)	1. remove backing wall
	2. set rock unit stage left (with Dean)
Dean (stage left)	1. latch door on wall unit #1
	2. set rock unit stage left (with Kirsten)
Craig (stage right)	1. remove sink unit
	2. remove wing chair (with Valerie)
	3. clear books from floor
	4. set kite and blanket

Fig. 12. The shift plot

to—heading for the mall with a credit card—it also means being able to hold on to something. If you can "get purchase" on a line, you can grab it hard enough to pull it. The purchase line, then, is the part of the counterweight system that you actually grab onto and pull. The purchase line is attached to the bottom of the arbor, so when you pull down on it, the arbor comes down as well. Since the arbor is coming down, the scenery will start going up and voilà! You're flying.

The purchase line is not just attached to the bottom of the arbor, though. It is actually a loop from the bottom of the arbor, down through your hand, through the lock, through a pulley on the floor, back to the grid, and down to the top of the arbor.

This setup means that the counterweight system can do one trick that the hemp system couldn't: It can pull the scenery *down* as easily as it can pull it *up*, even if the counterbalancing weight is not exactly right. With the hemp system, the counterbalance had to be kept a little lighter than the scenery. Otherwise, when the scenery flew out, it wouldn't come back in. When you look at the lock rail on a counterweight system, however, you should see *two* ropes, one in back of the other. The *back* one is hanging from the arbor, so pulling that one brings the arbor down (and the scenery up). The *front* one is attached to the top of the arbor, so pulling that one brings the arbor up (and the scenery down). The rule is, *the front rope does whatever the scenery does*. If the front rope is going up, so is the scenery, and vice versa. Still can't keep it straight? Try this: "The *F*ront rope *F*ollows the scenery."

The whole kit and caboodle—batten, lines, sheaves, arbor, and purchase line—is called a **line set**. Technicians often talk about the capacity of a flying system in terms of how many line sets it has: the more line sets, the more individual things that can be flown.

The Backstage Survival Guide to Scene-Change Choreography

Gripping, rolling, and flying are all possibilities when moving scenery around. No matter how you have it set up, though, you still need to take some time before tech rehearsal to work out who does what and when they do it. All this information should appear on a shift plot, like the one shown in figure 12.

Scene changes don't just happen: They require planning, forethought, and as much choreography as a dance number, especially if they are done *a vista*, or in front of the audience. Here then, are some things to remember when choreographing your scene change:

- *Try not to use the actors.* People are often tempted to get away with fewer technicians by having the actors move scenery around, but I try to talk them out of it. Having actors involved in a scene change can lead to mistakes. Actors aren't stupid, just preoccupied. After all, they have a lot to think about—lines to remember, characters to develop, movements to perform—all the time trying not to bump into the furniture and wondering if they remembered to zip their fly. I say, whenever possible, let the actors be the actors and let the crew be the crew. The exception? Actors with one-line, walk-on parts. Scene changes keep them from getting bored.
- *In general, move flying things first and last.* The order should be: Old flying scenery goes out, then old rolling and gripped scenery goes out,

then new rolling and gripped scenery comes in, then new flying scenery comes in. This way, the flying scenery is clear of the rolling scenery and the moving people for as long as possible, making it less likely that something will get tangled or somebody will get bopped on the head.

- *Don't run.* Speed is important, but so are accuracy and safety. With practice, a good crew will achieve a swift yet controlled speed that never appears rushed, but gets the job done quickly. If your scene change is *a vista,* keep something happening onstage all the time. A well-choreographed shift can be a treat for an audience, giving them a "behind the scenes" feeling and, if the shift is really clever, adding to the magic of the show. If you are going to do it, though, give the audience something to watch throughout the shift. If there is nothing visible happening onstage, the audience will think the shift is over. When the action doesn't start right away, they will get impatient.

- *Never have anyone onstage doing nothing.* An extension of the previous rule. Even if someone has to wait for something else to happen before they can do their job, have them wait in the wings. An idle person onstage makes the audience wonder: "Why is he just *standing* there?"

- *Don't take too long.* Obviously, make it as short as possible. As a general rule, get your shift down to under thirty seconds. That's still a long time, but an audience will sit still for that, especially if they can watch (and you have music playing). If you are doing a musical and have a pit orchestra to play during the shift, you can get away with a little bit more time, but if the shift goes over a minute, you'd better be prepared to sell popcorn (if not drinks) between scenes.

- *Be sensitive to the pace and the subject matter of the show.* This one is best illustrated by a story. One of the worst scenic mistakes I ever made was during a show called *For Benson, at the Height of His Career,* an original musical for which I designed scenery at Brown University. Toward the end of the show there was a funeral scene, complete with an ornate black casket on a marble slab center stage. The next scene was down left in a pool of light, where a narrator spoke, tying up the last threads of the show. During the narrator's monologue, the stage had to clear completely, since he was supposed to exit through the now-empty stage. The casket was big and bulky, but not too heavy. Since we did not want to see technicians onstage during the show, I decided to fly the whole thing out, slab and all. It sounded like a fine idea during the build and even through tech week. It wasn't until the resounding laugh from the audience on opening night that we realized that the sight of the casket "flying up to heaven" after the funeral just wasn't going to work. So, be aware of the moments before and after the shift as well as the general pacing of the show. You don't want to come on like gangbusters when the next scene is a lullaby.

- *Use your intermissions.* They are gold mines of time—at least ten minutes when the audience is not really paying attention. You can also get away with making more noise during intermission. Don't just think about the next scene, either. Use the intermission to set up anything else that you can. Playwrights, take note: If you must have huge scene changes, put the biggest one during intermission. Whether or not you are the scene-change choreographer, here's one rule that everybody in the theater should pay attention to:
  - *If it doesn't work at first, don't freak out.* It always requires several tries to get it right, and the shift will get faster every time. The crew and their chief should constantly be on the lookout for ways to speed things up:
    + Is somebody standing around for a moment with nothing to do?
    + Could something move faster if an obstacle were removed?
    + Would it work better to do things in a different order?
    + Could things that travel together be attached to each other?
    + What else can we do ahead of time?
    + How about attaching wheels to something that's being gripped?
    + Can any offstage changes be put off until after the scene starts?
- *Listen to the crew,* right down to the lowest ASM. They may have suggestions that will speed things up. Most of all, remember, there is not a crew in the world who will do it perfectly the first time, and some of them won't even come close. With practice, however, speed will probably increase dramatically. So, if it looks impossible at first, don't despair. Take a deep breath. This is fun.

Playing with the Audience: Special Effects and Illusions

Just in case you haven't yet picked up my feelings on the matter so far, let me say as clearly as I can here: There is no greater effect than a well-crafted script and no greater illusion than fine acting. No amount of fog or fire or strobe lights will ever save you if the basic show itself is faulty. So, don't look in this chapter for quick fixes, and for God's sake, don't *start* here. This stuff is the frosting. Make sure your cake is more than half-baked before you start choosing the decorations.

Now that I have that out of my system, there are several simple effects that people can (and do) use all the time.

Magic Disappearances

When it's time for Dracula to make his exit in a puff of smoke and a whir of bat wings, it is probably time for a **counterweight trap**. This nifty little device is a small lift, or trap, built into the stage and painted to match the rest of the floor. Under the stage is an arbor full of weight that matches the actor's weight. The lift and the arbor are mounted on either end of a long lever, which can be easily moved up and down when the actor is on board. If the effect is a disappearance, the actor steps onto the lift onstage, the lock is removed and the stagehand moves the lever so the weight goes up and the actor comes down. The actor steps off the lift, it flies back up to seal the hole in the stage and is locked in place. Alternatively, another panel can slide in from the side to fill the hole in the stage. It can all happen very fast and, with a puff of smoke and a light cue, the audience will never know what hit 'em. Obviously, for a magic *appearance*, you do the reverse.

Note that a counterweight trap can be hazardous to your health, so it should only be constructed by experienced technicians.

Fire

Real flames, like real running water, seem to have an almost magical effect on an audience. It is almost as if, up until the flame is lit, the audience has just been playing along, like benevolent parents. Suddenly, the real flame appears and the audience realizes that the kids weren't just playing around: They actually put something *real* on stage.

Real fire on stage can range from a single candle to giant propane-fired torches. Unfortunately, I can't go into much depth in this area because of the great differences in fire regulations throughout the country. What is acceptable in one state may be unheard of in another. When I went to work at Seattle Rep, I was amazed to see a prop brazier on stage with flames a foot high jumping out of it. In Illinois, where I attended grad school, any flame at all (even a candle) required a fire inspector's visit and a crew member stationed on each side with a fire extinguisher. Local fire laws and their application are usually a function of history. If the theater business in a particular area has a good safety record, fire laws tend to be more relaxed. If, however, there has been a large disaster in the past, the laws (and the inspectors) are a good deal tougher. In 1903, the Iroquois Theater fire killed over a thousand people in Chicago, causing all of that state's fire laws to be strengthened. Even now, over a century later, the fear of another disaster remains deeply rooted in the local consciousness.

The reader should not interpret the above, however, to mean that fire safety should only be maintained to the limit of local regulation. On the contrary, it is up to us to protect the performers and the audience at all times. If you are thinking about using a flame on stage, contact the local fire authorities to find out what the regulations are. Any time a flame is used, fire extinguishers should be readily available on both sides of the stage, with crew members standing by them.

In any case, it is highly recommended that you maintain a positive relationship with your local fire department inspectors. Remember, they do have the ability to shut you down, a possibility that should not be taken lightly. More than that, though, you should consider this relationship to be a partnership, the outcome of which should be the safety of everyone in the theater. There is no compelling reason whatsoever to put performers or audience in a potentially dangerous situation and the fire department can help you avoid doing that.

If you make the very logical decision to fake a fire effect on stage, there are several ways to go. Silk flames are a longtime theatrical tradition. This effect is created by tying pieces of red and yellow silk to a fan buried in a fireplace. When the fan blows the silk up in the air, the effect is rather remarkable, particularly if you light them from beneath. Disney has been using this effect in the *Pirates of the Caribbean* ride for almost fifty years. There are several lighting-effect companies that market commercial forms of this effect as well.

If you just want to fake the light coming from a fire, you can invest in a **flicker generator** a nifty little device that flashes red, white, and yellow lamps in a random series, creating a believable flicker that makes you want to get out the bearskin rug. This effect can also be created by combining several chase effects on a computer lighting console.

Look in chapter 5 ("Lighting Design") for other ways to fake firelight.

Smoke and Fog

I treat these two different effects together because they are so often confused with each other. When theater people say "smoke," they mean something that hangs in the air; fairly evenly distributed throughout the stage. When they say "fog," they are talking about a colder-than-air substance that hugs the ground. Smoke rises and fills the air while fog stays on the ground. The two effects require different processes to create.

Smoke is fairly easy. Rent or buy a commercial **smoke machine**, fill it with fluid (often, confusingly, called "fog juice"), plug it in, wait for it to heat up, and then push the button. Whoosh! Smoke fills the air. Smoke machines come in different sizes, and they are rated by how many cubic feet of smoke they put out. For most applications, a 1500 smoke machine will be adequate, unless you want a *lot* of smoke. There are smoke machines large enough to fill a gymnasium, but these are used more often to train firefighters than for the stage.

If you are using a smoke machine, make sure you allow yourself enough time to let it warm up. Some machines take up to an hour to really get up to speed, but for most, ten to twenty minutes should be adequate. Make sure you test the machine in rehearsal with all of your air-handling equipment (heating, ventilation, air conditioning) operating as they will be during the show and with all the stage lights on. Lamentably, between the ventilation blowing through the house and the hot lights over the stage, smoke has a tendency in most theaters to flow out into the audience. You may want to consider using fans to keep it on stage, or even a low-tech solution like a stagehand waving a sheet of cardboard in the wings. Also, try opening a few doors backstage. Experiment. Adjust the airflow any way you can until the smoke goes where you want it to. Most machines also let you alter the rate at which smoke comes out, so play with that as well. Smoke is tricky stuff sometimes, and it can have a mind of its own. Of course, when you get a full audience of people in the theater, the smoke may decide to go someplace else entirely. Be aware that, even though stage smoke is not toxic, there is a strong psychological reaction that causes many people to cough when smoke rolls over them. If you let a large billow go out into the house, you may be treated to the sound of a chain smoker's convention.

Finally, a trick: If you are using smoke for the beginning of a scene and the curtain is down before it, pump the smoke into the air a few seconds before the curtain opens and then have a technician run through it right before the curtain goes up. The audience will be treated to a swirling cloud of smoke that will seem to have a life of its own. Pretty cool.

Sometimes, instead of billowing smoke, you just want a hazy atmosphere that will show off the lights. For this purpose, you want a **hazer,** a little electrical device that continually puts out a very light stream of particles that disperse evenly throughout the theater. Get it going thirty minutes or so before the show and you will be rewarded with a dusky mist that will show off the beams of light, particularly those coming from upstage. The downside of a hazer is the light, oily film that covers everything in sight by the end of the night.

Unlike smoke, fog lays on the ground, well away from the eyes and mouth, so it won't prompt the coughing reaction. It does, however, have problems of its own. Fog is created by heating up a container of water and then dropping **dry ice** into it. The dry ice, which is actually frozen carbon dioxide, vaporizes in the water and produces a colder-than-air fog that flows out of the machine and crawls across the floor like a passing vampire. A **fog machine** (which you can rent, build, or buy) is a fifty-five-gallon drum with a heating coil in the bottom to keep the water warm and a fan on top to blow the fog out. A fog machine is bulky (usually about the size of a large oil

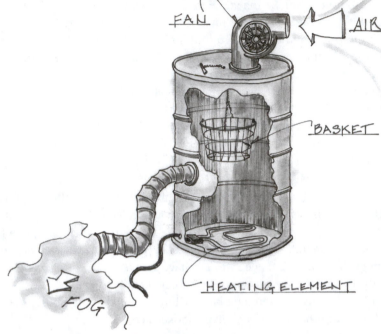

Fig. 13. A fog machine

drum) and must be kept plugged in since the water must be constantly heated. If the water is not constantly heated, the effect will last just a few seconds because the intense cooling effect of the dry ice will cause the water to rapidly lose all its heat. If you only need a few seconds, you might be able to get away with dropping the ice into a pan of hot water, but the effect will be ultra brief. Even with a proper machine, the effect will gradually fall off since the heater coil in the bottom of the drum can't keep up with the dry ice. Fog is best used to create an impressive opening to a scene, and then to add a little atmosphere as the scene goes on.

Besides getting the machine, you will also have to get hold of the ice itself. There are two places to get it: ice companies and welding supply houses (dry ice is used to quickly cool metal that has been welded). Dry ice is not expensive, but you usually have to buy it in thirty- to fifty-pound blocks. Even though you'll only need a few pounds every time you do the effect, you'll need to buy a new block every two days or so, because the remainder will melt away. You can slow down the melting process a little by placing the ice in a cooler or some other insulated space but, basically, dry ice is so cold that, no matter where you put it, it won't stay cold enough to prevent melting. Don't put the dry ice in your freezer, either, or everything else in there will become a solid block of ice and be ruined. Believe me. I've tried. If you are going to use dry ice, plan on getting a fresh supply every other day or so.

The other problem with dry ice is handling it, but I'd better say this emphatically.

_____

SAFETY ALERT! Dry ice is much colder than ordinary ice and it can adhere to your skin and burn you. When handling dry ice, never let it touch your skin! Use gloves whenever handling it and keep it away from children and animals.

_____

Operating the fog machine is relatively simple. Take out a chunk of dry ice about the size of a cantaloupe and break it up into golf-ball-size chunks. The more surface area you provide, the faster the ice will vaporize and the more fog that will be produced. *This theory should not be taken to extremes.* I know of one technician who completely chopped the ice into dust and threw it into the hot water. It produced so much fog that it blew the fog machine's heavy metal top twenty feet straight up in the air. It became known as the "Orville Redenbacher" effect and was not repeated. Keep the chunks between golf-ball and baseball size and things will go smoothly.

Fill the basket with dry ice, close the lid, drop the basket, and be prepared for a big "whump!" as the machine begins to spit out fog. Depending on how small you chopped the ice, and how hot you are keeping the water, the result could be anywhere from an anemic little puff of fog to a ground-eatin', actor-chillin', Hunchback-of-Notre-Damein' fog fest that folks will talk about all year. As with all effects, E-X-P-E-R-I-M-E-N-T.

Two other ways to get fog are with a **cool fogger** and **liquid nitrogen**. A cool fogger uses both fog juice and carbon dioxide to produce chilled smoke. This effect is halfway between a theatrical smoker and a dry ice machine. It works well, but is the most expensive of the do-it-yourself options, because the machines are expensive and you have to get both the fog juice and the carbon dioxide.

Liquid nitrogen, or LN_2, is *not* a do-it-yourself option. It is dangerous to handle and should only be handled by trained technicians. It's also very expensive. It is, however, the most visually impressive effect. Liquid nitrogen vaporizes even more spectacularly than dry ice, producing a cloud of low fog that would put the entire city of London to shame. The effect is produced by spraying liquid nitrogen out into warm air, using valves that are specially designed to handle both high pressure and extreme cold. Sometimes this stream will be combined with a blast of steam for maximum effect. If you see a huge, billowing cloud of low fog in a film or at a theme park, you are probably looking at liquid nitrogen.

Breakaway Glass

Breakaway is a general term for anything that has to break, or appear to break, on stage. **Breakaway glass** bursts easily into hundreds of tiny pieces without sharp edges. For some reason, breakaway glass (also called "candy glass") is always depicted in the theatrical supply catalog as beer bottles being broken across a cowboy's head. I guess the barroom brawl is a necessary part of every Western. Breakaway glass, however, is available in lots of different styles, including bottles, glasses, and plates, and can be purchased from a theatrical supply house. It has two problems: cleanup and expense. Because it bursts into so many pieces (sometimes almost like dust), it is tiresome to sweep up (particularly during a darkened scene change). As far as the expense goes, be sure to check out the price before you commit yourself to the effect. If the expense is too great, *do not be tempted to use real glass.* I spent one rather unpleasant evening driving to the hospital with an actor who had sat on real broken glass on stage. The sight of this poor guy kneeling on all fours in the backseat, bloody rump to the sky, made me determined never to make that particular mistake myself (even if it did lead to the longest continuous string of butt jokes I have ever heard in my life). Don't skimp. If you cannot afford the breakaway glass, then cut the effect, fake it, alter the scene, or do without. It is not worth the risk.

Rain

Ninety-five percent of the time, rain on stage is done with just a sound cue. The sound of a thunderstorm outside can go a long way toward giving the audience the idea that it is raining. (Does everybody know that you can get the sound of rain by recording bacon frying?) Now and then, however, you do need real rain, either because a scene takes place outside (*Singin' in the Rain, Night of the Iguana*), or the set has a window and the rain needs to be seen through it. Either way, the effect is basically the same. A pipe is perforated with lots of holes on one side. Then, the pipe is installed over the stage with the holes facing upwards. A hose is connected to one side and a catch basin is put underneath it. Water is pumped into the pipe, where it flows up out of the holes, dribbles around the pipe and rains off the bottom. Because the holes are pointed up, the water flows everywhere over the pipe and comes down in irregular drops, instead of steady streams like a showerhead.

Large-scale installations, like *Singin' in the Rain* on Broadway, use recirculating pumps to send the same water back up and through the system. Great

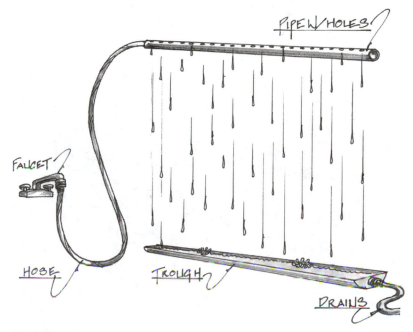

Fig. 14. Making rain

care must be exercised with water effects on stage since they will easily short out lighting and sound systems.

Snow

Technology is moving forward in wonderful ways, and one of those ways is snow. Up until recently, the only way to get convincing snow was with a snow bag, which we'll talk about below. Now, however, you can actually buy or rent a **snow machine**, which spews out "flakes" of wet soap that look and feel just like snow, right up until you taste them. They work in any temperature, both inside and out, making them perfect for "Christmas in July" parades or an indoor production of *A Christmas Carol*.

There are three downsides to snow machines. One is that they are expensive and require a constant supply of snow-making juice from your local theatrical supplier. The second is that they have loud fans, which are clearly audible, even over music. Finally, all that soap leaves a slippery, gunky residue on things if you let it run for awhile. It can also stain fabric. For outdoor shows or plays with smooth floors, this problem is solved with a hose or a mop after every show, but that might not work if you are trying to make it snow over carpet, plush seats, or, most importantly, dancers.

Dance presents a more difficult problem for snow. Snow machines will

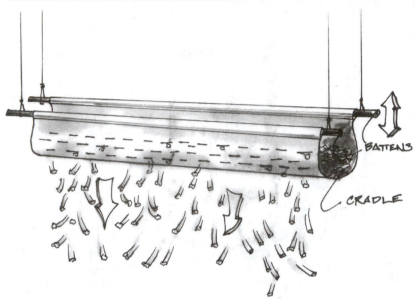

Fig. 15. A snow cradle

make a dance floor slippery, especially for ballet shoes. If you're doing the "Waltz of the Snowflakes" in *The Nutcracker*, for example, a snow machine might be a ticket to a sprained ankle. The best dance-friendly snow effect requires a flying system, so if you are in a theater without movable battens, you can't do this one. Do the "Waltz of the Sunspots" or something. People will marvel at your creativity.

If you do have movable battens, then you need a **snow bag** and two adjacent battens. A snow bag is not really a bag; it is a piece of canvas about two feet wide and as long as your battens. The canvas has holes cut in it about a foot from one side and tie lines along both long edges. Tie the bag between the two battens like a long cradle (some people refer to this as a "snow cradle").

Next, the bag is filled with snow. (I recommend that you spring for commercial snow: It is flameproof, it flutters beautifully, and it even looks good sitting on the stage.) Then the cradle is gently rocked, causing the snow to sift through the holes on one side of the cradle and gently float down to the stage. This technique is whisper-quiet, won't stain the stage, and is not as slippery as soap, although the dancers should step cautiously around those little slips of paper. The best way to avoid falls is to rig the snow bag either all the way upstage or downstage, avoiding the main dancing area.

By the way, keep in mind that sweeping up paper snow takes some time and is almost impossible to do during a fast scene change. If you really *are* doing *The Nutcracker,* though, you're in luck: Tchaikovsky was no fool about technical theater. The "Waltz of the Snowflakes" is the Act One finale, and you've got the whole intermission to clean it up.

Most scenic effects have two things in common: First, they work best if other distractions are reduced, and second, combinations are the most effective. Take away as much other stimulus as you can: Get rid of all the unwanted light and sound so that attention is focused on the effect. Then, try combining the effects—sound with light, smoke with projections, and so on. Unlike virtually everything else in the theater, in scenic effects, more is more.

CHAPTER 5

Lighting Design: Illumination, Mood, and Focus

Because our society is becoming increasingly oriented toward movies and television, it often works to think about stage lighting in terms borrowed from those media. One of the main differences between the theater and movies is that, in the movies, there is a huge piece of technology between the performer and the audience: the camera. The camera directs our view of each scene; it tells us when, where, and how closely to look. Not surprisingly, the person who decides where the camera should go is called the "director."

In the live theater, it is the lighting that performs this "direction." It can broaden to include the whole stage, or focus in (just like zooming a camera lens) to bring our attention to one person or thing. The lighting can also affect our mood, determine time of day or season, and move the play forward by separating the scenes and telling us when the show has begun and ended. Lighting also discriminates between where the show is happening and where it is not. Lighting is the opposite of masking. It says, "Look here. This is the show." If you are a director, you should know as much about lighting as Steven Spielberg knows about the camera.

Of course, the most important job that lighting does is to provide *illumination*. The audience must be able to see the performers and the scenery clearly. Once we can see clearly, we can think about time, place, mood, atmosphere, and other luxuries.

Illumination: First and Foremost

With all the things that lighting can do, as well as all the training we have
from watching music videos, it is not surprising that we sometimes forget the
basics: *We have to be able to see the performers clearly and comfortably* or we are
not going to care what they do. Watching a dark or unevenly lit show can
cause eye fatigue. Your eye muscles are like any other muscles in your body—
they get tired when you overwork them. Peering through the gloom at a dark
stage wears them out, making you want to close them or go to sleep. The
opposite is also true: Looking at a stage that is unremittingly bright can wear
out your eyes as well. What the eye wants is even, comfortable illumination
with some slight variations to keep it interested. If you give the audience a
brief blackout, for instance, they might be able to watch the next scene with
more energy. Conversely, bringing the lights up bright "stresses" your eyes a
little, making it more relaxing to watch darker scenes afterward. Of course,
all this should be looked at within the context of the script. Lighting must
conform to what the script, the director, and the action require.

Many people believe poorly lit actors are also more difficult to hear. In
other words, when our eyes are working harder, our ears suffer the conse-
quences. This may be a psychosomatic reaction, or it may be that actors
speak more softly when lit less brightly. Whatever the case, many people
swear by this phenomenon so it is worth taking note of it. Lighting is the art
of perception: People see whatever they think they see.

Good illumination, besides being the most important thing that lighting
does, is also one of the most difficult things to achieve. Even the best lighting
designers still struggle with it, and most of them spend years developing
techniques.

Why is it so difficult? Why do directors find themselves looking at the
same spot on the stage night after night, the spot where they *told* the designer they needed more light, and it never seems to get any better? Why
do designers put their heads in their hands every time an actor hits a dark
spot, the same dark spot that has been there for the last three rehearsals and
refuses to go away?

Well, like most things, there is not one central reason. A lighting designer is
fighting a battle against the senses: As I said, people see what they think they
see. No matter how much light you are pumping into a scene, if people think
it is dark, then it is dark. The lighting designer is a slave to the human eye.

Time for an exercise: Go out to your living room, your lobby, or your
reception area—anywhere with natural light. Look around. Notice how the
light flows evenly over all the surfaces. Notice how all the colors look pure
and clean. Notice how the shadows are sharply defined, but also notice how
you can see objects that are not directly lit. Look up at the ceiling. It proba-

bly is not getting any direct light at all, but chances are you can still see it clearly. Look at the features on people's faces—they will probably be easy to make out.

The sun is one heck of a lighting instrument. It is the lighting instrument that lighting companies have been trying to imitate for years. They make progress all the time, but they are still light-years (sorry) away from imitating Mother Nature.

Why is the sun so terrific?

Well, first of all, the sun is an *extremely* bright light source.

Brightness is measured in "foot-candles," a pretty straightforward unit of measurement. The amount of light produced by one candle, measured from one foot away, is one foot-candle (in theory anyway). A sixty-watt bulb in the ceiling of a light-colored room produces about twenty-five foot-candles. The sun, on a clear day in summer, produces about 250 foot-candles, ten times as much. If you have ever walked out of a bright, sunny day into a room with no windows, you know that your eyes need a moment to adjust to the new space, regardless of how brightly the room is lit. The sun is putting out a lot more light than our stage lights.

It does not help that the light coming out of a lighting instrument falls off very quickly as you move away from the instrument. This makes it hard to create an even amount of light everywhere on stage. Imagine that there are two actors, one standing ten feet from a light source, the other standing twenty feet away. Due to something called the "inverse square law," the person standing twice as far from the light source only gets one-quarter as much light. Since the sun is so much farther away, it really does not matter if one person is ten feet farther away (or ten miles, for that matter). The light on them will be the same. On stage, however, people can get different amounts of light depending on how close they are to the lighting instrument.

Unfortunately, there are difficulties with using the sun to light our shows. For one thing, it is outside, and we are in. For another thing, a lot of our shows have scenes that take place at different times of the day, and the sun doesn't respond very well to commands like, "Proceed to five o'clock, please," let alone, "Fade to black."

What to do then? How do we provide all the benefits of the sun—its brightness, its evenness, its accurate rendition of color—with the equipment we have available?

Back in the infancy of lighting, when most of the theaters we now refer to as "Broadway" were built, theater designers were only concerned with providing a place for lighting that had as direct a shot at the stage as possible. Therefore, they installed a pipe running across the front of the balcony and put all the lights there. Because of the shape of the theaters, the **balcony**

rail, as it is known to this day, was almost level with the stage, providing a horizontal angle of light. The performers were brightly lit, but they looked flat, like animals caught in the glare of oncoming headlights. With light only coming from one direction, their faces were not "modeled," that is, they had no three-dimensionality, and features were hard to distinguish. The actors had to wear very heavy makeup so that the audience could make out their expressions.

This situation persisted until the fifties when a new movement appeared in stage lighting. This movement was best encapsulated by a man named Stanley McCandless, who published a book called *A System of Stage Lighting,* which, quite simply, changed everything.

The 45 Degree Concept

McCandless pointed out, as artists and photographers have known for years, that the most attractive angle of light for the human face was about 45 degrees up, much higher than the balcony rail. Furthermore, the face was best illuminated by two lights, one to each side, both coming in at a 45-degree angle.

McCandless also took note of the fact that, when illuminated by any light source, faces take on two different colors, one on the side toward the light source and another in the shadows on the side away from the light source. He felt that the audience should see light on the stage looking like real sunlight, moonlight, or room light. Whatever side the "real" light was coming from was called the **motivational side**. The color hitting the actors from that side would be the color of the "real" light source: bright and warm for the sun, cool and blue for the moon, yellow for candlelight and so on. The color coming from the other, "nonmotivational" side would be the color of the light bouncing off the walls, the trees, the ground, the sky, and so on. Does this phenomenon really hold true in reality? Opinions about the McCandless theories vary widely. One good place to look is in paintings. Rembrandt knew a lot about the color of shadows. Remember, however, lighting is subjective. The audience sees what it thinks it sees.

Anyway, McCandless's book gave birth to the "warm/cool" idea in stage lighting. The two 45-degree lights that we talked about previously would be colored with filters: one warm, one cool, depending on which one was on the motivational side. The contrast between the two colors, along with the more attractive angles, would provide the modeling effect on people's faces that would help the audience distinguish features.

There have been a lot of changes over the years since McCandless's book first appeared in print, and these days his system is viewed as somewhat dated. Nevertheless, the 45-degree angle is still considered the most flattering angle for front light, and we still try to choose a motivational side. Most designers stay away from a strict interpretation of the "warm/cool" system, since it tends to make actors change color as they turn and move on stage, but the general idea of using groups of lights placed at 45-degree angles is still in constant use, as is the use of color to create modeling.

Rim Light

Front light is only the beginning of illumination. If you think back to your field trip to the natural light laboratory, you will recall that in a well-lit room, there is light coming from many directions. The same is true of a well-lit stage.

When performers and the scenery behind them are only lit from the front, they will tend to fade together. When viewed from the front, the performers will melt into the scenery, particularly if the colors are similar. It is necessary to add some **rim light**, that is, light that comes from the side or the back to illuminate the "rim" of the actor—the shoulders, the top of the head, and the sides of the costume. This "halo" of light will help separate the performer from the background, and give the stage more depth. Back light and side light should be applied to the acting areas just like front light, so that each acting area has its own instruments.

Acting Areas

McCandless also suggested that the stage be broken up into **acting areas**. The designer divides the stage into small blocks of space and designs a set of lights to illuminate one area—two front lights, a back light, and two side lights, for example. Then, he will replicate that set of lights for every area on the stage. This way, the light on every part of the stage would be coming from the same angle, plus, the actors would always be about the same distance from a light. This idea is still very much in use.

How do you decide how many instruments to use for each acting area, and which angles to put them at? Now you know how lighting designers earn their fees. Most designers have their own favorite formulas, systems, and magic books for determining the best arrangements of lights, but you can fake your way through it.

The simplest system for an acting area would be two front lights, evenly placed 45 degrees off the center line and a single back light. This gets the job done in a basic way. By adding two more front lights, you have a second set of colors for the night scene. Adding side light gives you more rim light and better illumination. These are only some of the possibilities. What about a light coming straight down? Very dramatic. You might decide to emphasize light coming from one direction (perhaps the scene is in a dungeon, and the

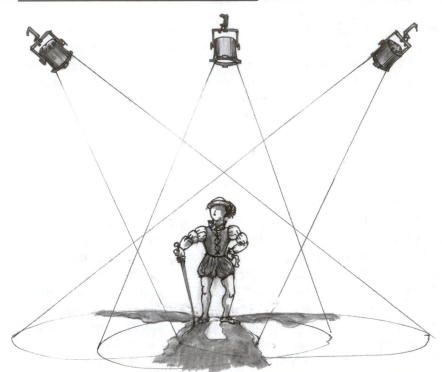

Fig. 16. Lighting an acting area

only light is from a high, barred window), or your theater may not have the right positions, or there might be scenery in the way, or you may simply discover a system that you like better.

How do you decide? And what do you do when you just want to survive? A few simple guidelines will help. Here are the three rules that I use:

- Each acting area should be lit from at least three different angles. By using three different angles, you can achieve the modeling effect, and give the audience something comfortable to look at. You can, of course, use more than three (something I would highly recommend), but three is the absolute minimum.

- At least one of those angles should be *downstage* of the performer. Whether or not you choose to use the flattering 45-degree position, you should light the performers from downstage so the audience can see them. If you are going for a "realistic"—not stylized—look, then you will probably want to use at least two different angles of front light. You may wish to only light performers from the back for an "effect" moment, but be aware that the audience will quickly tire of looking at an actor with no front light, so do your moment and then show the performer's face to the audience.

- At least one of those angles should be *upstage* of the performer. As I said above, you need to get some "rim light" on the stage in order to make the performer stand out from the scenery. This can be straight from the back, from the side, or anywhere in between, but you will need it to keep things from looking flat.

So far you have divided the stage into acting areas and devised a system for lighting each area. Now what?

Wash Light

While the acting area system outlined above will cover most of the bases, it is not enough in most applications. For one thing, lighting instruments are not perfect. The beam of any instrument (especially those with a few miles on them) will be uneven, with hot spots and dark spots. Even brand new instruments will be brightest at the center and dimmer toward the edge of the beam. Furthermore, the designer may want the light from some instruments to be limited with **shutters**, movable metal blades inside the instrument that cut off part of the light. He may do this to keep the light off the scenery or the proscenium, or he may do this so that light from one area doesn't spill into another. Shutters cut off the light, but they often create hard shadows, which will show up as **shutter lines**, dark shadows crossing actors' faces as they move from area to area.

In order to address these ills, as well as a hundred others, it is a good idea to include some **wash light** in a lighting plot. A wash is a set of soft-edged instruments, all pointed in the same direction, that provide a smooth, broad wash of color over all the areas. Washes can be used to regulate the overall color of the scene as well as blending the acting areas into one another, covering the gaps.

The combination of well-designed acting areas and appropriate wash light will provide comfortable illumination.

Motivational Light: Time, Place, and Season

By now you know that motivational light is not the head speaker at a lamp convention. Actually, *motivation* is a term stolen from acting. Actors use it to refer to whatever is happening in their character's life that "motivates" them to take whatever action they are taking. For us, motivation refers to the light source that is apparently causing the room to look the way it does. **Motivational light** is the light that would be illuminating the scene if it were in a real place: the moon for a forest scene, for example, or fluorescent lighting in an office scene. Whenever you are working with a lighting designer, one of the first questions she is going to ask is, "Where is the light coming from?" The set designer may provide part of the answer by incorporating lamps, overhead lights, a fireplace, or some other light source into the set. The playwright may help by choosing when and where the scene is taking place. Here are some of the things that the designer will want to know about the motivational light:

- *Where is the light in the room supposed to be coming from?* Sometimes the answer is easy. If the scene is outside, then you are primarily interested in the sun or the moon. There might also be streetlights, neon signs, Joan of Arc burning at the stake, or other types of additional light. If the scene is indoors, the sources may be lamps, candles, fluorescent lights, and so on. Sometimes the lighting will be a combination of indoor and outdoor sources, as sunlight or moonlight may be coming through the window.
- *What time of day is it?* This is a critical question, as lighting conditions change all day long. Sometimes they will need to change within a scene, as the sun goes down, for instance, or a character turns a light switch on.
- *What time of year is it?* Like time of day, time of year determines a great deal about lighting. The sun is cooler and lower in winter, brighter and higher in summer and sometimes playwrights use this for dramatic effect. Chekov's *The Cherry Orchard,* for instance, uses the approaching fall as a dramatic device to comment on the impending "winter" that is about to befall the Russian aristocracy. A good lighting designer can do a lot with this sort of detail.
- *Where is the play taking place?* Light is different by the seashore than in the mountains, different in the city than on a farm.

A good lighting designer spends a lot of time looking at the world, and so should you. What color is the light in the room where you are sitting right now? What is the "motivation" for the light in the room?

Mood and Atmosphere: Angles and Color

Angles in lighting are divided into five categories: front light, side light, back light, down light, and up light, and they all have their uses and meanings. I say "meanings" because each angle seems to come with a certain emotional baggage, which you can either exploit or ignore.

- **Front light**: The best light for illumination, the most "natural light," best delivered from around 45 degrees up. When delivered from straight ahead, it is "deer-in-the-headlights" light, useful for sudden realizations or the arrival of the police.
- **Side light**: The best light for illuminating the body and for giving the figures on stage sharp outlines. Side light builds excitement and "show value."
- **Back light**: Essential for separating the figures from the scenery. Used alone, it is great for sinister villains and dark shadows in the door. A subset of back light is the **silhouette**, where figures are seen against a brightly lit background without any light on themselves. This seems to have a connotation that is more "dramatic" than "sinister."
- **Down light**: Makes for awkward rim light, as it not only lights the rim, but also the nose. Better to use it alone for a dramatic opera procession or an unusual dance. Good scene-change light. Will get you a laugh if used alone with a booming, divine voice.
- **Up light**: Light coming up through a grating gives the "industrial" look. Foot lights can give an olde-time theatrical look or a bizarre, Fellini-esque glare that is distinctly ominous.

Color in lighting is often more difficult to talk about than color in scenery or costumes. Color in lighting is rarely seen in isolation. Designers use a combination of colors to achieve a "balance" of color on stage—a general, overall range of colors that center around a particular part of the color palette.

Color is part of what makes each lighting moment distinctive. Light changes color continuously throughout the day, more pink in the morning, tending toward yellow in the afternoon, a warmer orange in the early evening, falling off toward blue as night falls. Light changes color when it reflects off objects as well. Light in a forest is a different color than at the beach.

Like everything else about lighting, color is subjective: An audience sometimes expects to see something that is not really there. Firelight is one of the better examples of this. Next time you are sitting around a campfire, look at the color of the light that hits people's faces. If you are burning normal, dry wood, the light will be a yellowish white. Any good lighting designer, however, knows that audiences expect to see *red* light coming from a fire, and will filter it accordingly. People see what they think they see. As a theater artist, you have the choice of whether to play the game or not.

Color in lighting is also at the mercy of sets and costumes. There is a common belief, basically true, that it is easier to change the color of the lights than those of the set and the costumes. Sometimes, a lighting designer will choose a color that (pardon the pun) shows a costume in an unflattering light. In *Hedda Gabler,* Hedda kneels over the stove and, page by page, burns the manuscript written by her rival. Because of the glowing fire, I lit her in deep amber. Unfortunately, the costume designer had dressed her in purple. Purple cloth plus yellow light equals brown dress. I lost that battle, as lighting designers invariably do. It's easier to change a lighting filter than to make a new dress.

The colors in the lights need not be stagnant throughout a show. In fact, in many cases, it is essential that they change over time, just as the color in real light does. Colors will change as the motivational light changes, as the sun goes down, for example, or as the room light changes. Sometimes color will become less saturated, as in the famous confrontation scene between Stanley Kowalski and Blanche DuBois in *A Streetcar Named Desire.* Blanche tries to hide her suffering behind a mask of gaiety and nonchalance, choosing a colorful Japanese lantern to light her dingy room. Stanley rips the colored paper off the light and holds the stark white bulb up to Blanche's make-up-smeared face:

> *Stanley:* There isn't a damn thing but imagination, and lies, and conceit, and tricks. Take a look at yourself in that worn-out Mardi Gras outfit, rented for fifty cents from some rag person.

The absence of color in the light makes a powerful point about Blanche's refusal to confront reality.

One final note about color: Since the primary job of a lighting designer is to provide illumination, and what we are illuminating primarily is people, it is very useful to know which colors are best for which skin tones. Most of the time, for most actors, the oddly named "Bastard Amber" is a good bet. Bastard Amber gets its name because it is not really amber—more of an orangey pink. (There is also a color called "Surprise Pink," because, Surprise! It isn't pink.) Very light blues are all right as well, but they will make actors look a little pale. If you are lighting for video, however, stay away from saturated colors entirely. That romantic blue moonlight that looked so good on stage will look like little blue men from Alpha Centauri on television. Keep it white for TV.

Creating Focus: Specials and Follow Spots

Okay, so you are doing *When Ya Comin' Back Red Ryder?* It's a tense but quirky drama that follows a pile of offbeat characters playing out their lives in an Arizona diner. The waitress in the diner—a shy, portly girl named

Angel—never leaves the stage during the show and the director wishes to make the point that, after all is said and done, all these people have really been living in her world.

You decide to leave Angel in a pool of light for a brief moment after all the other characters have gone. A brief, lyrical moment. A blackout. Applause.

Enter the **special**, a single lighting instrument that lights one particular place on the set. Specials are generally a less saturated color than the rest of the lighting, allowing them to "punch through" the rest of the color. Often, they have no color at all. Specials are usually **ellipsoidals** because you want to have precise control over where the light goes.

When you really want to add emphasis and your subject is moving, there is nothing like a **follow spot**. A follow spot is any lighting instrument that is capable of being moved by an operator to follow an actor on stage. They come in all shapes and sizes. Follow spots may be hard-edged, super bright spotlights, or they may be more subtle and soft-edged, almost blending into the rest of the lighting. The subtle, soft-edged spot is very popular in opera, where the designers want to emphasize the lead singers without destroying the overall ambience.

Generally, choosing to use a follow spot means choosing to enter the visual style of musical theater. An audience is usually unwilling to accept that light is following an actor unless that actor is singing. I guess two departures from reality cancel each other out. The image of an actor standing in a follow spot is so strongly associated with musical theater that putting a follow spot on stage virtually declares, "We are doing a musical show." An actor standing in a follow spot is one of our cultural icons, so make sure that icon fits your show before you do it. I welcome rule breaking, but be sure you know which rule you are breaking before you do it.

Lots of theaters have a built-in position for a follow spot toward the rear of the theater. Unfortunately, this creates a flattened-out look that can be unattractive. Follow spots are just like acting area lighting—the most attractive angle is around 45 degrees. Of course, if your spots are built in, then you must live with what you have.

Spots do not come only from the front. Back-light spots occasionally show up as well. Look for them in large musicals and rock-and-roll shows.

Where the Show Is (and Isn't): House Lights and Actors in the Audience

House lights serve a practical purpose—they help the audience to find their seats and read their programs. They also serve an aesthetic purpose—they tell the audience when the show is starting (by turning off) and ending (by turning on again). The line between house lights and stage lights also helps the audience to know where the show is taking place. Sound like I am stating the obvious? Not necessarily. Sometimes, a director wants to have an actor go into the audience area. It can be problematic to light an actor walking through the audience because the lighting positions are in the wrong place. (Lighting positions are designed to light the *stage,* after all . . .) In this case, someone usually makes the suggestion that the house lights be used to light the actor. This is a difficult issue.

In the first place, there are very few theaters that have specifically focused house lights that can be turned on individually. Usually, when you hit the house-light switch, the entire house is lit. Right away you lose the primary raison d'être of lighting—to provide focus. Once you have brought the house lights up, the audience has a lot to look at—namely, itself.

When the house lights come up, the audience becomes part of the show. Fair enough, but the reverse is also true: The actor becomes part of the audience. That is, the actor ceases, in some ways, to be his character and he becomes a real person who is trying to portray a character. The audience's willingness to accept the actor as the character is strained. It is no longer clear what is the show and what is not.

Some productions want to do exactly that! Some directors want to play with these issues, and that is fruitful ground. As with follow spots, it is important to be aware of the conventions before you break them. Unless you are trying to make a point, however, use stage lights, with their capacity to be focused and directed, to light an actor in the audience. Of course, if you are in the musical theater style, you can always use a follow spot.

If you are using a space where you have to hang your own house lights, keep these suggestions in mind:

Use very unfocused lighting instruments, like big scoops, without lenses. If you are using fresnels, take the lenses out (be sure that you store them carefully). Add soft orange filters to give them warmth. Dim them down halfway. Hang them slightly behind the audience, pointing a little toward the stage. This keeps them from getting in the audience's eyes, yet allows easy reading of the program.

Moving the Show Forward: Cues, Timing, and Blackouts

Besides helping the show move around the stage by steering the audience's eyes, lighting also helps the show move through time by separating the scenes and defining the beginning and the end.

Every time the lighting changes, it is referred to as a **cue**. Cues are numbered, starting with cue number one, the lights that are on stage when the audience enters. Cue two is usually the light change that happens as the show begins, often a blackout. Cue three is the light that begins the first scene, and so on.

Each cue is a list of which lights are on and how bright they are. Besides these levels, each cue has a time. This time tells how long (in seconds) it takes for the lights to fade to the levels written in the cue.

The timing of lighting cues is critical, and it is one of the most important things that a designer does, along with providing clear, steady illumination. The most important times are the ones at the ends of scenes, particularly if you are going to a blackout. A long, slow fade at the end of a scene can cause the emotions of the scene to become deeply internalized by the audience, as they slowly take in what has just happened on stage. Fast blackouts, or **snap-outs**, can be a stunning punctuation, leaving the audience with an after-image impressed on their retinas. Of course, in comedy, the blackout is a critical part of the show's timing. A second or two can be the difference between getting the laugh you so richly deserve and actors stumbling off the stage in uncomfortable silence.

Unfortunately, lighting equipment does not always go to black as quickly as we would like. Even with a snap-out, there is always a slight glow on stage for a few seconds after the lights go out. The problem is the filaments in the lights. When the lights are on, they are glowing white hot (that's what makes the light, after all). When the power to them is cut, it takes a moment for them to cool enough to stop putting out light completely. This takes longer for a stage light than it does for a household light because the stage light has a much bigger filament.

Actors should always hold their positions on stage for a few seconds after the lights go to black. Look at the filaments in the lighting instruments. If they are still glowing, the audience can probably see you. Count to three before you move. If you are not sure if you can be seen after blackouts, ask someone who is sitting close to the stage during a rehearsal if they saw you move.

In some cases, a scene will be followed by a scene change. The crew moving the scenery will need some light, so the designer will create a dim **scene-change light** (typically some blue lights or a dim back light) to allow them to see. This cue needs to be dim enough so that the audience recognizes it for what it is and does not believe that there is a scene going on. If you are doing a scene-change cue, make sure you "button up" the previous scene by going to black first. Once you are in blackout, the actors can exit, the audience knows the scene is over, and the scene-change cue can come on. Likewise, do not fade directly from a scene-change cue to the lights for the next scene. Go to black first. It buttons up the scene change and tells the audience that the "show" is starting again.

Lighting for Dance

Lighting actors means lighting faces. Lighting dancers means lighting bodies. Some time after the middle of the twentieth century, somebody (lots of people take the credit) figured out that lighting dancers from the front, like actors, did not fully reveal their bodies in three dimensions. Sure, it was great for their faces, but dance is less about facial expression than the shape of the entire body. That discovery, along with the need to keep light off the large fabric backdrops that dance used, brought dance lighting around to the side of the stage. The wings became full of instruments stacked up on tall booms from the floor to high in the air, offering a variety of angles to light the dancers from the side.

All these angles have names: The lowest light is called a **shinbuster**, because that is what it does when you run into it. Next up is the **crotch light**, which is just what it sounds like. After that come the **mids**, so called because they are in the middle of the side-lighting boom. Above that are the **heads**, or **tops**. Above them are instruments called **pipe-ends**, because they are actually hanging on the end of the batten and not on the **boom** at all. (Pipe-ends are somewhat romantically referred to as "high suns" or "high moons," by the old-school ballet designers.) All of these instruments may be doubled or tripled to give the designer more color options. Dance lighting is literally composed of a wall of side lighting. A side-lighting boom in a first class company may have fifteen or twenty instruments on it.

Another way to get more colors is to change the filters between numbers, either by manually changing the ones that can be reached from the floor, or by using mechanical **color scrollers**. These little wonders have long scrolls of different colors in them, allowing crew members to change from one color to another by remote control.

As a more abstract medium, there are far fewer "rules" in dance lighting than in straight drama. Basically, you can get away with anything that the choreographer lets you try. Lighting designers tend to like doing dance because of this freedom.

With more freedom, however, comes more pitfalls. Lots of lighting changes can distract from good dancing, and it will *never* save bad dancing. Dance lighting should amplify and reveal the movement, and the designer should pay close attention to the music. If you are a choreographer working with a designer, send him the music first. Let him play it and have reactions to it before you begin discussing the dance. Let him know if there are specific moments in the music that you would like to emphasize. You do not have to be overly specific—it is okay to talk in generalities, even metaphor. As in the spoken-word theater, it is always helpful to show paintings or pho-tographs that are in line with the message that you are seeking to create. As

HEADS

MID'S

CROTCH
LIGHT

SHIN
BUSTER

Fig. 17. Lighting instruments on a dance boom

a side note, since so many choreographers ask me, I must tell you, no, it is *not* possible to light your dancers to make them look thinner.

Dance productions tend to have little scenery, both because they need the stage space to dance and also because, in dance, the human body acts as its own scenery. Dance will often have a single backdrop or a cyc behind the dancers. Hence, one of the biggest decisions that the designer will have to make is what color to make the background. Of course, it does not have to be a single color. It can change over time. It can have patterns or slides projected on it. In theaters with cyc footlights, the bottom and top of the cyc can be different colors. Do not be afraid of white! Or black, for that matter. It is very dramatic to have dancers perform in front of a black drape, particularly if a show has many separate pieces. Staging a dance in front of a black drape is a dramatic break from all those other pieces that simply pick a new color for the backdrop.

What dance productions *do* have is costumes. Lighting designers will often lobby for costumes that have more fabric in them than just the leotard. Having folds of fabric on the dancers creates more interesting lighting surfaces. I encourage all choreographers to explore fabric, not only as a costume but also as props or scenery. Give the lighting designer a surface on which to perform her magic.

Lighting for Musicals

Musical theater is a peculiarly American art form. In the classic fifties-style show, there is dialogue, which furthers the plot and leads up to some sort of conclusion. Then the action stops and someone turns to the audience and sings about what just happened. It makes no sense. It shatters every theatrical convention about acting as if the audience were not there. And everybody loves it. Why not? It's fun, it's emotionally cleansing, and you can walk out humming the tunes.

This alternating structure affects the lighting choices. When the dialogue stops and the singing begins, the lighting should reflect the change. Because you are already shattering the "reality" of the show, it is possible to make more "unrealistic" choices in lighting the number. The stage as a whole can get brighter (for an upbeat dance number) or darker (for a ballad) for no apparent reason. Pools of light or follow spots can appear out of nowhere. The idea that you must pay attention to the "motivational" light can be put aside. Musical theater lighting can be more emotionally expressive than lighting for spoken-word theater.

Musical theater lighting is full of conventions. I present them here to alert you to the presence of cultural stereotypes, not to tell you what to do. You must decide whether you will follow them, thereby making your audience comfortable, or ignore them, thereby challenging your audience's perception.

Follow Spots

Perhaps the most traditional part of musical theater lighting, follow spots, are used during musical numbers to focus attention on the characters who are singing. If the number is upbeat and several different characters are singing at once, the spots may be omitted, since there is no need to single out one performer. The size of the spot depends on how much the character is moving (bigger spots for characters that move more) and how upbeat the number is (smaller spots focused on the head and upper body for slower, more introspective numbers). The size of the spot may change through the number as the character dances or as the number becomes more introspective. This is called **irising in** or **irising out**.

Generally, follow spots do not come on when the music is not playing. This is in line with the convention that the musical numbers are expressions of inner thoughts or emotional states and therefore subject to dramatic liberties.

Level Changes

The overall light level on stage will change at the beginning and ends of numbers. For slower numbers, the lights will drop (allowing the follow spots to be more obvious). Big, upbeat dance numbers generally require an increase in light. For a song that alternates between verses sung by a single character and choruses sung by the entire ensemble, the light levels may bounce up and down.

In any case, most upbeat numbers end with a **bump cue** that pushes the lights just a little bit brighter for a little flourish at the end (often on the last note). Quiet numbers often end with the lights fading gently to black. For extra tears, try irising in the follow spot as the lights fade away.

If the number doesn't end the scene, the designer will do a **restore** after it. This means that the lights come back to the "reality" level they had before the number started.

Side Light

For shows that have big choruses and/or lots of dancing, you will want lots of side light for emphasis. Costumes with lots of glitter and sparkle need side light to really shine. Dancing bodies, as we noted in the "Lighting for Dance" section, are also best illuminated from the side.

The "God" Light

Singers need to see the conductor. So do musicians in the orchestra pit. In order to make him visible, the designer may have to hang an instrument straight overhead to light the conductor. Putting white gloves on the conductor helps, too.

Lighting for Fashion

Lighting fashion means lighting clothing, and it almost always means lighting a runway. Ordinarily, putting light on clothing and the body would mean a generous use of side light, as in dance. On a runway, however, side light is out of the question because it would blind the audience on either side. Even 45-degree light, which we use in straight drama, will end up flinging light into somebody's eyes.

For fashion shows, we end up going back to the basics of three-angle lighting. Every performer should be lit from at least three directions, in order to reveal shape and avoid flattened faces. In lighting fashion, then, we must fall back on the only three directions we have to work with: front, top, and back.

Fashion lighting starts with strong front light, aligned with the runway. All the instruments are ellipsoidals so that the shutter lines can be cut sharply to the edge of the runway. Then, the designer covers the runway with as much top lighting as possible, again, shuttering sharply to the edge of the runway. Finally, she floods the runway with back light, going as far downstage (toward the end of the runway) as possible without blinding the poor souls seated at the end.

This front-top-back configuration causes the runway to pop out of the audience and stand alone, like a bright, razor blade of light. Runway models are very focused onstage, rarely breaking the "fourth wall' or interacting with the audience. Containing them in their own sharply defined rectangle of light enforces this sense of separation and, more importantly, focuses attention on the stars of the evening—the clothes.

Furthermore, for most of the audience, this configuration is seen from the side, which means that it really turns into the dance-like side light we wanted in the first place. The important exception is the camera position, which is invariably set directly downstage of the end of the runway. If the front light comes down at a good 45-degree angle, however, you can get away with it.

The second trick in fashion is to stay away from colors in the lights. Fashion calls for lots of bright, clear light. The last thing a fashion designer wants is for the lighting designer to go changing the palette of the clothes. Let them be what color they are. If you want lots of color, throw it on the set.

If you are a fashion designer talking to a lighting designer, let her know what the color palette is like for each section of the show. The designer might want to change the lighting on the set to accent the clothes.

Lighting designers sometimes want to use moving lights for fashion, but rarely on the models themselves. The moving lights can be used for accents on the set or the audience, or as playful eye candy between scenes. Once the clothes are onstage, the distractions should fade away.

Models: Be aware that the lighting designer is pumping in lots of light to make the clothes look good, and adjust your makeup accordingly.

Video Lighting

When lighting for video, always remember that what you see is not what you get. That is, the way it looks to the naked eye is not the way it looks to the camera. Now that you have put a piece of technology—the camera—between the audience and the action, you must now do everything to serve that technology.

Lots of Light

Our lighting must now serve the camera, and the camera is a greedy master. It wants light, and I mean LIGHT! Video cameras require almost three times as much light as the human eye to get a good image. Light levels are measured in foot-candles, and a brightly lit stage might have around 50fc. The human eye is amazingly adaptable, able to make out shapes in light levels from a single foot-candle up to hundreds. Video cameras can record detail down to 20 foot-candles or so, but, for a really good image, they want something north of 60fc. Lower light levels will cause the video image to be grainy. To the naked eye, a stage that is lit for video might feel too bright. You may feel that some of the intimacy is lost from the darker scenes because the overall light level had to be brought up for the video camera.

White Balance

Not only do video cameras need a lot of light, they need a very specific color of light. Television **lighting directors** (note the different job title) spend a lot of time talking about **white balance**. Contrary to what you might think, there is no clear standard in lighting about what "white" light is, especially since your eyes are capable of identifying lots of different colors as white, depending on the surrounding visual context. As countless detergent commercials have shown us, you may think you have a white shirt on until you see one that is "whiter and brighter." In stage lighting, you may think that you are looking at white light until you see it on a video monitor and it looks pink or orange or blue. Video cameras must be told, "This color is white." Once they have identified "white," they can adjust the rest of the colors accordingly. This process of training the camera is called "setting the white balance" and videographers must do it before they shoot, generally by training the camera on a white card and pushing the "white balance" button.

Color Temperature

Lighting directors also talk about **color temperature**. They are not talking about how hot the lights are—once again, they are talking about white light. The term *color temperature* comes from the way a piece of metal changes color as it heats up. It starts yellow, then becomes orange, then red, then finally blue-white and "white-hot." The color temperature scale goes by the temperature of the metal. Normal incandescent light is around 2,500 degrees Kelvin, by the color temperature scale. Sunlight is around 5,300 degrees. Video likes anything over 3,500. To change a lower color temperature light to a higher one, you don't heat it—you put a special color filter in front of it. Watch the video people as they set up—they will be putting sheets of light blue color in front of some of the lights. They are trying to make all the lights the same color temperature.

Lighting for Rock-and-Roll

When I say "rock-and-roll," I do not mean only head-banging, blood-spitting, guitar-raging rock-and-roll. I mean any kind of live music that is not classical. The visual style of rock-and-roll music has spilled over into country, jazz, pop, funk, rap, and everywhere else.

PAR Cans

For years, the primary instrument in the world of rock-and-roll has been the **PAR can**. Basically an automobile headlight with a color filter holder in front of it, the PAR can is very bright and very durable. You can knock it around in the back of a truck for five hundred miles, throw it up over the stage with some color in it, point it roughly in the right direction, and you're rocking. Subtle it ain't. It has no shutters and it cannot hold a template. The beam is rough-edged and not even round. It's a lot of light and that's about it.

Intelligent Lighting

While we still rely on PAR cans, many other kinds of exotic instruments have appeared to make rock-and-roll one of the most visually exciting shows around. One of the most sweeping changes was the introduction of **intelligent lighting** by the Vari*Lite company in the mid-eighties. Vari*Lite created a spotlight that could spin, zoom, tilt, and change color on cue. Pretty cool. It caught on because rock-and-roll is extremely dynamic. The Vari*Lite allowed the lighting to respond to the music in a heretofore unattainable way—it allowed the light beams to move in time to the music. The beams of light could actually dance. The rock band Genesis was so taken with the idea that they invested heavily in the Vari*Lite company and equipped their entire touring rig with movable spotlights, completely dispensing with PAR cans. It was radical, beautiful, and very, very expensive. Since that time, the field has broken open and a whole string of companies have appeared with amazingly feature-packed lighting instruments that can create cosmic light shows that are like, whoa, dude. Today, most large-scale rock shows carry a combination of cheap, simple PAR cans and expensive, intelligent spotlights.

Rock-and-Roll Lighting Consoles

Rock-and-roll requires a very dynamic lighting design. The look is always changing, and the operator needs to be able to highlight the sections of the song, emphasize certain musical moments, and follow the beat. The goal is always to increase excitement and provide a visual style that matches the music. Programming a series of simple cues won't cut it. A good rock-and-roll console is designed especially for this task. The designer will create a series of preprogrammed "looks" and assign them to bump buttons, so he can bring up an entire bank of lights with one-button ease, right on the beat.

Prehung Trusses

Large-scale touring rock shows carry their own lighting instruments (unlike touring theater shows that use whatever is there or rent locally). This is primarily because rock shows do a different venue every night and there is no time to set up the house system or deal with a rental company. The lights will be prehung on a trusswork of pipes that gets pulled off the truck and hung over the stage the day of the show. This kind of a setup is essential for movable spotlights, since the lighting instruments are preprogrammed to hit particular parts of the stage. As long as the truss is in the same place relative to the stage, the lights do not have to be reprogrammed every night.

Special Effects

Besides intelligent lights and PARs, you will also see some other exotic lighting instruments in large-scale shows, including **lasers** and **ACLs**. You probably know what a laser is, but ACLs might be less familiar to you. They shouldn't be. You see them all the time. They are *AirCraft Landing* lights—headlights for planes. If you see a plane landing at night, look at the lights stuck in the wings. That lamp appears in rock-and-roll all the time. You can recognize it by its bright, narrow beam. ACLs are often used in groups to create a spray of light beams.

Other special effects that tend to land in rock shows are strobes, fog, smoke, pyrotechnics, and **audience blinders**. That last one usually consists of a bank of nine PAR lamps mounted in a three-by-three square and pointed, you guessed it, right at the audience. They are usually brought up toward the end of the show, so that the band can choose a date for the evening. OK, just kidding. They are brought up to put a momentary, brilliant wash of light on the audience for the sheer thrill of it.

Video

Most large rock shows these days travel with video screens, so everything I said above about lighting for video applies here. Brighter and whiter, basically. There is also a trend now toward putting video into the surface of the stage itself, under a protective layer of clear acrylic or Plexiglas. This actually presents fewer lighting problems than you might think, because these screens are LED screens, which can still produce a clear image, even when bright stage light shines on them. Normal video screens, with an image from a projector, would be washed out by stage lighting hitting them.

Follow Spots

Like musicals, rock-and-roll depends heavily on follow spots. In this case, however, there are two groups of spots: **front-of-house spots,** which are hung over the audience, and **truss spots,** which are up inside those trusses over the stage. The truss spots provide a brilliant back light to performers that is particularly important when that performer is shown on the video screen.

Rock-and-Roll for the Rest of Us

But what if you are doing rock-and-roll on a smaller scale and you don't have the money or the staff to handle intelligent lights and lasers? What if you have a band coming to your convention's closing dinner, or you are trying to light a small club stage? Never fear. You can have exciting rock-and-roll lighting on the cheap.

Rock-and-roll lighting rule number one: Get as much light on stage as you can. This means, get as many instruments as you can afford. PAR cans are cheap to rent, so get a lot of those and never mind the more expensive ellipsoidals and fresnels. Rule number two: Use lots of color. Hang sets of colored lights, like a group of red back lights, that you can turn on together. Try to get as many different sets of color as you can, to increase the variety. Rule number three: Use lots and lots of back lighting and side lighting. You will not need much front light—just a few white lights to hit faces. If there is a drum set, make sure that you get lots of side and back light on it. All those brass cymbals will really shine. Back and side light will provide dynamic color and you can flash them to the beat to create an exciting stage show. Speaking of flashing the light, Rule number four is: Get a control console with bump buttons, just like the big boys. The bump buttons on the cheaper boards won't have all the features you'll see on the larger boards, but who cares? Use the buttons along with the other control features of the board (presets, masters, etc.), to follow the flow of the songs. You don't have to be flashing and bumping continuously, but try to emphasize beginnings and endings of songs, as well as marking verses and choruses with appropriate changes. Close counts. Remember, there's a reason why stagehands say something is "Good enough for rock-and-roll!"

CHAPTER 6

The Tools of Lighting: Now You See It . . .

$\mathbf{L}$ighting is really just electricity made visible, so we will start by trying to understand what electrical power really is. Then we will follow the flow of electricity through the theater, past the dimmers and the control console, through cables and plugs, and into the instrument itself, where it will change to visible light inside the lamp. Then we will bounce off reflectors, pass through lenses and color media, and finally land on the stage and provide illumination for the show.

The Birds and the Bees: Where Does Power Come From?

What is electricity?

Okay, an analogy: When I lived in Seattle, we used to go down to the fish market where all the tourists hang out and buy fresh fish. The shops had these long tanks full of fish and whenever somebody wanted one, the sales guy would reach in with his bare hands, yank one out and toss it over the heads of some surprised tourists right into the hands of another guy by the cash register who would wrap it and sell it, singing in Sicilian the whole time. It was pretty impressive, but even more impressive when you consider that is how electricity works. Imagine a long tank full of fish. I mean, really full. Imagine a tank so full that you could not put one more fish into it. Absolutely jammed. Now imagine that the sales guy down at one end reaches in and pulls one fish out. With one fish removed, there is room for another fish. Now imagine there is a fisherman who pulls up to the other end of the tank with his catch of the day. He sees that there is room for one more fish in the tank, so he dumps a fresh one in. Only he does not stop there. He keeps trying to force more fish into the tank. No matter how hard he pushes, though, he will not be able to get another fish in the tank until the sales guy down at the other end pulls one out. The fisherman keeps trying, though, and every time the sales guy pulls a fish out, the fisherman succeeds in getting a new one in. Sometimes, the fisherman pushes so hard that, when the sales guy reaches into the tank, he comes up with not one fish but two, or three. In fact, if the fisherman pushes really, really hard, the sales guy might be overwhelmed by fish when he reaches into the tank.

This is electricity.

Confused? Of course! Okay, the fish are electrons, and they are swimming around inside the fish tank, which is a cable. The fisherman is the source of the electricity, which means that he is the power company. The sales guy is the **load**—the thing that is using the electricity. He could be a stereo, a toaster, a clothes dryer, or a theatrical lighting instrument. It does not matter. A load is a load. The load (the sales guy) is pulling electrons out of the cable. He is using electricity. (The guy at the cash register singing in Sicilian does not figure into this analogy. I only put him in for local color.)

This analogy breaks down in one place. Power requires a round-trip ticket—a circuit. There must be a complete path from the power source to the load and back again to make a circuit, and there must not be any breaks along the way. If the circuit is broken at any point, no power will flow, no matter how hard the fisherman pushes or the sales guy pulls. The simplest way to break a circuit is something we do every day—turn the light switch off. Turning a switch off creates a physical break in the circuit and interrupts the flow of power. I could improve the analogy, I guess, by having the sales guy throw the fish back into the ocean for the fisherman to catch and bring back to the market, but let's not split hairs.

There are three terms we use to describe how the fish move through the tank, or how the electrons move through the cable. The **wattage** is how many fish (electrons) the sales guy (the load) can pull out at a time, and it is a function of how big he is. All loads, whether they be lighting instruments or toasters, are rated in watts. A small load cannot pull out as many electrons as a big load. A two-hundred-watt lamp cannot pull as many fish as a five-hundred-watt lamp.

The **voltage** is how hard the fisherman (the power company) is trying to push fish into the tank. Voltage describes how much pressure is put on the electrons in the cable and, in turn, on the load. More volts mean more pressure. If the voltage is too high and the load is not strong enough to deal with it, it may be overwhelmed, as the sales guy could be overwhelmed by the fisherman pushing too hard. When this happens, the load may burn out. All

Fig. 18. How electricity works

lamps will burn out sooner or later, but higher voltage shortens their working life. If the voltage goes really high, the load will burn out instantly.

Every load is designed to work with a particular voltage. In the United States, the power company is pushing around 115 fish, uh, volts, so lamps sold for use in this country are designed accordingly. In Europe, the power company is pushing around 220 volts, so the lamps must be built to handle more power. This is also why you have to take a voltage adapter with you when you travel with appliances that are made for use in the United States. The adapter sits between the power company and your hair dryer and takes some of the pressure off.

The third term describes how quickly the fish are moving through the tank. This is **amperage**. The cable (the tank) is rated by how many amps it can handle at one time. If the voltage goes up (the power source is pushing harder), so will the amperage. Likewise, if the wattage goes up (the load is pulling harder), that also forces the amperage up. No matter how far up the wattage goes, the power source will just keep throwing more electrons into the cable as fast as the load pulls them out. This can lead to an overload situation, where the power company and the load are pushing and pulling so hard that the cable itself is in danger of being damaged. This can result in the cable breaking down, and it is a major cause of fires. That is one reason why we have **circuit breakers** and **fuses**. These two devices work differently but they basically do the same job: They monitor the flow of power and, if the flow of power gets too high, they shut down the system by breaking the circuit. We will talk more about fuses and circuit breakers in a minute, but for right now just remember that fuses and circuit breakers, like cables, are rated in amps.

These three terms—wattage, voltage, and amperage—are related to each other by a simple formula known as the "West Virginia" law. It says: Wattage equals Voltage times Amperage, or $W = V \times A$.

Let's try a few problems: Say you have some 100w lamps plugged into a circuit with a 15a fuse (a common size in most houses). How many of the lamps can you plug into the circuit before the fuse blows? Fill in the formula (remember, the power company in the United States provides 115 volts):

$$W = V \times A = 115v \times 15a = 1,725$$

You can put 1,725 watts into the circuit, so you can plug in seventeen 100-watt lamps with a few watts to spare. The eighteenth one will trip the fuse.

How about trying it from the other direction? Say you have three 250w lamps and you want to know what size cable you need. First, add up the loads:

$$3 \times 250w = 750w$$

Now, solve the formula for amps. (Come on . . . you did it in tenth grade):

$$W = V \times A$$
$$A = W/V$$

Fill it in:

$$A = 750w/115v$$

Do the math:

$$A = 6.5217391304$$

Yeesh! Save me from that kind of number. Of course, you can round off your answer to find you need a 7a cable, but you still have to carry a pocket calculator around to do the long division (at least, I do).

Or, you can do the whole problem an easier way.

You still have to use the West Virginia law, but with a slight change. If you are in the United States, just assume that the power company is putting out 100 volts. It will make the numbers come out a little high, but that is okay, since it will make us a little more conservative. Look what substituting 100 volts does to the problem above:

$$A = 750w/100v = 7.5$$

When you divide by 100, all you have to do is move the decimal two places to the left, and you are done. Now your answer says that you need a 7.5a cable, which is a little bigger than before, but we can call the difference a safety margin. So, we now know that, rather than bothering with the formula at all, we can just add up all of our loads and move the decimal place two spaces to the left to get our answer. Try it again. Let's say that you have two 500w lamps and you want to know how big a cable you need:

Add up the loads:

$$2 \times 500w = 1,000w$$

Now, move the decimal over two places to the left. Your answer is 10 amps. 1,000 watts equals 10 amps.

So, if you know how many watts you have, just move the decimal over two places and you will know how many amps you need. Likewise, if you know how many amps you have, just move the decimal two places to the *right* to find out how many watts you can plug in. You can also just say "hundred" after you say the amperage, that is, if you have an 18-amp cable, you can plug in 18 "hundred" watts.

Of course, like any kind of mathematical formula, this one gets much easier after you work with it for a little while. Besides, lighting is standardized, so there are some amounts that you will get used to. For example, most stage cable is 20-amp cable, so you can plug 2,000 watts into it. Or how about this one? Many stage lights are 500 watts, so that means they need 5 amps apiece. Are you with me? Great!

Last one: Suppose you are doing a show in a hotel ballroom and the hotel electrical guy tells you that he will put a 30-amp power strip out in the room for you to plug your lights into. You call the lighting rental company and they say that they have lots of 500w instruments and how many do you need? Using the "West Virginia" rule, figure out how many instruments you can plug in that power strip. The answer's at the bottom of the page.*

Enough math! (Don't worry, it gets easy with a little practice.)

Protecting Yourself

Time for another field trip. This time we are going to a **circuit breaker panel**. If you live or work in an older building, you might have a genuine **fuse box**. Otherwise, you have a circuit breaker panel. You can tell immediately when

---

*Using the simplified formula: $W = 100$ volts $\times 30$ amps $= 3,000$ watts, so $3,000/500 = 6$ instruments

Fig. 19. The power commute

you open the box. If it is a fuse box, there will be rows of round metal fuses with little glass windows staring at you. If you have breakers, there will be rows of switches, usually black. Let's talk about fuses first.

The old-style round **fuse** is the original no-brainer electrical device. It consists of a thin wire built into a metal and glass enclosure that screws into a socket in your panel. This wire is carefully designed so that a power surge above a certain amount will cause it to melt. When the wire melts and separates, the circuit is broken and no power will flow. There are two things that will cause a fuse to blow. The first thing is a **short circuit**. A short circuit means that the wires going to the load somehow get connected, or "shorted" to the wires moving away from it, thereby cutting the load out of the circuit entirely. This means that there is now an uninterrupted path from the power company, through the cables, and right back to the power company—without any of the power being "used" by a load. This can happen if a cable gets damaged, or if you stick a paper clip into both sides of an electrical outlet. (*SAFETY ALERT! Do not do that.*) Electrons are like Ferraris on the Autobahn—they do not pay attention to speed limits. When a short circuit is created, the jubilant electrons start whipping through the circuit at light speed, causing an unrestricted, almost infinite, flow of power. If the circuit is not cut off, *right now,* you are in danger of the wires heating up and catching fire. The wire in the fuse is built for just such a contingency, and it will immediately sever, breaking the circuit. Whew.

The second thing that will fry your fuse is an overload—when you have too many things plugged into one circuit. Remember our West Virginia formula? Most household fuses are 15 amps, so how many watts can you plug into the circuit?* If you try to plug too many things into the circuit, the wire will heat up and, eventually, melt. The fuse can save you in this situation as well.

Fuses are a one-shot deal, however. Once they blow, they have to be replaced. This is one reason why electricians moved on to circuit breakers. Here is another one: Fuses are not as precise as circuit breakers. Even though you may have a 15-amp fuse, if the power is brought up gradually, a fuse may let it stay on a little higher before cutting off the circuit. Because of this lack of precision, electricians prefer circuit breakers for most applications. Fuses do have one advantage: Once they decide to blow, they blow more quickly than circuit breakers—an important consideration when short circuits or other massive power surges are happening. This is why you still see a few of them around—inside your stereo, for instance. There is probably a big fuse buried inside your breaker panel as well. Look up toward the top for a tube shaped like a small soda can. This protects your house from a massive power surge if, for example, a telephone pole down the street gets hit by lightning.

A lot of theatrical equipment (dimmers, for instance) have both fuses and circuit breakers. The fuse protects against short circuits (when you need a fast cutoff), while the circuit breaker watches for overloads (because it can monitor them more precisely).

Aside from the one big fuse, however, your panel at home probably has circuit breakers. Take a look at the panel now. A breaker panel is like a freeway interchange. It is a way to split up the incoming traffic into lots of different, smaller roadways. Most breaker panels have a door that you can open to see the breakers, but to really see the insides, you have to unscrew the front of the panel. *Do not remove the cover yourself.* There is more than enough power inside the panel to kill you if your fingers do the walking down the wrong streets. Either get someone who knows what she is doing to open it for you, or wait until an electrician is doing repair work and peek in.

Whether or not you are looking inside the panel right now, let's talk about what happens there. There are three big wires coming into most breaker panels (four or five if you are looking at a large industrial panel). These are the hot line, the common line, and the ground line. (In large panels, there are sometimes additional "hot" lines.) The hot line brings the

---

*100 volts × 15 amps = 1,500 watts

power in and the common line takes it out. The ground line is there to "soak up" extra power that might be released by a short circuit.

The hot line, which can be upwards of 200 amps (quick: how many watts?), runs right down the center of the panel. Sticking out from it are a number of "exits," little metal tabs that are connected to one side of all the circuit breakers. The circuit breakers are smaller (15–30 amps), so each circuit can only handle a small portion of the available "traffic." The power leaves the hot line, passes through the breaker, goes out of the panel, travels through the walls of your house, and finally hooks up to one side of an electrical outlet. When you go into your bedroom and plug in your clock radio, the plug takes the power and sends it up to the clock where it passes through a bunch of electronics and makes those little numbers change. Then the power goes back down through the cord, into the other side of the outlet, and back to the breaker panel. All of these returning lines are collected together at a long metal strip, where they are attached to the common line that is heading back to the power company. As long as the breaker in the panel and the clock radio in your bedroom are on, there is a complete circuit from the power company, into your house, through your clock radio, back to the panel, and out to the power company. Just one big power commute.

You also might notice a few breakers that are double-size, that is, twice as big as the rest. These breakers take up two "exits" from the power freeway, and they are there to provide power for some of the big power eaters in your house, like your hot water heater, or the dryer. You might also have a really big breaker that shuts off the whole house.

Circuit breakers and fuses are not the whole protection story, though. If you have electronic devices like computers, stereos, televisions, and so on, you should also include two other kinds of protection in your system: **surge protection** and **spike protection**.

While the level of power coming from the power company is pretty reliable, there are inconsistencies, and sometimes the power will float a little above or below 115 volts. Circuit breakers guard against fluctuations in amperage, not voltage, so they won't guard against this problem. Surge protection guards against these annoyances. If you have a lot of really critical electronic equipment, you should explore **power conditioners**, which take whatever is thrown at them and put out a steady, precise 115 volts. This is unnecessary for most of us, but critical computer installations, sound studios, and other highly electronic environments should invest in them.

Besides these small fluctuations, there might also occasionally be a large, fast, jolt of power caused by a lightning strike or some other momentary problem in the power grid. These "spikes" can go as high as 10,000 volts, if only for a fraction of a second, and they can easily take out a computer, so a spike protector is a good investment.

Surge and spike protectors usually come bundled together in the same device and often are built into a multi-outlet power strip. Their quality and reliability varies, however, so spend some dough and get a good one. It does not make sense to trust a $1,000 stereo to a $10 spike protector.

Highways and Byways: Outlets and Plugs

We can get this one out of the way in a hurry, and a good thing too. Boring.

Plugs and outlets go together, so let's deal with both at once. In the modern American theater, there are three types of plugs. The first one—the **Edison plug**—is the one you see in your house. It is easy to plug in, commonly available, and cheap. It lacks toughness, however, and it cannot handle a huge amount of power, so it is limited to smaller uses, like toasters and televisions.

Most theater applications use one of the other two kinds of plugs. If you are using rental equipment, it is important that you get all of one kind, because they are not compatible. The first is the **stage pin plug**, also called the "three pin" or "stage plug."

Stage pin plugs are tough, durable, and can handle lots of power. I highly recommend taping stage pin connectors together with gaffer's tape. Do not use duct tape or masking tape—it will melt, and then you'll have gooey glop all over your pretty black plugs.

The other—and, in my opinion, best—kind of plug is the **twist-lock plug**. These are durable, can handle large amounts of power, and best of all, they do what the title says: They twist and lock into place, so they will not come apart. No taping required.

One caution about twist-locks: They did not come onto the market with the same degree of standardization that Edison and stage pin plugs did, so there are several different kinds of twist-locks out there. If you are renting or buying instruments to use along with your existing equipment, make sure the plugs match. You may have to take one of your plugs down to the supply company to be certain. It is easy to get cynical about these kinds of compatibility problems until you realize how amazing it is that all the electrical outlets in all our different houses fit all the electrical plugs on the ends of all the different clock radios that are sold all over the country. Now that is something to be happy about. I can deal with the occasional odd twist-lock.

One final note about plugs and outlets: The end of the cable where the prongs of the plug stick out is called the male end. The end that has the holes that the prongs stick into is called the female end. That is what they are called—I did not invent it and I do not want to get any letters about it.

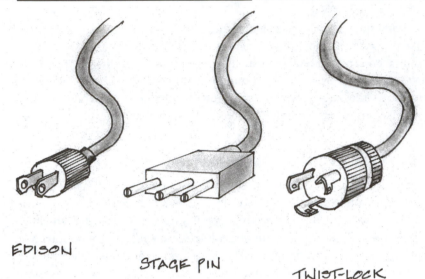

EDISON   STAGE PIN   TWIST-LOCK

Fig. 20. Different kinds of electrical plugs

Taming the Beast: Dimmers and Control Consoles

As useful as electricity is, sometimes you want a little less of it. In fact, some-times you do not want any of it at all.

There have been a lot of schemes over the centuries to make lights dim up and down on stage. Back when they used candles to light the stage, some clever entrepreneur invented little cans that slipped down over the candles to partly cut off the light. When gas lighting came in, technicians invented complicated mechanisms called gas tables that routed gas to little burners all over the stage. Most of the gas-lit theaters burned down, and now you know why.

Dimmers

When theaters went to electric power, the first dimmer that took over was the **resistance dimmer**, so called because it dimmed the lights by creating resistance to the electricity. Basically it just wasted the extra power. Resistance dimmers were mounted in big piano-sized modules with Frankenstein-style levers on them. Every six dimmers had its own "piano box" and it took a score of technicians to run them all. (The crew at Radio City Music Hall are reputed to have worn roller skates.) All that resistance created a lot of heat as well. Legend has it you could cook breakfast on the dimmers after an all-night rehearsal.

Today, through the miracle of science, we have solid-state, electronic dimmers, called **SCR dimmers**, to do the job. (That's Silicon Control Rectifier, and aren't you glad you asked.)

In most lighting setups, the dimming is handled in two different pieces: The dimmers themselves sit in a closet backstage, while a control console sits in the light booth and tells the dimmers what to do. If you are renting dimmers, they might come in two separate units—the dimmer pack and the controller—or as an all-in-one dimmer/controller combination.

Dimmers are rated in watts. The most common size is 2,400 watts, often abbreviated as "2.4K." You will also find 1K (1,000-watt) dimmers. Dimmers often come in packs of six. Control consoles are listed by how many dimmers they can control and, since dimmers come in sixes, so do control consoles. Look for six-, twelve-, twenty-four-, or thirty-six-dimmer boards. You also get to choose between manual or computer boards, but we will talk about that in a minute.

Time to Plug It In

Okay, so you have some lighting instruments, you have a theater, you have some dimmers, and you want to plug it all together and make it work. Great. What now?

Well, the next part is kind of like that children's game, the one that goes: "The hip bone's connected to the thigh bone. The thigh bone's connected to the knee bone," and so on. It goes like this:

The instrument is connected to the circuit.

The circuit is connected to the dimmer.

The dimmer is connected to the channel.

The channel is connected to the master fader.

From the top: A theater is full of *circuits*. A circuit is an outlet, a place to plug the instrument in. A theater might have only a few, or it might have hundreds. These circuits are connected to a cable that travels through the walls of the theater back to a panel in a room somewhere, not unlike how the cable from your clock radio travels back to the circuit breaker panel in your house. The panel in the theater, however, is slightly different. It's called a **patch panel**, because it is here that circuits are "patched" together with dimmers. Most theaters have more circuits than dimmers, so you use the patch panel to determine which dimmers will send power to which circuits. Some fortunate theaters are wired **dimmer per circuit**, which means that there is a dimmer plugged permanently into each circuit. In this case, there is no patch panel. The rest of us, however, must slog through patching.

There are several kinds of patch panels, but they all serve the same purpose: They let you decide which dimmers are going to control which circuits. You may decide to let all the odd-numbered dimmers control all the lights on stage left and vice versa, or you may decide to have all the dimmers that end in "0" control special effects, or whatever. Every designer has his own system. If you are using a rental system, the patching is done by plugging the cables from the instruments right into the side of the dimmers themselves. In-house patch panels sometimes look like those big telephone patch panels that old-time operators used to use, or sometimes they are rows of little sliders that you slide across to make connections, but the principle is the same: You take a cable that leads to a particular circuit and plug it into whatever dimmer you want to control it. Of course, you should be keeping track of what you are doing. Figure 21 is one example of a chart, called a **hookup chart**, that stores all of the information.

In a larger theater, or in a theater that is wired dimmer per circuit, you will end up with a lot of dimmers, maybe even hundreds. For this reason, many computerized control consoles have another level of organization—the **channel**. With these boards, it is possible to assign groups of dimmers to a single channel and control all those dimmers at once. For example, let's say you have a large group of instruments set up to look like sunlight flooding through a window. They are all the same color and you know that you are going to want to bring them all up and down together. They are plugged into circuits all over the place and controlled by a whole bunch of dimmers. By assigning them all to the same channel, you only have to remember one number. Every time you bring up that channel, all the dimmers will bring up all the instruments at the same brightness. Magic.

One confusing thing about this setup is that, while dimmers and circuits are real physical objects, channels only exist in the computer's brain.

The final step in the control process is the **master fader**. Every control console in the world—computerized or made out of yak skins—has a master fader that controls all of the dimmers or channels. Fade the master down, and all the lights fade out. This is the best way to create a blackout on stage.

Many control consoles have a **blackout switch**, which turns all the lights off with a flick of a tiny switch. I suppose light board manufacturers include it for those people who want really quick blackouts, but for my money, it is not much faster than just slamming down that master fader. Plus, it has "problem" written all over it. Brush against it, and the stage goes black. People are always calling rental companies to say that their rental board does not work, only to find out that the blackout button was down. If I were in charge of worldwide theatrical lighting, I would ban blackout switches. My advice? Tape it over. Next time you take your board in for service, have them remove it.

Sweet Matilda! *Hookup Sheet*

POSITION	NUM.	TYPE	CIRCUIT	DIMMER	COLOR	FOCUS
1st Beam	1	6x9 ellipsoidal	3	1	Lux 03	Acting Area 1
	2	6x9 ellipsoidal	6	2	Lux 03	Acting Area 2
	3	6x12 ellipsoidal	2	30	No Color	CD special
	4	6x9 ellipsoidal	3	1	Lux 08	Acting Area 1
	5	6x9 ellipsoidal	3	3	Lux 03	Acting Area 3
	6	6x9 ellipsoidal	11	2	Lux 08	Acting Area 2
	7	6x9 ellipsoidal	3	3	Lux 08	Acting Area 3
1st Electric	1	8" Fresnel	21	4	Lux 03	Acting Area 4
	2	8" Fresnel	27	5	Lux 03	Acting Area 5
	3	8" Fresnel	29	6	Lux 03	Acting Area 6
	4	8" Fresnel	26	4	Lux 08	Acting Area 4
	5	6x9 ellipsoidal	23	31	No Color	phone special
	6	8" Fresnel	32	5	Lux 08	Acting Area 5
2nd Electric	7	8" Fresnel	24	6	Lux 08	Acting Area 6
	1	8" Fresnel	34	11	Lux 54	backlight
	2	8" Fresnel	37	12	Lux 54	backlight
	3	8" Fresnel	35	13	Lux 54	backlight
	4	8" Fresnel	41	14	Lux 54	backlight
3rd Electric	1	Borderlight	45, 46, 47	34, 35, 36	Lux 27, 81, 90	cyclorama
	2	Borderlight	45, 46, 47	34, 35, 36	Lux 27, 81, 90	cyclorama
	3	Borderlight	45, 46, 47	34, 35, 36	Lux 27, 81, 90	cyclorama

Fig. 21. A hookup sheet

Manual Control Consoles

The **control console** sits in the light booth and communicates with the dimmers through a thin control cable. The power that is flowing to the dimmers never goes through the console itself. The console is not controlling the power, it is controlling the dimmers, and the dimmers are controlling the power.

As I mentioned earlier, the moment-to-moment operation of lighting is organized into **cues**. Every time a new cue comes along, it may mean that dozens of dimmers are all moving at the same time. On a manual console, there is a slider for each dimmer, but unless you have dozens of fingers, you're not going to be able to move them all at the same time. That's why, on manual boards, we use **presets**.

Let's say that your theater has thirty-six dimmers (a fairly common number). Your control console will have thirty-six sliders on it to allow you to control each of the dimmers individually. Underneath those thirty-six sliders, though, there are thirty-six more sliders, identical to the first set. Down to

Abby and the Alderman   *Lighting Cue Sheet*

CUE #	PRESET	TIME	1	2	3	4	5	6	7	8	9	10	11	12	13	14	15	16	17	18	19	20	21	22	23	24
1	x	3	7	7	7	7	7					F				3	3	3						8		4

CUE #	PRESET	TIME	1	2	3	4	5	6	7	8	9	10	11	12	13	14	15	16	17	18	19	20	21	22	23	24
2	y	5					B	L	A	C	K	O	U	T												

CUE #	PRESET	TIME	1	2	3	4	5	6	7	8	9	10	11	12	13	14	15	16	17	18	19	20	21	22	23	24
3	x	0		8	8	8	8	8	8	8	8	8		5	5	5	8	8	8			F			8	4	8

CUE #	PRESET	TIME	1	2	3	4	5	6	7	8	9	10	11	12	13	14	15	16	17	18	19	20	21	22	23	24
4	y	3					5	5	5	5		F				3	3	3							F	

CUE #	PRESET	TIME	1	2	3	4	5	6	7	8	9	10	11	12	13	14	15	16	17	18	19	20	21	22	23	24
5	x	7		8	8	8	8	8	8	8	8					3	3	3			F	F	F	8		4

Fig. 22. A cue sheet

the side, there will be a big slider marked "X" on the top and "Y" on the bottom. As long as the big slider is up, the top row (the "X" row) of sliders is controlling the dimmers. If it's down, then the bottom row (the "Y" row) is controlling the dimmers. This big slider is called a **crossfader**.

Why bother with all these sliders?

Well, if the top row is on, then you can set up a new group of dimmer readings (a new cue) on the bottom row. Then, when the time comes, you can slide the crossfader from the top to the bottom, thereby gradually shifting control from the top group of sliders to the bottom group, and changing all the dimmer levels simultaneously. Then, when the bottom line is on, you can reset the sliders on the top one and, at the appropriate moment, fade back to it. This kind of a board is called a "two-scene" preset, and it is the foundation of how we control lighting equipment. Back before computer control came into operation, it was not uncommon to see five- or even ten-scene preset boards that would allow an operator to work several scenes ahead of the action on stage.

Computerized Control Consoles

Computer control simply automates the process I talked about above. Instead of having to set up all those dimmer readings by hand every night, you simply set them up once and the computer remembers what they were. It also remembers how fast you want the lights to change. When you want a

Fig. 22. A two-scene preset lighting control board

cue to occur, you push the bright green button that says "GO." The computer changes all the levels from the previous cue to the next one. Because it's a computer and it doesn't have anything else to do with its brain, it will run the cue the same way every night. In addition, it can do a few tricks that a human would find difficult or impossible:

- **Split fades**, which means that the cue fading out is fading at a different rate than the one fading in. You might decide, for dramatic reasons, to fade up the lights for a scene in a new part of the stage, before an earlier scene in another part of the stage is done.
- **Run multiple fades at once**, such as when you have a sunset going on outside, plus an actor comes in and turns on an overhead light switch, plus car headlights appear in the window, etc., etc. . . .
- **Chase effects**, like movie marquees, or the slowly changing flickers of a fireplace. A chase cue is a series of cues that the computer will cycle through, one at a time, at whatever speed you choose.
- **Run cues really fast**, as in a rock-and-roll show or an up-tempo musical. A computer can run cues as fast as you can hit the "GO" button.

DMX-512

Ultimately, no matter what you tell it to do, the control console has to communicate with the dimmers. We've been through many different styles of communication over the years but these days, most people have settled on **DMX-512**. Back in the eighties, engineers from a group of lighting companies, working under the auspices of the United States Institute of Theatrical Technology (USITT), a nonprofit industry working group, got together to come up with a standard, digital way for lighting consoles to talk to dimmers. Previously, control boards controlled the dimmers with analog "control voltage" cables, but that was susceptible to electronic "noise" and had limited functionality. The designers came up with a way for a lighting console to control 512 dimmers at the same time, by "multiplexing" the information. *Multiplexing* means having a lot of different conversations at the same time. The computer spends a fraction of a second talking to dimmer #1, then another fraction talking to dimmer #2, then #3 and so on, right up to dimmer #512. Because the computer is switching between the dimmers so fast, the data seems to be flowing to all 512 dimmers pretty much simultaneously. The computer can communicate with all the dimmers in a fraction of a second, but send them all different information.* Like MIDI, each stream of information was called a "channel." Thus was born *D*igital *M*ulti-ple*X*ing for 512 channels, or DMX-512.

DMX (the 512 is dropped in everyday conversation) can also talk to other things besides dimmers. Intelligent lighting instruments, strobe lights, color scrollers, fog machines, and other devices can all be made to work with DMX. Thus, your computer lighting console can control different kinds of devices all over your theater.

DMX does have some limitations. As it turns out, even 512 channels aren't enough. In some cases, particularly where intelligent lights are concerned, a good-sized lighting system can use up all 512 and still need more. Intelligent lighting fixtures use one channel of DMX for each controllable attribute, like size, shape, color, pan, and tilt. Once you start adding up all the things an intelligent light can do, this list can get pretty long. Check out this example from the High End Systems Cyberlight:

Channel 1:	Pan (coarse adjustment)	11: Rotate mode
2:	Pan (fine adjustment)	12: Zoom
3:	Tilt (coarse adjustment)	13: Focus
4:	Tilt (fine adjustment)	14: Iris
5:	Color wheel position	15: Special Effects
6:	Amount of Red	16: Frost
7:	Amount of Green	17: Shutter
8:	Amount of Blue	18: Dimmer
9:	Static litho (gobo)	19: Motor Speed
10:	Rotating litho (gobo)	20: Control Commands

This one lighting instrument has just gobbled up twenty DMX channels. Hang twenty-five of these and you have just burned up your first DMX

*This is also how the phone company uses one phone line to carry dozens of different conversations.

universe. For some shows, twenty-five intelligent lights is nothing. The most recent Rolling Stones tour used over *three hundred*. Now that is some serious DMX. System designers have gotten around this one by creating **DMX universes**, each of which has 512 channels. Lighting boards that are so equipped can send information out to more than one universe, although each universe needs its own plug on the back of the console. One, two, or three universes is common.

One advantage of DMX is that it can run for long distances, so using it to control instruments or dimmers that are hundreds of feet from the booth is no problem. In fact, DMX can be sent wireless. Parade-float designers do this all the time. It allows the lights on a float to be controlled in sync with the lights beside the route. The float carries its own dimmers, but gets control information via wireless DMX. Pretty neat.

If you do not have a computer board, you will suffer some limitations about what kind of cues you can run and how fast you can run them. You may encounter particular difficulties when you try to run cues too close together or if you are trying to have two different things happen at once. Some operators are better than others. Of course, having a computer board will not make your life a bed of roses. Any computer comes with its own set of problems. It is important to remember that a computer will not save you time. It will simply allow you to do more things.

If you use a computer, this is the most important rule I can tell you: *Back up your files.* Right now. I repeat, *back them up* or, I guarantee—beyond any shred of doubt—you will be sorry. Maybe not today. Maybe not tomorrow. But someday, and soon, and for the rest of your life. It's not a question of whether your board will crash, it's a question of when. There are two kinds of computer operators, those who have lost large amounts of data and those who are about to. Enough said? Probably not.

The Real Workers: Lighting Instruments

At last, something that puts out light!

Contrary to what you've been told all your life, all of those metal things hanging up there above the stage are not called lights. Light is what comes out of them. The things themselves are called *lighting instruments,* or simply, instruments. People do call them "lights" now and then (even I say "bring up the lights!"), but I recommend the term "instrument" when you talk about them individually.

Inside the instrument is a glass and metal assembly that actually puts out the light. Contrary to what you've been told all your life, this is not called a

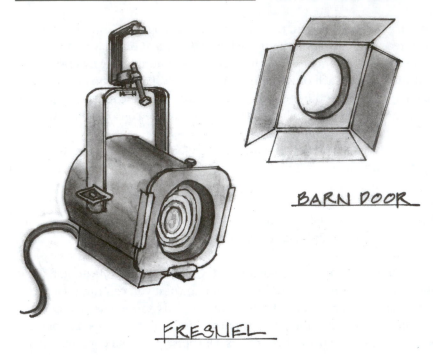

BARN DOOR

FRESNEL

Fig. 23. A fresnel with barn doors

bulb. This is a **lamp**. The glass part of it, exclusive of the metal base and the filament, is the bulb. The whole thing is a lamp.

Lighting instruments are usually mounted on pipes. The standard mounting clamp is called a **C-clamp**, because it looks like one. The C-clamp is attached to a U-shaped **yoke**, which straddles the instrument and attaches on either side. To turn the instrument left and right, you loosen the bolt on the side of the C-clamp. In newer instruments, there is a little handle you can grab onto, but on older ones, you have to put a wrench on it. Be careful! It's easy to twist that little sucker right off and then the clamp will be frozen forever.

To move the instrument up and down, loosen the bolts that hold the yoke to the instrument itself. Newer units have handles; older ones have bolts. Regardless of what you are working with, the tool of choice (and one of the things all show people should own) is an eight-inch adjustable Crescent wrench.

On the front of the instrument, there is a color frame holder. It's nothing complex—just a slot in front of the lens. Some instruments will have a little spring-loaded flap that you have to pull open to slide the frame in. Other instruments will only have a slot on three sides, so be careful that it is pointed the right way when you hang the instrument. The open side should point up, or the color frame will fall out.

Lighting instruments generally fall into two categories: soft-edged and hard edged.

Soft-edged Lights

Everyone has seen the image of the crisp, hard-edged spotlight piercing the dusty air to light the emcee downstage, and a lot of people believe that all stage lights look like that. A lot of them do, but many do not. When you are using a lot of instruments to light a stage, you do not always want that sharp, clear stab of light. As a matter of fact, more often then not, you want the lights to blend together as seamlessly as possible, forming a smooth wash of light. For this kind of application, a soft-edged light is the instrument of choice. By far the most common kind of soft-edged light is the fresnel (pronounced "fur-nell"), named after the distinctive ridged lens invented by Augustin Fresnel, a French physicist who spent his life developing a number of important optical formulas and preparing the way for the theory of relativity. You can always tell a fresnel from any other kind of instrument by rubbing your hand over the outside of the lens. A fresnel lens will have ridges in it. Anything else will be smooth. Actually, Fresnel developed his famous lens for lighthouses.

Besides its impressive pedigree and unusual lens, the fresnel has a number of other positive features. It is a cheap way to get a lot of light on stage and its beam has a nice soft edge that blends with the light from other instruments. The fresnel beam is also adjustable in size, from a large circle to a small one. Making the beam larger is called **flooding** it; making it smaller is called **spotting**. These adjustments are made by sliding the lamp closer to or farther away from the lens.

Fresnels come in lots of sizes but the two most common in the live theater are six-inch and eight-inch (the number refers to the diameter of the lens). Film sets use lots of fresnels as well, in larger diameters. A fresnel is great for lighting stages where you still might need to isolate smaller areas. Sometimes, however, you have a large expanse, like a drop or a cyc, and you need a large, smooth wash of light. For these uses, the best choice is a **strip light**, also known as a **border light**. Strip lights are long, narrow metal enclosures with rows of lamps set into them. They provide large amounts of unfocusable light, usually in several colors. A strip light may have one circuit of red, one of green, and one of blue, for instance. Since the lights are soft focus, it all mixes together on the drop, creating one solid color. By varying the mixture, the designer can change the color on the drop. This is how designers create sunsets, for one thing. They light the top of the cyc with various shades of

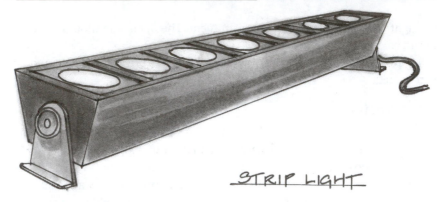

STRIP LIGHT

Fig. 24. A strip light

dark blue, while lighting the bottom with everything from red to orange to lavender. With a computer board or a skilled human operator, those colors can be changing and blending continuously, giving the audience a visual treat. When the sun finally goes down, you could turn on the stars that are sewn into the cyc and then . . . whoops, sorry. Got carried away.

There are two other types of soft lights you might run into. First, you may encounter **scoops**, which are just what they sound like, big ice cream scoop–looking things with a large lamp in them. Since they have no lens and no optics to speak of, they are cheap, but the light that comes out of them is difficult to control. They are best used to light large areas (in a single color) or as work lights.

Finally, there's the instrument that has changed the face of rock-and-roll: the **PAR can**. Basically an automobile headlight mounted in a metal can, the PAR can (it's written in all caps because it's an abbreviation—Parabolic Anodized Reflector—and no, you don't need to know that) is bright, intense, and durable. It is not a subtle instrument. It cannot be focused, spotted, or given any kind of sharp edge. Even so, many theater and dance designers have been lured to it by the intensity of the beam. It makes great sunlight, among other things. As I said before, most rock-and-roll shows are packed with PAR cans.

With all soft-edged instruments, it is good to remember that the light from them is more difficult to control than that from hard-edged instruments. This can be significant if, for instance, you are using them in a front-of-house position, where it is important to keep the light off the proscenium arch, or if you need a tightly focused pool of light. A small piece of equipment, like **barn doors**, which fit into the color filter slot on the lighting instrument, can help you control the light better. Barn doors have two or four little wings that can be swung in front of the lens, masking off part of the light. This masking does

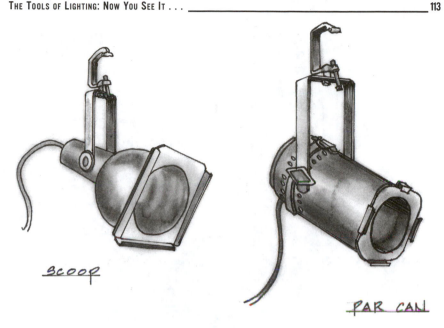

Fig. 25. A scoop light   Fig. 26. A PAR can

not produce a sharp edge, but it will get a lot of light off the scenery, the audience, or whatever. (If you are hanging fresnels pointing anywhere near an audience, barn doors are a necessity.) If possible, all fresnels should be hung with barn doors. One good reason not to use barn doors: If you are hanging the instruments on battens that have scenery moving next to them, barn doors are notorious for catching draperies, corners, moldings, and just about anything else that goes by. I swear, they reach out and grab them.

Hard-edged Instruments

When you need to have greater control over the light, the instrument of choice is usually an ellipsoidal reflector spotlight, also called an **ellipsoidal**. The ellipsoidal is sometimes referred to as a **Leko**, but this is actually a "Kleenex" word—a brand name that has become the general term for something. Like Kleenex, Jello, and Muzak, these words have entered the lexicon in a way that brings great joy to the original manufacturer. People will know what you mean if you say *Leko*, but I recommend that you use the more general term *ellipsoidal*, both for the sake of clarity and in fairness to all of the other fine manufacturers of stage lighting equipment.

Ellipsoidals are actually capable of being either hard- or soft-edged and, all things being equal, I usually prefer to use them over the more finicky fresnels. All things are not equal, however, because the ellipsoidals, with

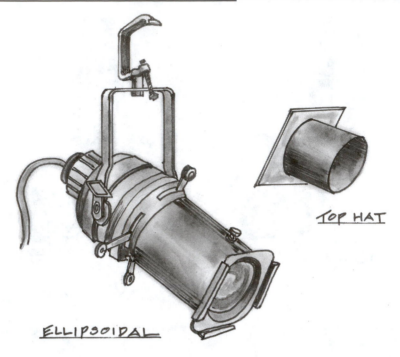

Fig. 27. An ellipsoidal with a top hat

their more complex optics, are considerably more expensive to own and rent than their soft-edged counterparts.

Not that operating an ellipsoidal is some kind of rocket science. An ellipsoidal reflector spotlight is so called because (are you sitting down?) it has a reflector shaped like an ellipse. This style of reflector has the useful property that it focuses the light more precisely, making it easier to manipulate. From there, a slightly more complex lens system collects the light and sends it out the front.

One way that light is manipulated in an ellipsoidal is with **shutters**, little metal blades that push in from the side of the instrument and cut off part of the beam. Using the shutters, you can give the beam a sharp edge that, for instance, follows the line of a drape, the bottom of a flat, or the edge of a podium. Ellipsoidals are also designed so that you can slide in a **template**, a piece of metal with a design cut out of it. The template, or **pattern**, or **gobo** (short for "go-between") allows the instrument to act as a sort of shadow projector, projecting whatever shape is cut out of the metal. Templates are a great way to get creative with lighting. You can cut your own simple patterns out of pie plates, or you can select from the constantly growing selections offered by several different companies. Ask your dealer for a catalog. Remember, though: If you are going to use templates, you must have an ellipsoidal spotlight. Fresnels cannot handle templates.

I mentioned earlier that an ellipsoidal is capable of being either hard- or soft-edged. This is possible because an ellipsoidal has all of its lenses mounted in a movable barrel that can be slid back and forth. If you want to make your ellipsoidal more "fuzzy," that is, get rid of the sharp line, just "run the barrel" forward or backward until you like it. Likewise, if you are inserting a template and you want the image to sharpen up, run the barrel back the other way.

Ellipsoidals are referred to by two numbers: the diameter of the lens and the **focal length**. The focal length is the distance between two mystical points in the optical system, and the only thing you need to know is that the longer the focal length, the narrower the beam that comes out the front.

There is also a class of ellipsoidals called **zoom ellipsoidals**. These handy instruments have an adjustable focal length, so you can make fairly radical changes to the size of the beam without hanging a different instrument. Why not use them all the time and have more flexibility? There are two trade-offs: cost—predictably, zooms are more expensive—and amount of light—zooms tend to be less bright than the fixed focal-length units, because they waste some light inside the instrument.

Follow Spots

Follow spots come in many shapes and sizes, but there are some things that are common to all of them. Follow spots are designed to put out a bright, crisp circle of light, much like an ellipsoidal (in fact, you can bolt a handle onto the back of an ellipsoidal and have yourself a low-tech follow spot). The size of the circle of light is determined by the **iris**, which is operated by a sliding handle on the top or the side. A spotlight will also have **shutters** that shut off the light by sliding in plates from the top and bottom. Many spots can also dim the light out gradually with a **douser**, two plates that swing in from the sides to gradually block out the light. These controls—the iris, the shutter, and the douser—are often right next to one another. On most spots, they are on the top.

A follow spot will generally have a number of different **color frames** that may be pushed in one at a time or together to put a **color filter** in front of the light. These color frames are controlled by a series of levers on the side of the follow spot. Pushing one color frame in knocks the previous one out.

Finally, many spots have a lever, called a **trombone**, that you can push back and forth to adjust the focal length, just like a zoom ellipsoidal. Pull it back to shorten the focal length and produce a wider beam; forward to do

Fig. 28. A follow spot

the opposite. Unlike the iris, shutter, and douser, the trombone is a "set it and forget it" control that the operator will only need to mess with once.

Different size theaters need different size follow spots. In order to determine which spot you need, you need to know the **throw distance**. This is the distance from the follow spot to the stage. Thirty feet is quite short; a good distance for a converted ellipsoidal or a "club" spotlight. These spots use lamps similar to those in regular lighting instruments. Some of them even use "MR-16" lamps, the low-voltage slide projector lamp I mentioned before.

As spots get bigger, the light sources start to change. For throws approaching one hundred feet, use a metal-halide, or **HMI** lamp. This highly specialized lamp has no filament. It produces light by forcing electricity to jump a tiny gap, sort of like a miniature arc welder. It packs a real wallop though, and it is often used for rock-and-roll. If you go to a rock concert and see follow spots mounted on the truss directly above the stage, they are probably HMIs. They make excellent spots for clubs, fashion shows, and theater as well. An HMI spot comes with a twelve-pack-size piece of equipment that sits on the floor under the spot. This is called a **ballast**, and it is required to keep the lamp burning, so make sure you do not forget it when you rent the spot. One caution about metal-halide: Once you turn it on, do not turn it off until the end of the show. HMIs will not restart if they are hot, so if you turn it off at the beginning of intermission, forget about getting it back on for the second act. You must let it cool for a couple of hours before you can use it again.

For extra long throws (200 feet and up) in large theaters or stadiums, technicians use another type of spot. This kind of spot uses an arc like the HMI, but the arcs are much bigger and the light is much brighter. There are two varieties: the **carbon-arc spot** and the **xenon-arc spot**. Both of these spots require permanent installations and external venting to accommodate their large size and noxious fumes. Carbon-arc is a much older technology and is gradually disappearing. It requires a fair amount of skill to operate because the light is produced by arcing the light between two carbon electrodes, called **trims**. These trims slowly burn away, increasing the gap between them. If the gap gets too big, the arc will stop and the light will go out. If it gets too small, the trims will fuse together and the light will go out. If the gap is only slightly too big or too small, then the light will smoke, flicker, and look terrible. It requires a skilled operator to maintain the proper amount of space between the two trims. Furthermore, the trims only last about forty-five minutes to an hour, so right in the middle of the show, they have to be replaced with fresh ones, which is called "retrimming." It used to be that rock-and-roll shows had a period of about a minute built right into the show when all the spots could be shut down to retrim.

There is a general trend in theatrical equipment toward making things easier to use, and the carbon-arc spot is a welcome casualty of this movement. Replacing it is the more sophisticated xenon-arc spot. The concept is the same: Force an arc to jump across a sizable gap and it will produce light. The xenon arc, however, is enclosed in an airless glass envelope and the electrodes do not get used up in the process. Xenon lamps do occasionally have to be replaced or adjusted, but the adjustment happens every few years, not every few minutes.

Intelligent Lighting Instruments

It was a warm spring evening in 1980, when a team of designers from Showco Productions sat the rock band Genesis down outside a barn in rural England. On that day, they showed the band the prototype for the first practical, roadworthy, and cost-effective intelligent spotlight. The band's manager, Tony Smith, coined the name "Vari*Lite" and rock history was made.

The first Vari*Lites were shrouded in mystery. Until recently, they could not be purchased—only rented—and they came with their own technicians. On tour, local stagehands were shooed away from the lights and they were never opened in public. Because of their popularity, however, it wasn't long before other companies—among them Morpheus, High End Systems, Martin, and Clay Paky—released competing products. Together, they changed the visual image, not only of rock-and-roll, but of theater, industrials, fashion, award shows, and even permanent architectural installations. Today there are dozens of different moving lights, falling into two general categories: **moving yoke** (or moving body) and **moving mirror** (or moving beam).

Moving Head versus Moving Mirror

In a moving head (the more common term for moving yoke) fixture, the lamp, optics, color wheels, gobos, and all accessories are built into a moving case, which is panned (moved up and down) and tilted (moved side to side) by two motors. The combined motion of the pan and tilt motors can point the unit in almost any direction. Moving head fixtures tend to have a greater range of motion than moving mirror lights.

Unlike the moving head fixture, the moving mirror fixture stays in one place, while a mirror redirects the light beam. The mirror uses two motors— pan and tilt again—to throw the light where the designer wants it. What the unit gives up in range of motion, it gets back in speed. Because the mirror is so much smaller and lighter, it is easier to reorient, giving the designer almost

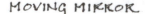

MOVING MIRROR

MOVING YOKE

Fig. 29. Moving head versus moving mirror

instantaneous movement. The Clay Paky Golden Scan 3, for example, can go from one end of its pan to the other in less than half a second. That's fast.

Spot versus Flood

Intelligent spotlights are similar to ellipsoidal spotlights. They can be focused and shuttered with a hard-edged beam and they can project a shadow pattern from a gobo. Intelligent floodlights are kind of like fresnels, with a soft-edged beam that blends well into other lights but cannot be fitted with a gobo.

The Light Source

Almost all moving lights use a short-arc light source* that produces light by jumping electricity across a tiny gap between two electrodes, creating a tiny "point source" of light. A smaller source means smaller optics and a sharper beam.

Different intelligent lights have different features, depending on their function and their price range. Here are some of the features you will see, depending on how many samoleons you want to drop on a fixture.

Color Filters

Intelligent lights have the color filters built into the body of the fixture so they can be manipulated more quickly and easily. Unfortunately, that puts them next to the extremely hot light source where plastic or Mylar media would be instantly melted. Moving light color filters are made from **dichroic** glass that reflects away the unwanted frequencies instead of absorbing them, thereby staying cool and extending the life of the color media. There are two kinds of color systems: In the simplest, a dozen or so dichroic glass filters are mounted in slots on a moving wheel and the designer dials up the one she wants. The second color system, known as CMY mixing, consists of three wheels, generally cyan, magenta, and yellow. Each of these wheels is graduated from a fully saturated color at one end to clear at the other. By rotating the wheels in front of the beam of light, the unit can create virtually any color. Some fixtures may have diffusion filters or even "black light" filters.

Gobos

Intelligent spotlights are fitted with at least one gobo wheel, that is, a moving wheel with slots where the designer can insert preselected gobos. More expensive lights may have as many as four wheels, with at least one of them capable of spinning the gobo in its holder. Spinning gobos can produce

---

*As of this writing, Vari*Lite has come up with an ellipsoidal spotlight that uses the same type of tungsten lamp as a conventional, nonintelligent fixture.

flickering fire, water ripples, or other psycho-spacey effects. You can also order custom gobos with text, logos, or other artwork.

Focus, Zoom, and Iris

Some units allow control over the focus of the unit, from hard to soft focus, just like moving the barrel of an ellipsoidal back and forth. The zoom function moves the light source itself, making the beam of light larger and softer.

Shutters

Another way to control the light is with shutters, either hard-edged or soft-edged. A soft-edged shutter produces a frost-like effect, while a hard-edged shutter gives a sharp edge.

Other Effects

Depending on the fixture, the manufacturer may include a strobe effect (produced with lightning-fast shutters), prisms that multiply the image, or an iris to alter the size of the beam.

Dimming

Short-arc lamps cannot be dimmed like filament-based lamps, so they require mechanical dimming, generally a metal door that closes over the light beam before it hits the lens. Because the beam is out of focus at this point, the door reduces the overall light output instead of creating a hard edge, like a shutter does.

Control Systems

The original Vari*Lite system had its own proprietary control language and control boards. These days, however, intelligent lights all use the DMX lighting protocol. DMX is actually a poor choice for controlling intelligent lights, because it only allows one piece of information to be sent on each channel. For example, if you want to mix red, green, and blue color wheels to produce a color, you must use three DMX channels to send the information—one for red, one for green, and one for blue. A complex moving light may require dozens of channels of DMX control, one channel for each gobo wheel, color wheel, focus mechanism, shutter, and so on. The need for a common standard was strong, however, and DMX was already familiar to light professionals. In the absence of a better idea, it was adopted by default.

The Downside

Despite the best efforts of instrument designers, there remains a downside to using intelligent lights. The most obvious is cost. Intelligent lights cost thousands of dollars, although healthy competition and cutting-edge technology are slowly bringing that cost down. The fact that many off-the-shelf control boards can now handle moving lights helps keep the cost down as well. Maintenance may also be an issue. Be aware that if you invest in moving lights, you will need to get some training about opening the lights and cleaning the optics from time to time. Supplying power can be a challenge because some lights require greater voltages than the standard 115 volt. The other downside: noise. Besides the motor noise, many moving lights have internal fans that can be clearly audible in a small, quiet theater. Many companies have made great strides in quieting down the fans, but listen before you buy.

Fluorescent Lighting

Time now to talk about a few kinds of lighting that you will find in the "real world." Fluorescent light is produced by sending an electrical current through a gas contained in a tube. The gas is excited by the current and begins to glow, or "fluoresce." They are cheap to operate and they put out an even glow in all directions.

Fluorescent lighting has several major drawbacks when used on stage. First of all, it is almost impossible to dim; it has only two settings—full on and full off. For that matter, if it is slightly out of adjustment, it may not even turn on instantly, but may flicker a couple of times before snapping on to its full brightness. An undimmable light may be a major stumbling block onstage; you generally want to begin and end your show with a nice smooth fade to a blackout.

Besides the dimming problem, it is difficult to control where the light from a fluorescent lamp falls on stage. Since the light comes from a long tube, without the benefit of a lens system, the light tends to splay out in all directions, hitting people, scenery, and everything else.

Finally, most people find fluorescent lighting hard to look at for long. It has a harshness that can be difficult to withstand. Of course, if this is the effect you are trying to achieve, then go for it, but think it over carefully before you commit.

Because of these three reasons, fluorescent lighting is generally avoided on stage unless the designer is seeking a specific effect.

Sodium Vapor and Mercury Vapor

I have always had a deep appreciation for the 1973 oil crisis. During America's campaign to use less power, most cities switched from fluorescent street lighting to sodium vapor or mercury vapor. Almost overnight, travelers flying over cities saw them change from bright white to soft orange and green. A definite improvement.

While these instruments were a boon for our streets (and our electric bills), they are a horrible thing to inflict on a theater. The reason is simple: They take too long to turn on. When you flip the switch, you see a tiny glow in the heart of the lamp right away, but it takes *forever* for that little flicker to become usefully bright. It can take up to fifteen minutes for the lamp to come to full bright. This is acceptable in a streetlight or even in a gymnasium, but not in a theater.

You may be stuck with some of these lights if you are doing a show in a gym or a cafeteria, so take note of them. You may have to rig another set of house lights unless you want the audience to sit in the dark for five or ten minutes after the curtain call.

Special Effects Lighting

As with scenery, special effects in lighting will never carry a show. Nevertheless, sometimes you need to throw something unexpected or strange or attention-getting at your audience. The following special effects can be very useful when the story, the mood, and the characters call for them.

Ultraviolet, or "Black" Light

For many years, ultraviolet, or "black" light was out of fashion, considered by most to be an outdated refugee from the seventies, when it was used primarily to illuminate black-light posters of Elvis and Gollum. It actually has many uses in the theater, however, not the least of which are puppetry and strip joints. Black light will cause some colors, most notably neon shades of green, yellow, and orange, to shine brightly. It also makes white fabrics glow in the dark. Very dark fabrics, such as navy blue and black, will not reflect black light at all, making anything covered by these colors disappear completely. Hence, puppeteers sometimes use it to bring focus down to a brightly colored puppet, while making a darkly dressed puppeteer invisible. Designers of strip-joint lighting (if there are such people) install it because it doesn't show skin blemishes, yet it highlights what there is of the dancers' costumes.

There are also special paints and makeups that can only be seen under black light. This is useful if you want an image to fade away and reveal another image inside it. The next time you ride "The Haunted Mansion" at any of the Disney themeparks, look for paintings that turn into skeletons as the lights fade down. This is ultraviolet paint at work.

Black light comes in fluorescent tubes, which can be put into an ordinary fluorescent light fixture. You can also get stand-alone fixtures that put out considerably more light (and cost a lot more). Either way, the bulbs emit very little visible light, and provide almost no illumination by themselves. What light these bulbs do provide comes from the reflections off other surfaces. Black light is also very annoying to look at for any length of time (as any stripper can tell you), so I don't recommend putting it anywhere the audience will be staring straight into it.

Strobe Lights

Any time you see a light that is flashing on and off very quickly, going from completely on to completely off instantly, you are probably looking at a strobe light. The light from a strobe is caused by a tiny arc of electricity from one pole to another. There is no filament to warm up or cool down, so the flash is instantaneous. Strobes are useful whenever you want an instantaneous flash of light, or a quickly flashing, "moviola" type of effect. One of the most interesting uses I've seen was an imitation "supernova" in a planetarium. (That one was a BIG strobe light.) A strobe also makes a great lightning effect, either by itself or inside a specially prepared lighting instrument.

SAFETY ALERT! When using a strobe, you should warn your audience ahead of time. Some people, notably epileptics, will suffer severe physical reactions after seeing a flashing strobe. Put a notice in the lobby of your theater warning the audience that a flashing strobe light will be used during the show. What you lose in surprise, you will gain in audience comfort and happiness.

Lightning

As I said above, a lighting instrument adapted for a strobe and fitted with a lightning-shaped shadow projection makes a great lightning bolt that you can project on the cyc, but if you don't have the time and expertise, there are other solutions.

If you are lucky enough to live somewhere that has great thunderstorms (I really miss them out here on the West Coast), watch one go by some time. You don't have to stand in a field and get electrocuted—just turn off the lights and look out the window. Look at the world around you when a bolt of lightning strikes. What kind of light is it? A flash from a lightning bolt is instantaneous, much faster than an incandescent light. Try turning a room light on and off as fast as you can. See what I mean? Incandescent lights, like the ones in your house, take time to warm up and cool down, so they will never flash like lightning. Up until recently, the only way to really make convincing lightning was with a **lightning box**, which was basically an arc welder in a case. With the development of better strobes, however, you no longer need to go to the trouble and expense of having a lightning box. Strobes can be controlled with DMX, so they can be reliably and safely run from the lighting console. Note that you will need a real theatrical strobe, like the Dataflash from High End Systems, and not a disc jockey–style strobe from the corner party store. But let's go back to that storm.

What else do you notice? You may notice that the light is bluish, and that it often seems to flash several times, sometimes from several different directions at once.

All these things can be recreated on stage. The best lightning effect is several large strobes coming from different directions, fired very quickly, one after another. You can get away with two, as long as you fire them off several times in a row at irregular intervals. Put some light blue filters in front of the lights to get the proper color. Sound complicated? Well, it can be, but persevere. Get two big strobes and put them on opposite sides of the stage. Set them to fire for different lengths of time and at different speeds. The irregular combination of flashes will really sell the effect. Most importantly, get rid of as much normal stage light as you can while the lightning is flashing.

If you can't get strobes, here's a *really* low-tech solution. If you have worklights backstage, try flashing them for the lightning effect. Worklights usually have very small bulbs, so they come on more quickly than stage lights. If you turn down the rest of the stage lights, you might get away with it.

Several lighting companies make metal patterns that can be inserted into lighting equipment to make a projected "lightning bolt" on the sky, but I would counsel against using them, unless you have the aforementioned strobe-light adapter for your equipment. As I said, incandescent lights don't flash quickly enough to imitate lightning. Rather than trying to project the lightning bolt itself, concentrate on the *effect* of the lightning on the ground.

Flames, Water Ripples, and Other Lighting Tricks

As I said in the scenery chapter, silk and a fan can be used to create believable fire effects, but you can also get more high-tech. To create the look of flickering flames on a wall, you can use **gobo rotators** or **film loops**, both of which slide into the gobo slot on your ellipsoidal spotlight. Gobo rotators are just what they sound like—a small motor that rotates a gobo. It is usually possible to put one gobo in the regular slot where it stays still while you rotate the other one with the motor. Depending on the choice of gobos and color media, you can get flame effects, water ripples, or really stoney disco effects. If you have more dough, you can rotate the gobos in an intelligent lighting fixture to create this effect as well.

Film loops are a continuous metal strip, cut out with a flame or water pattern. The motor pulls the film across the gate in the ellipsoidal where the light comes through. When combined with a stationary gobo, this makes the most believable flame effect.

Of course, the absolute best water-ripple effect is the low-tech version. Put a big pan on the floor with about a half-inch of water in it. Put a mirror in the bottom of the pan. Shine an ellipsoidal into the pan and tap the pan gently to make ripples. The ripples will bounce off the mirror and be projected up onto the set. Ah, romance.

Color My World: The Joy of Filters

The last thing the light beam sees when it leaves the instrument and heads out on its trip to the stage is a color filter.

Terminology time: Color is produced by stripping away a part of the light. To the physicists, this is called "subtractive mixing." To us it means that filters do not add color to a light beam—they take it away. If you put a red filter in front of a beam of light, that filter will strip away all the light that isn't red. It is sort of like that old joke: How do you make a sculpture of an elephant? Just get a piece of rock and carve away everything that doesn't look like an elephant.

The first color filters that appeared were actually made out of gelatin, an animal byproduct. The term **gel** has persisted to this day, even though filters are now made out of various types of high-tech plastic. Likewise, the piece of metal that holds the filter is often referred to as the **gel frame**. Since we are in search of accuracy here, let's give them their proper names: the **color filter** and the **color frame**.

Color filters are available from lots of different companies. Filters are always referred to first with the name of that company and then with a number. For instance, Lee 120 is a dark-blue filter put out by the Lee company. RoscoLux 27 is a primary red from Rosco Laboratories. GAM 385 is a light amber put out by Great American Market, and so on. All of these colors have names as well, but those names mean about as much as the names people give paint or lipstick. "Steel Blue" for example is a color that everyone carries, but Rosco's Steel Blue is a different color than Great American's. There are thousands of colors available from many different manufacturers and they are all unique. Each company puts out sample books (persistently called "gel books") and lighting designers spend a lot of time experimenting and keeping track of what is available. In the end, most designers develop a palette of favorite colors that they use whenever they design a show. This list of favorites is part of what gives each designer her distinctive style. As you learn more about lighting, you may also develop favorites. You may learn, for example, which colors look good on your own skin, and then you can really drive designers crazy by insisting that they use them.

Color is sold (you cannot rent it) in large sheets, usually about eighteen by twenty-four inches, which will give you six pieces for a six-inch ellipsoidal or fresnel, or four pieces for an eight-inch fresnel or a PAR 64. Excess scraps can be taped together with Scotch tape to make more pieces if you're strapped for cash.

Color filters absorb a lot of frequencies, which means they absorb a lot of heat. This can cause the filter to fade, warp, and even melt over time. Darker colors absorb more frequencies, which means they absorb more heat and fade faster. Dark blues are particularly short-lived.

It's a good idea to poke some holes in the color filters to let hot air pass through them. Make short, quarter-inch long cuts with a razor blade or, to be truly cool, buy a "pounce wheel" from a fabric store. A pounce wheel is a little spiked wheel that you can roll over the filter to make a series of tiny holes. (The costume shop uses it to mark fabric, but do not steal theirs unless you want the crotch in your next costume sewn shut.) Do not worry about white light sneaking through the holes—unless the holes are huge, the light beams will mix together and hide any white light.

If your show is going to be running for a long time, you might want to invest in glass **dichroic** filters. Because dichroic filters *reflect* the unwanted frequencies instead of absorbing them, they remain cooler and last longer. In fact, they last forever. All this durability comes at a price, though. Dichroic filters are anywhere from five to ten times more expensive than plastic filters, so they are really only worth it if the cost of maintaining your filters is more than the cost of buying dichroics in the first place. Because of this equation, dichroics tend to show up in semipermanent applications, like theme parks and architectural lighting.

To install color in a lighting instrument, get a color frame for the instrument you are coloring. (Make sure it's the right one—color frames from different manufacturers are frustratingly incompatible.) Using the frame as a guide, cut a piece the right size. Open up the frame and insert the color, making a filter sandwich. Most color frames have a small hole punched in them so you can insert a brass paper fastener through the whole assembly to keep it from coming apart as you carry it up the ladder. Otherwise, put some tape around the edges to keep it together. Slide the color frame into the little shelf on the front of the instrument. It does not matter which side of the filter faces front.

Besides color filters, lighting companies also make a line of **diffusion filters**. These highly useful filters look just like color filters except that they

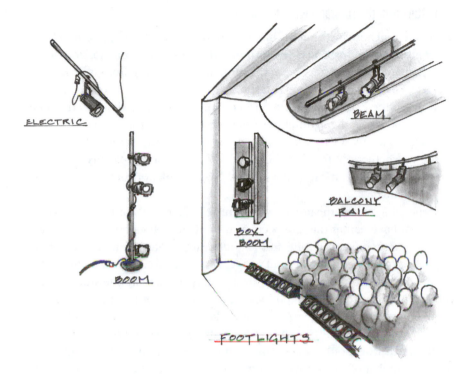

Fig. 30. Common lighting positions

are white and frosty, sort of like the glass in your bathroom window. They are designed to spread out the light in various ways. Some of them just soften the light a little bit, getting rid of shutter lines and hard edges, while others spread the light out over a large area. Some diffusion filters only spread the light out in one direction. This is useful if, for example, you are trying to spread the light across a drop. You can combine diffusion with a color filter in the same frame, but be sure to put some holes in both filters so the heat can get out (otherwise the filters may melt together). Diffusion comes in lots of varieties, so play around.

Color filters are especially fun to use with templates. Try cutting two different color filters in half and taping them together in a single frame. This is called a split color and it can do fun things with an intricate pattern.

This may be stating the obvious, but since I have seen people try it, I must tell you not to try putting color into the slot where the template goes. It will melt faster than you can say . . . too late, it's gone.

Putting It in the Theater: Lighting Positions

There are probably instruments hanging all over your theater, in a number of different **lighting positions**. The **batten** (remember? the long horizontal pole hanging over the stage) that instruments are hanging from is called an **electric**. Electrics are numbered starting at the proscenium arch and moving upstage, so the closest one to the proscenium is called the **first electric**. Out over the audience, the lighting positions are called **beams**, or sometimes, **coves** (particularly if they are built into the ceiling). Any vertical lighting position, whether out front or backstage, is called a **boom**. Beams are horizontal, booms are vertical. Still with me? Take a look at figure 30 if you need to get oriented.

Depending on the theater, there are lots of other kinds of lighting positions that have names that are peculiar to individual theaters. For instance, there was a set of short booms in the auditorium at San Francisco State that happened to be located over a set of speakers. They were always referred to as the "Speaker Box" lights. There was probably more than one student who went to his first professional job looking for the Speaker Box position. That term, however, was unique to that particular theater.

Many theaters have lights in a small position to the side of the apron, pretty much where our speaker box position was, and that position goes under a number of pseudonyms: **side coves**, **juliets** (because of their resemblance to the famous balcony), and often **box booms**. That last one is relatively common and is descended from the old Broadway theaters. When the theaters were built, the architects included box seats in the side wall of the auditorium for the gentry to sit above the madding crowd. These boxes were well to the side, almost over the stage itself, and they didn't have much of a view. They did, however, give the audience a great view of whoever sat in them, which was more the point. As time went on (and the price of theater tickets went up), people became more interested in seeing the show than being seen by the audience, and that, combined with a greater emphasis on lighting, caused the boxes to be overtaken by lighting equipment. Today, any lighting boom in that position, regardless of whether or not there was ever seating there, may still be called a box boom. Incidentally, if you ever buy Broadway show tickets that are labeled "restricted view," they might be selling you seats alongside the lighting booms in the old boxes.

Costume Design: Character, Period, and Function

To me, there always seems to be a kind of divine madness about costume designers, and no wonder. They spend much of their time mucking about in character's brains, peering at their everyday life, thumbing through mythical closets and faraway dresser drawers. As costume designer Celestine Ranney puts it, "I make clothes for imaginary people."*

While scenic design focuses on Grand Statements and lighting builds Mood and Atmosphere, costume design takes a more personal, more individual road. Costumes depict Character. The costume designer is trying to give the actor a home for the character, a place in physical space, a garment that restricts and reveals the actor as it would the character. The costume should help the actor move as the character would move, giving the actor another tool with which to create the role. "Clothes make the man," the saying goes, but perhaps it is more accurate to say, "Clothes reveal the man." Costumes take the inner workings of the character and put them on the outside. They are like X-ray machines.

Costumes must also knit together well with the other design elements. If the set, lighting, and costumes are not of the same "world," the show will feel disjointed, although the audience might not know why. Furthermore, the color in these three elements must be complementary, so the actress in the beige dress doesn't end up in front of a beige wall and completely disappear.

Of course, all the design arts exist to tell the story, and costumes are no different. It is not enough to see an eighteenth-century nobleman wearing an

---

*Quoted by Tara Maginnis on *Costumes.org*.

embroidered waistcoat. We must see a desperate eighteenth-century noble-man who has lost his fortune and donned his last threadbare waistcoat as he comes courting, seeking a bride's dowry that will reverse his fortunes and make him a true man once again, a force to be reckoned with, a courtly presence unmatched in power and influence.

Or something like that.

The work doesn't stop there. Even more than scenery (and way more than lighting), costume design expresses a certain snapshot of historical time: a Period. When signing up to a new project, one of the very first questions from the costume designer will be, When is it set? The silhouette, shape, texture, and accessories of any garment are dependent on fashion, and fash-ion goes hand-in-hand with time. Costume designers, therefore, tend to be history buffs. They must know general trends in clothing—like bustles, top hats, and skirt lengths—plus tiny little details like the fact that purple dye used to be very costly and was, by law, forbidden to everyone but the emperor. They must know that the opening of King Tut's tomb sparked an explosion of Egyptian-themed clothing. Costume designers have to know about revolutions, scientific discoveries, cultural traditions, and all sorts of other phenomena that affect the design of clothing. Therefore, researching the period of the play is of tremendous importance.

Of course, every aspect of design has its practical side as well, and the cos-tume designer's work is grounded in the reality of the human body. Every piece of art the costume designer makes must be displayed on a pre-existing shape. It must fit that shape, reveal or hide that shape as necessary, and not impede any of the actions that shape wants to take in the course of arguing, sword-fighting, wrestling, lovemaking, eating, or doing jumping jacks. Some characters dance, some sing, some strip, some climb stairs or ladders, some have to fit through doors and some have to change clothes in an awful hurry. Costume designers, therefore, must design clothes that serve whatever Function is required of them by the play.

Let us take a look at how costumes reveal character. Then we'll talk history and, finally, we'll get practical.

Character

The playwright's words are the beginning of everything, so, like every other designer, the costumer starts with the script.

How to Read a Play Like a Costume Designer

Like the other designers, a good costume designer will read the play through once without worrying about the practical details, simply letting the emotions of the play flow out of the text. Once she has a handle on the overall story, she will go back and begin to answer specific questions:

Where does the play take place? What country are we in? What city? Are we indoors or out? Which rooms are we in? People might dress differently in the bedroom than in the kitchen.

When does the play take place? What year? What *time* of year? What time of day? Is it a warm summer evening or a crisp fall morning? What is the weather like?

What is the world like where the play takes place? What kind of government? What kind of church? What are the character's social beliefs about everyday conduct, relationships, marriage, sex, children?

What happened before the play began?

What type of action does the play call for? Will the characters be tumbling around on stage? Is there fighting? Food? Sex?

What kinds of clothing references are in the text? These might be very direct, as when a maid asks a gentleman for his hat, or they might be inferred if, for example, a character remarks that someone looks "all dressed up."

Who should the audience be focusing their attention on? Who are the protagonist and antagonist? Who are the supporting characters? Visualize the scene in your mind and think about where you would want the audience to be looking at any moment. It is the lighting designer and the costume designer that direct focus around the stage. The lighting designer does it with intensity of light; the costume designer with color and style. When Mame enters on the arms of ten black-tuxedo'd gentlemen, the last thing you want to do is put her in a black evening gown. A bright red dress lets the audience know they should be looking at her.

Therefore, when creating costumes for each character, you should know the following:

- Age
- Social class
- Financial position
- Marital status
- Health

- Moral beliefs
- Job
- Mental state
- Education
- Country of origin

All of the above information can determine what they would wear and how they would wear it. Costume designers must understand how these characters choose to reveal themselves to the world—their habits, their place in society, their career, health, education, and so on and so on. They will do much of the same research as the actor, and may end up knowing as much about the character as the actor who plays him. The director should also be sharing his ideas for the character early on, as the designer will want to build on them. This relationship is most useful when it goes both ways, of course. A costume designer will often discover tasty details in her research that may influence the director's conception.

Costume design often dips into metaphor, whether the audience notices it or not. One production of *Hedda Gabler* envisioned her trapped in her fate like a prison inmate, so her costumes were all tightly laced like straitjackets and decorated with thin stripes. Whether or not the audience understood the metaphor directly, the costumes confined and restricted the actress, giving her a valuable tool to create this tortured character. These sorts of metaphors often hit the audience on a subconscious level as well, though they rarely realize it.

One way that a costume designer can influence a performance early on is with the introduction of a costume prop. Costume props are things like umbrellas, pocket watches, boas, canes, and so forth. If the prop is an interesting choice, it can become the center of a great deal of business in the hands of a creative actor and a clever director. These sorts of props need to be provided early on, so they can grow in personality throughout rehearsal. Give Mame that boa early on, and you may find her weaving the male chorus line into it by opening night.

Costume designers are often looking for a "keynote" piece for a costume: a single element that expresses the inner workings of a character's mind. It might be Madame Arcati's exotic turban in *Blithe Spirit* or Henry Higgins's frumpy, slightly out-of-fashion suit coat in *Pygmalion*. It could be as simple as a piece of jewelry or as elaborate as a suit of armor. This single signature piece can offer guidance throughout the design period, much as a single piece of scenery or furniture can keep the scenic design process on track.

The director generally comes up with an overall stylistic theme—"a flashy carnival spectacle," "a bizarre Fellini film," "a fascist diatribe," "a wacky comedic romp," "a passionate romance novel," and so on. This helps the designer get a sense of style for the show. This shared style helps hold the visual style together onstage, so that all the characters look like they are part of the same story.

Besides revealing a character's inner workings, costume design can often help the audience to follow the story. If a play is packed with characters, a designer may create a sort of color-coding for the players. This set of lovers is in blue, that one in orange, and so on. The usefulness of this technique is in direct proportion to the potential for confusion in the story.

An Exercise

I think you know where this is going. That's right, to a closet. This exercise is best done with a friend, because it can be hard to see yourself objectively.

Have your friend reach into her closet and pull out twenty articles of clothing: shirts, dresses, pants, skirts, bathrobes, underwear, whatever. Tell her to get a good assortment, but concentrate on the ones that she wears most often. Lay them out on a bed, the floor, or a couch so you can see them all.

Take a good, hard look at these clothes. What do they say about her? Do you see a common color palette? Are there shapes and textures that run through them? Try answering the following questions about your friend based on her clothes:

- How old is she?
- What is her financial status?
- Is she married?
- What does she do for a living?
- What is her attitude about her own body?
- Is she involved in a romantic relationship?
- Is she shy? Confident?
- Where did she grow up?

Ask yourself: If she were a character in a play, how would these clothes reveal her personality to the audience?

Period

Choosing a period has a tremendous influence on the costume but, interestingly enough, getting it a little wrong isn't a disaster. Costumes serve characters who, in turn, serve a story. Unless you are doing *The Abe Lincoln Story*, you can fudge the years a little in most cases. Period is not just about historical accuracy. It is about putting the play in a place in time that fits the story. It's not enough to say *when* the play is taking place. You must answer the question, "Why then?"

In some cases, period is determined for you by historical events depicted in the story. If the family owns slaves, it will be challenging to set the play after the Civil War. (Actually, now that I think about it, that might lead to some interesting political theater.) In other cases, a play will set itself in a period because of a style of language. Nobody really talks like Noel Coward these days (more's the pity) so setting *Hay Fever* in the present might be a bit unsettling.

What really sets a play in a period, however, are the issues that are treated in the text. When Orson Welles directed his brilliant *Julius Caesar* in 1937, he set the play in the then fascist Italy, not because he liked the uniforms, but because he wanted to make a statement about the abuse of power and the ultimate failure of political will among the liberal ranks. Shakespeare's plays seem to endure being set in all sorts of periods, in fact. Seeing an Elizabethan *Hamlet* these days is almost a novelty.

Because of her historical knowledge and clothing sense, a costume designer can actually be a great deal of help in choosing a period. Smart directors will consider including her in this decision.

There are also times when it is useful to strategically ignore the period. For example, if you are setting *The Merchant of Venice* in the Italian Renaissance where Shakespeare envisioned it, you might discover that all Jews were required to wear a bright yellow hat at that time. Personally, I don't recommend putting your lead character, Shylock, in a big yellow hat. People will think you are doing *Curious George*, and speculate during intermission if Shylock's mischievousness at the zoo is what got him in trouble. In this case, ignore the period and find another hat for your lead.

From time to time, a director will throw the idea of period out the window, insisting that "This play takes place in no particular time." This is a problematic decision, for two reasons. First, it often turns out that the director *does* have a particular period in mind for most of the characters, but wants to cheat mightily with a single character to make a point.

Tweet! Five yards for not trusting your designer.

If you want to plop a French maid costume in the middle of a prison camp, it's your call, but don't yank the entire work out of period to do it. Challenge your designer to embody the idea of a French maid costume into a prison uniform. If you provide her with the tools she needs—a clear understanding of the character being paramount—you will be amazed at what comes out of some people's sewing machines.

The second reason that "no period" is problematic is that it sometimes means "no clue." Directors will decree that a play is about "universal themes" that transcend time and place, and thus each character should wear what suits him individually.

Tweet! Fifteen yards for delay of production while you figure out your concept.

Sure, love, hatred, passion, jealousy, rage, and all other emotions have been with us since time began, but that doesn't mean that they have always been felt and treated the same way. These emotions do not make a theme by themselves. Plays are about relationships—between people, between people and places, between people and society, between people and time. When you ignore period, you risk setting your play adrift, not only in time, but in concept.

I didn't say you couldn't do it. I didn't say you shouldn't. I just said it's tough.

A period doesn't necessarily have to be a particular year, however. It could be the world of a particular painter, for example, or a fantasy book. Vincent Van Gogh's late paintings have no particular year, but they do have a particular look and feel. The same might be said of *The Hobbit*.

Now that I have that out of my system, let's look at what the past gives us to work with. While history does not always give us the benefit of clearly defined periods, Western historical style basically breaks down as follows:*

- Prehistoric and Babylonian
- Ancient Egyptian
- Ancient Greece
- Ancient Rome
- Byzantine
- Barbarian Europe
- Medieval Europe
- Italian Renaissance
- Sixteenth Century/Northern European Renaissance
- Seventeenth Century
- Eighteenth Century
- Regency and Empire
- Victorian Era
- Edwardian Era
- 1911–1920
- 1920s
- 1930s
- 1940s
- 1950s
- 1960s
- 1970s
- 1980s
- 1990s
- 2000s

Note that, in this list, historical periods tend to get shorter as we move further forward in history. As it gets closer to the present day, the periods tend to subdivide more. If you are doing a show in the Edwardian Era, you don't have to worry so much about the differences between early Edwardian and late. If you are doing a show in 1982, however, you can get busted for rolling out an outfit that didn't make its appearance until 1988.

First and foremost, period determines the **silhouette** of the costume, that is, the overall shape of the garments, irrespective of color, texture, and fabric. In any given period, there is a choice of silhouettes. The designer will pick the one that is appropriate for a character, then build it with one of the fabrics that she has chosen for her palette.

Function

Actors move. There's no way of getting around it, and we wouldn't even if we could. It is the dynamism of the live performer that makes theater a wonderful experience.

*Thanks to Tara Maginnis of *Costumes.org* for this list.

That dynamic performance, however, can create some headaches for the costume department. As I said in the introduction, a costume can be a tool, even a toy, for an actor to use and play with to discover a character. Those toys, however, should be built to match the level of punishment they are going to get. You wouldn't play baseball with a long-stemmed rose, and you shouldn't stage a fistfight in costumes that weren't built for it. One designer I know always goes by the rule, "Dress up singers, Strip down dancers," which basically expresses a general philosophy about how clothes must serve the action.

Here's what the costume designer wants to know about how a costume will be used:

- *Does the actor need to dance, fight, climb ladders, or otherwise move in a highly physical way?* In this case, the seams may need to be strengthened. The costume may also need to be cut with more room around the joints, so the actor can move smoothly. Long trains on dresses may want to be reconsidered. Obviously, different types of dancing (tap, ballet, folk, etc.) will require different shoes.
- *Does the actor need to sing?* Singers need more room around the diaphragm, and may find it difficult to sing in corsets.
- *How big are the doors?* Women have worn some pretty bulky stuff through history, and you really don't want your rehearsal to grind to a halt because the four-foot-wide bustle skirt won't fit through the three-foot-wide door. The same goes for furniture. Ever seen what's underneath a hoop skirt? You will, if the actress sits down on a chair that's too small.
- *Is there food or drink involved?* Will this actor eat? Do they need to spill anything on themselves, have a food fight, or laugh so hard they shoot milk out their nose? These types of messes may affect which fabrics can be used. Protein stains will not wash out of some fabrics, and there may not be time or money for constant dry cleaning.
- *Will there be blood?* Never depend on the costume shop reading the play. They do, of course, but you should still let them know who gets stabbed and whom they will bleed on.
- *Will there be fast changes?* This is something the costume designer should be aware of well ahead of time, but it doesn't hurt to confirm it. People have different definitions of "fast," but I believe that any time an actor is in two consecutive scenes with two different costumes, it should be considered a fast change.
- *Does the performer need to dress or undress onstage?* This could happen for various reasons, from lovemaking to dressing for a joust. Any time

a garment is put on or removed in sight of the audience, the costume shop needs to know. For one thing, the fasteners that hold the clothes together must now be historically accurate. There were no zippers in Renaissance Verona. The costume shop can also do things to make the costume easier to remove or put on.

- *Does the costume need pockets?* Finding out during tech week that a costume needs a pocket makes costumers grumpy, and for good reason. It's always easier to install a pocket when a costume is being built.

You can address many of these issues ahead of time by putting the actors in **rehearsal clothes**. Most costume shops can provide rehearsal skirts for period plays, as well as corsets, hats, and other period pieces that will seriously affect the actor's ability to move. In the vast majority of cases, you won't get the actual costume until dress rehearsal, but you should get something that approximates the size and weight of the actual item. Male actors should plan on wearing their own suit coats and everyone should plan on providing appropriate footwear for rehearsal. The shop can and should provide costume props, like fans, pocket watches, cigarette cases, and so forth, particularly if those props are involved in **business**, a bit of action that is meant to draw the audience's attention.

The most important thing about all these issues is ASK EARLY. It is far easier to accommodate all these things when you are still a month from dress rehearsal.

The Costume Sketch

All of this design work is of no use if it is not communicated to the director and the costume shop. Costume design is communicated in a series of sketches that start with rough thumbnails during the design period and culminate with a fully realized costume rendering that is delivered to the shop for construction. In the world of scenery, the rendering gives a sense of what the final product will look like while the set is built from drafted plans. The costume designer depends entirely on the rendering to communicate her design both to the director and to the shop.

The rendering should depict the costume on the actor in a standing, full-body pose. Earlier versions that are done for the director will not include construction details, but the final version must contain all the information that the shop needs to build the costume. A rendering will often be accompanied by swatches, to show which fabrics will be used.

CHAPTER 8

The Tools of Costume: Shopping, Draping, and Stitching

Let's get one thing out of the way right off: costumes are not sewn. They are *built*. Saying a costume is sewn is like saying that sets are hammered; sewing is just one of the skills employed in modern costume construction.

As a costume design is coming together, the designer must make a decision between four avenues for each piece of clothing: *building, buying, renting,* or *pulling.* Costume designers choose between these four paths by employing the same formula that all designers do: money versus time versus available skills. Actually, it's all about money.

Buying is the most common option where contemporary clothes are involved. The options are limited to what is in the store, of course, but once you've found it, you've got most of your work done. Once you own the garment, you can also distress or alter it to your heart's content. Renting is a great option when you are doing period shows on a budget, but you can't change what they send you and it can be difficult to make rental clothes match clothes that are built or bought. Pulling a costume from stock is fast and easy, plus you can mess with it however you want. If you don't have it, though, you can't pull it.

Regardless of which path each costume is on, the first thing a designer does after a design is finalized is go shopping. A costume designer must have intimate knowledge of every clothing store, fabric store, secondhand store, and notions shop in a fifty-mile radius (not to mention the ones in New York and Los Angeles).

Let's go through these four paths, one at a time.

Building

Depending on how expensive your labor is, building is either the least or most expensive way to go. In an academic production, where labor comes in the form of credit-seeking students, both the cost and the skill levels may be low. If a professional shop is involved, both the costs and skills will be much higher. Building gives the designer the greatest control over the final product, as well as the sturdiest construction.

If the costumes are being built, the first stop is the fabric store, where the designer will collect **swatches**, playing-card-sized scraps of fabric that she can mix and match to find the right collection of fabrics for a range of costumes. Most costume designers collect swatches regularly, even when they are not working on a show. This habit helps them create a stock of colors and textures they can draw from when rendering their costumes. There is an old costume shop joke about a costume designer who dies and wakes up in a gigantic warehouse full of shelves, all of which are groaning under thousands of bolts of fabric of every description. Dozens of people are wandering around these shelves, staring up in wonderment. As the designer gapes at the untold bounty, she stops a passerby and says, "This is incredible. Is this Heaven?" to which the passerby replies, "No, this is Hell. There are no scissors."

After the swatching is done and the designer is ready to purchase fabric, she must figure out the yardage that she needs. Fabric is priced per yard, so the yardage times the price equals the cost of the fabric for the costume. The variety of available fabric is stunning, so one way of breaking it down is natural versus synthetic.

Natural versus Synthetic

This is not nearly as clean of a distinction as we would all like it to be. Rayon, for example, which most people would call synthetic, is actually made from wood. In general, however, natural fibers are things like wool, cotton, and silk, while synthetic fibers are things like nylon, polyester, and spandex. You can generalize about these groups and say that natural fibers are more expensive, easier to work with, and harder to keep clean and pressed, but every costume designer who just read that sentence has got her hand up in the air right now to tell me about the exceptions. The fact of the matter is, this distinction is only useful to a point. With that in mind, let's look at general groups of fabrics. All of the groups listed here have natural and synthetic subgroups as well as stretchy and nonstretchy variants. Furthermore, there is a fabric in every group that is fabulously expensive and another that is shamefully cheap.

- *Animal Hair*: Many types of wool including Merino, Corriedale and Leicester; also cashmere, mohair, alpaca, angora, camel, and many others. Luxurious, soft, and expensive. Can get warm on stage.
- *Sheers*: chiffon, organza, lace, and other lightweight, gauzy, see-through fabrics. There are both synthetic and natural varieties.
- *Naps*: plushes, fur, corduroy, and other thick, fuzzy fabrics. Remember that many sets are HOT, so these may be uncomfortable.
- *Shiny*: satin, taffeta, silks, and other fabrics that catch a lot of light and look dressy. Also many synthetic fabrics such as acetate.
- *Cotton and blends*: cotton is lightweight, breathable, and easy to sew, but gains durability and lower cost when blended with fabrics such as rayon, acrylic, or polyester. Linen, which is made from flax, a vegetable fiber, is similar but more durable, better-looking, and pricier.
- *Synthetics*: Nylon, rayon, spandex, polyester, and many, many others. Most are harder to dye and not as luxurious to wear, but much cheaper and easier to care for.
- *Plastics*: Synthetics, like vinyl, look shiny and colorful on stage but do not breathe and can be a pain to wear for long periods.
- *Twinkles*: Metallics, sequins, glittery, and showy fabrics, there seems to be no end of variety.

Most designers will decide which kind of fabric they are looking for, then go looking for the color or pattern that fits what they have in their mind's eye. When shopping for a show, many designers will avoid searching for a particular fabric for a particular costume. Instead, they are looking for a fabric that is within the style of the show. As Tara Maginnis, head of the costume shop at the University of Alaska, puts it, "I am always looking for a fabric that says, 'I want to be in this show.'" Designers will stock up on fabrics that feel right for the show, then parcel them out later.

Once the fabric is bought, the designer faces another fork in the road: *patterning* or *draping*. Patterning means that the shop must create a pattern from which they will cut the clothes. Sometimes these patterns are designed by taking apart existing garments and copying them, but in most cases, the **cutter**—the costume shop person who specializes in this area—must be able to look at the costume rendering, visualize each piece of the costume in her head and draw it out using the actor's measurements. It's an impressive display of three-dimensional visualization, particularly since the cutter is imagining how the pieces will connect in her head, without the ability to see how it comes together until it is time to assemble the whole thing.

It is possible to build a costume using patterns that were actually used at the time, but in general, it is advisable to use contemporary patterns and adapt them to period costumes, rather than adapting period patterns to modern bodies and construction techniques. Recently, there has also been a trend from pattern companies, like Simplicity and Butterick, toward producing patterns for costumes. As fewer and fewer people sew their own clothes, these companies are trying to open new markets in theater companies and historical re-creationists. If you are building period costumes, check these companies' catalogs for useful patterns.

In order to drape a costume, the shop sets up a dressmaker's dummy that is the same size as the actor who will wear the costume. Some dummies are adjustable, and I'm just going to leave that joke alone. Draping is the process of laying fabric onto this dummy, building the costume up piece by piece, using the costume rendering as a guide. There is no pattern. The **draper**, as this person is called, must call upon her knowledge of clothing construction to determine which pieces go where. It's a bit like doing sculpture, and a talented draper is worth her weight in gold.

Both drapers and cutters often do the first version of the costume in muslin, a cheap but pliable fabric that can be used to make a mock-up of the costume without spending a fortune. Having a fitting in a muslin mock-up can be disorienting to an actor, who might walk into the shop expecting to be decked out in her Act Three ball gown, only to be unceremoniously safety-pinned into an itchy, off-white pile of fabric with extra pieces sticking out of it everywhere like Medusa's hair. Don't panic, it's only the muslin mock-up.

Once the draper has the costume looking like she wants it on the dummy and has checked it on the actor, she cuts the fabric into its final pieces, leaving extra fabric all around for the seams.

Whether the fabric pieces come from the cutter or the draper, the next stop is the **stitcher**, an expert in construction. Of course, in a small shop or one-person operation, one person might build the entire costume start to finish, but in a larger shop, these jobs are split between three people.

Buying

One might think that buying clothes would be the easiest way to do a show, but it ain't necessarily so. If you are buying costumes for a show, it generally means that the show is a contemporary one, and, when it comes to contemporary shows, everyone has an opinion. An actor might object strongly to a costume choice, saying, "My character would never wear that!" If you are doing *Merchant of Venice* in the seventeenth century, however, the designer can gently remind the actor that, yes, it looks a little strange to our eyes, but that collar was the style in Venice at the time. Research settles a lot of issues on the spot.

If you are depicting people in modern dress, you will sometimes be shopping for things that could be built in an historical style much more cheaply. If your character is a wealthy New York socialite, it might be cheaper to fake a nineteenth-century evening gown than to purchase a modern one. Modern dress means a tighter standard of accuracy.

If your run is short and your relationship with the community is positive, you can often borrow certain kinds of garments, such as police or military uniforms, lab coats, waitress uniforms, athletic equipment and clothing, choir robes, clerical outfits, and so forth. Naturally, the shop and the actors would need to treat these garments with extra care, so that they can be borrowed again next season and, of course, the lenders should be given credit and/or advertising in the program.

Secondhand and thrift stores can be a gold mine for costume designers, even if you are planning on building a costume. These days, the price of fabric is high enough that it can actually be more cost-effective to build a costume out of an old garment than to buy the new fabric. Find something that is close at the Salvation Army and then cannibalize the fabric for your new costume.

Renting

In some cases, it is best to rent a costume that has been built by someone else. This is most often, and most effectively, done when you are looking for an entire production, especially musicals and operas. It is best not to try to put rental clothes onstage with clothes that you have built. It can be challenging to make them look like they are in the same show, especially because you cannot alter rental clothes in any way. You can get away with putting rented uniforms or men's formal wear in an otherwise built show, however, because those things are pretty standard.

Rentals can allow you to save a lot of money, but you must be very cautious with the clothes. You have to tell *everybody* that the costume is rented and no harm must come to it. That means no spills, no tears, no alterations, no dyes, no nuthin'.

When you are setting up the rental, get a complete list of all the measurements that the rental house needs. You will need to take these measurements carefully from every performer who is wearing a costume and then hope that the rental house gets it close enough. If you are not familiar with taking measurements, the rental house can provide a diagram showing you where each of the measurements is taken.

Costume houses tend to gather out on the coasts, so look for one that is on the coast closest to you, either in New York or Los Angeles. If you are out in the heartland, it really isn't going to matter.

Pulling

Pulling clothes can be as much of an art as patterning, draping, or designing. A talented designer can look at a stock garment and see a world of possibilities. The ability to see the patterned waistcoat in the Renaissance tunic can keep your costs way down. If a show is going to be pulled, the designer will generally go through the stock before she does the renderings.

One of the most valuable kinds of stock that a theater can have is hats and shoes, because both are expensive to buy and shoes cannot be built.

The great thing about pulled clothes is that they are already yours, so you can disassemble, dye, paint, cut, and distress them to your heart's content. You can even stitch them together with other clothes, if you want. In this way, costume stocks keep turning over, year after year, providing season after season of Mercutios, Blanches, and Mames.

Fittings and Measurements

Very early in the production, the costume designer and her assistant will visit the actors to get measurements. This is more conveniently done at the first read-through, when the designer might also display the costume renderings. Measurement sessions can be a little nerve-racking for actors, especially those who battle their weight, but designers are firmly professional about taking measurements and it is usually over quickly. If you are an actor being measured, just stand still and let them do their thing. It is perfectly acceptable to ask that your measurements be taken in a private space.

Depending on the costume, an actor may have anywhere from one to five fittings, not counting the initial measurement session. The first one usually involves a costume that is not quite finished. Don't freak out if trim is missing, if the color is too bright, or if it doesn't fit you correctly. You are in the middle of an ongoing construction process and lots of things are going to change.

You are also, however, a member of the team that is creating this costume, so you should feel free to share information and make respectful requests. The shop wants to know how the costume fits you, so take the time in the fitting to move around with it on. Stretch your arms and legs out as you will onstage. If your character walks or sits, you should do that in the fitting, after first warning the crew. You don't want to find out the hard way

Fig. 31. The costume fitting

that there is a pin stuck in the butt of those pants. Let them know if the costume is binding you anywhere and if it is comfortable. The time for this conversation is NOW, not at dress rehearsal. It's a good idea to take a look at the costume rendering during the fitting, as the garment you are wearing might not resemble it yet.

One conversation that seems to take place a lot during the fitting starts with the actor saying "I wouldn't wear this!" First of all, remember, YOU are not wearing it; your character is. Second, remember that this design was agreed on between the designer and the director, so if you disagree, it might be because you have a different concept of the character than the director does. Ask respectful questions of the designer if you don't understand her choices, but serious disagreements should be taken to the director, not the designer.

Actors should also remember that the shop has a lot of fittings to get through, so try to keep the process moving.

Fabric Augmentation

Once the costume is built, the shop isn't finished. Besides attaching trim and fasteners, the costume artisans often augment the fabric by dyeing, painting, distressing, or otherwise texturing it.

Dyeing and painting both involve putting color onto the costume. Fabric dye actually seeps into the threads of the fabric and permanently colors it. Dyes and dyeing technique vary depending on what kind of fabric is being treated, so, if you are interested, get one of the many books on dyeing as a guide. Many dyes are hazardous to work with as well, so pay attention to safety warnings. Paint sits on the surface, which gives the costume more vibrant color but makes it less washable. Sometimes a costume is too bright on stage, so it must be dipped in a lightly brewed tea to "take it down."

Distressing is a general term that simply means to make a costume look older and more beat up. Costumers might grind dirt into it, wash it repeatedly, rough it up with rocks, slash it, or otherwise make it look like it's been through hard times.

Dealing with Hair

The first piece of advice I can give any actor is to forget about having a memorable hairstyle. The first thing they're going to do is make you cut it. Men, keep your hair a neutral length. Forget about dreadlocks, ponytails, shelves, mohawks, or any other unusual style. Insisting on keeping a style like that will shorten your list of possible roles considerably. Women may keep their hair long or short, but stay away from funky colors and braids. Musicians may (and should) ignore everything I just said.

If you are going to need a wig, remember that wigs come in synthetic and human hair. Synthetic wigs usually look more fake and are harder to style, but they cost much less. Human hair, however, can be a good long-term investment because it can be styled over and over for years to come. Above all, don't put human hair wigs on stage with synthetic. One will call the lie on the other. (The same goes for fur, by the way.) Any wig looks like a wig when it first comes out of the box, so they all have to be styled before they are ready for the stage.

One Final Note

For many actors, the most important person in the theater is their dresser and/or their makeup person. Like a lot of things in the costume area, this is an intimate relationship, dealing with issues of body, appearance, and ego. One longtime actress told me, "The dresser is either my enemy or my best friend." If you are an actor, recognize that this person is here to help you, and deserves your respect. If you are a dresser or a makeup artist, remember that it ain't gonna be you out there doing your thing in front of hundreds of people. Acting is hard.

CHAPTER 9

Sound Design: Audible Atmosphere

Sound is the most mysterious backstage technology. Something about it seems mystical and strange. You speak into a microphone and somehow that sound goes down a cable, goes into some black boxes, changes, gets louder, and comes out of a big speaker over your head. Magic.

People often assume that theatrical technology is more complicated than it really is. People shy away from scenery and lighting because they appear overly complex. They assume there are lots of complicated things they have to learn when, in fact, the actual process is fairly simple.

With sound, however, the opposite is often true: People underestimate the complication. They don't realize what it takes to produce really good sound. What makes this especially tragic is that good-quality sound is absolutely critical to a successful production. In its ability to stir emotions, sound has no rival. Furthermore, for a budget-conscious theater company, sound can be the financial miracle worker, producing the deepest experience for the least amount of money.

We'll start this discussion with an overview of the entire sound system, known as the **signal chain**. Then we will enter the system at the microphones, explore the mixer, get pumped up by the amp, and head back out into the air through the speakers.

The Signal Chain

"Sound" is something you hear. It is what your mouth produces and your ears pick up. When a sound enters a sound system (through a microphone, for example), it is translated into electrical energy, an energy that goes up and down as the sound gets louder and softer. This energy is called a **signal**. The signal continues through the system until it gets out the other side, where it is changed (in a speaker) from electrical energy back into audible sound. While it is inside the system, however, it is an inaudible electrical force—a signal.

Every sound system is a set of links, a chain that this signal moves through. This signal chain has four major links. Sometimes, one piece of equipment may do more than one thing. In a portable tape player or "boom box," for example, one piece of equipment does all four. Regardless of size or purpose though, all sound systems have all four pieces. They are:

- *Source:* The sound has to come from somewhere. If the sound is something audible in the outside world, then the **source** is the microphone used to capture it. If the sound is already recorded, then the source is the tape deck or the CD player that is playing it back. Somehow, the sound must enter the system.

- *Routing:* The signal has to be sent to the proper place at the proper volume. This is done by some sort of **mixer**. On your home stereo, you choose "tape" or "CD player" on the front panel and turn the volume up. Believe it or not, that huge mixer at the back of a theater does not do much more than what you did by hitting "tape" and raising the volume. It just does it better, more quietly and with more options. On a mixer, for example, you can have input from several sources playing simultaneously. Plus, you can set the volume for each one separately. Imagine that your home stereo allowed you to play the CD player and the radio at the same time, while also letting you talk over a microphone, setting a separate volume control for each one, and you can start to see what a mixer does.

- *Amplification:* The signal coming from the source (the microphone, the tape deck, whatever) is not powerful enough to drive the speakers. If you were to plug your CD player directly into your speakers, you would not hear anything. For the signal to be loud enough, you need amplification. On your home stereo, this is usually built into the same unit that routed your signal. In most theater sound systems, however, it is a separate unit that takes the output from the mixer and pumps it up to a strong enough level for the speakers.

- *Output:* There must be some way for the sound to get out of the system so that people can hear it: speakers.

As the signal travels through the sound system, it goes through some changes. Some of the most important changes it goes through are changes in strength, or **signal level**. A signal may appear in various places in the system at various levels. Let's look at the different levels:

- *Mic* (pronounced "mike") *Level:* When you speak into a microphone, the air pressure from your voice causes a small magnet inside the microphone to move, creating a tiny electrical charge. This electrical energy travels down the microphone cable to the mixer. This is an extremely low-level signal, a sort of electronic whisper. This **"mic level"** signal must be boosted by a **pre-amp** before it is useful to the sound system. That is why you cannot take a microphone and plug it in to the tape input on your stereo and expect it to work. The tape input has no pre-amp. If there is an input on your stereo marked "mic," then that input is equipped with a pre-amp, which boosts the signal up to a higher level.
- *Line Level:* Tape decks, CD players, and electronic musical instruments all put out line-level signals, so they do not need to be boosted when they get to the mixer. In fact, line level is the level that all electronic devices, except microphones, use to talk to each other. If you are plugging two electronic devices together, the signal that is traveling down the wire is at line level. The mixer may adjust the volume up and down, but the signal level that it puts out remains the same. This distinction may be hard to understand, because sound people sometimes use the terms "level" and "volume" interchangeably. Just remember, both mic level and line level refer to a range of volumes. A high mic level is still less powerful than a low line level.

Think of it this way: A high school teacher's salary may fluctuate up and down over the years, but it is still in the range of high school teacher salaries. The CEO of General Motors has a much higher salary, which may also fluctuate up and down. The range of the teacher's salary, however, will never be anywhere near the CEO's. (Then again, the CEO doesn't get three months of summer vacation. Some things are better than money.) In the same way, mic level, though it may fluctuate, will always be lower than line level.

On a mixer, there is generally a switch or a rotary knob by each input that allows you to select mic level or line level for that input. If you plug a microphone into a line level input, you won't be able to hear it. If you plug a line level signal into a mic level input, it will be so loud and distorted that you might damage your system. So don't do that. Simply turn the switch or rotary knob to "mic" or "line" as appropriate and the pre-amp will do the voodoo that it do.

- *Speaker Level:* Once you are done combining the signals and adjusting their volumes, the resulting signal gets sent to the amplifier. Here, it is pumped up to a level that will actually drive the speakers. This level is *way* above either line level or mic level, so you definitely don't want to plug the output of an amp to anything other than a speaker. If a line level signal is a CEO's salary, then **speaker level** is like the budget of the Pentagon. During a Bush administration.

Microphones: The Testy Toddlers of Sound

As I said above, the first thing you need in a signal chain is a source. The world of signal sources can be divided into two distinct groups: microphones and everything else.

If it were not for microphones, sound design would be the easiest dollar in show business. It is not that the rest of the equipment lacks complication. It is simply more predictable. Microphones are unpredictable to the point of rebellious. A sound engineer who can keep microphones happy is a valuable person indeed.

What's the deal? Why are microphones so skittish? Well, first let's explore what they are and how they work, and then talk about how to keep them happy.

At the heart, microphones are simple machines. Sound is created by movement. When an object (like your vocal cords) vibrates, it creates waves of air pressure—sound waves. The greater the pressure, the more volume the sound has. This wave of sound pressure bumps into everything in its way, and if the object it bumps into is delicate or light, the air pressure will cause it to move. In your ear, there is a sensitive membrane called your eardrum. When waves of sound pressure hit it, it vibrates. Those vibrations are transmitted to your brain as electrical impulses. This is how you hear.

A microphone is a mechanical ear. When sounds arrive from the outside world, they move a sensitive membrane called a **diaphragm**. The diaphragm is connected to a magnet. As the diaphragm moves, the magnet turns these vibrations into electrical impulses and sends them to the rest of the sound system.

A microphone is the ear of the sound system. It is how the sound system "hears."

Like your ear, the microphone converts sound from a wave of pressure into a series of electrical impulses. The mixer and the amp amplify the sounds, in turn, and pump them out to a set of speakers. The problem is that the microphone is innocent and naïve, like your basic toddler. And just like a two-year-old who doesn't know Cheerios from rat poison, a microphone will pick up whatever is around and happily put it in its mouth, sending it off to be amplified and broadcast. And, just like a toddler, some of the things that it will pick up are not good for it. If the sound system gets a taste of these unappetizing tidbits, it may respond with anything from persistent static to an ear-splittin', equipment-fryin', I-want-my-mommy wail. It is not without logic that Jimmy Thudpucker (*Doonesbury*'s fictional rock-and-roll star) considered naming his new baby "Feedback." If you don't go out of your way to feed your microphone only what is good for it, the whole sound system is going to call you a bad mommy.

Choosing a Microphone

If you have ten dollars, you can buy a microphone and still buy lunch. If you have ten *thousand* dollars, you can buy a different microphone and not have a quarter left for the parking meter. Microphones come in an almost incomprehensible variety, from the inexpensive ones at Radio Shack to the multithousand-dollar ones that studio engineers treat better than their girlfriends. There are microphones specifically designed to amplify guitars, drums, or saxophones. There are mics that attach to your body, to your clothes, and in your hair. There are even mics that sit on the floor and look like mice. Let's talk about what makes them all different.

Dynamic versus Condenser Mics

Dynamic mics are simple and robust: These mics have a lightweight, suspended diaphragm that vibrates when sound hits it. Dynamics are the tougher style of microphone and will put up with more abuse than the other kinds. Live music shows and speeches rely heavily on them and virtually every rock-and-roll show uses them exclusively.

Condenser mics are more sensitive and reproduce sound more accurately, but are less durable and convenient. Condenser mics use a more complicated mechanism that involves generating an electrical field inside the mic. Incoming sound creates disturbances in this electrical field, generating a signal. Because the electrical field is easier to disturb than the physical diaphragm, the mic is more sensitive. Condenser mics also require a power source, so they will usually have a power cord hanging off them. Some condensers can get power through the audio line, through a trick called **phantom power**, but the mixer must be equipped to handle it. Because of their fragile nature, as well as their need for external power, you will find fewer condenser mics backstage.

Low Impedance versus High Impedance

Impedance is a fairly mysterious audio phenomenon that even some professional sound engineers do not understand. They do understand its importance, however. Put simply, impedance is the amount of resistance an electrical circuit puts up to an incoming signal.

Why is impedance significant? Three words: Noise, noise, and noise.

Remember how I said a microphone is like a toddler crawling around stuffing sound into its mouth? Well, one of the unsavory things that it will wrap its chubby little fists around is electrical noise. Lots of backstage gear creates electrical noise: extension cords, lighting equipment, fluorescent lights, even wall sockets. Video monitors are particularly notorious, as are refrigerators. Where there is electricity, there is electrical noise. This noise isn't audible to us, but it can be deafening to a microphone circuit. Remember: Everything the microphone sends to the sound system is going to be amplified—first by the pre-amp, and then by the amplifier. Silent electrical noise will become clearly audible by the time it gets through the amplifier.

Here is a little secret, however: Electrical noise does not create sound pressure, so it is not really the microphone that picks it up. It's the cable. A mic cable operates like a big radio antenna, sweeping up any kind of electrical impulse it can get its hands on. Actually, it is not *like* an antenna, it *is* an antenna (the radio antenna on your car is just a cable), so do not be surprised when passing police cars start broadcasting into your theater.

Audio engineers shut out noise by using **balanced lines**. A balanced line is a microphone cable that sends the signal out on two wires at once, one running from the mixer to the mic and one running from the mic to the mixer. Any noise that the cable picks up gets sent in both directions at once, effectively canceling it out. An **unbalanced line** sends all the noise in a single direction: toward the mixer. Result: The noise enters the sound system.

The catch is, you have to use a low-impedance microphone to use a balanced line. Better-quality mics are always low impedance and it's easy to tell the difference. Look at the plug coming out of the end. A low-impedance mic will have a three-pin **XLR plug** coming out of it. This kind of plug is required for a balanced line, because a balanced line has three wires: one running in each direction, plus a ground wire.

A high-impedance mic will generally have a **phone** (or quarter-inch) **plug**. This kind of cable only has two wires; ergo, it is unbalanced. Without the balancing effect, the cables will tend to pick up extraneous noise. Bottom line:

- Low impedance = balanced line = XLR plug = better.
- High impedance = unbalanced line = ¼" plug = cheaper.

Don't understand it? You are not alone. Electricity boggles a lot of people's minds, including mine. Here's the *real* bottom line: *All mics should run on balanced, low-impedance lines using mics and cables with XLR plugs.*

And don't try to beat the rule by putting an adapter somewhere in the stretch of cable between the mic and the mixer. Any piece of unbalanced line will cause you trouble. Maybe not today, maybe not tomorrow...

All of this impedance and balanced-line nonsense only applies to microphone lines. Tape decks, CD players, keyboards, and many other kinds of sound equipment can be happily plugged in with quarter-inch plugs on unbalanced lines. Because this equipment operates at line level, it tends to wipe out the noise.

Types of Microphones

Here are some questions to help you decide on a mic, whether you are renting or buying. Knowing the answers to these questions will help you talk intelligently to a salesperson or a sound designer:

- *What are you mic-ing?* Some mics are specially designed to pick up voices. Some are better for instruments. Some are better for picking up sound from a large group, such as an orchestra or a chorus. Some mics are built for specific uses, like **lavaliere mics** that attach to your clothing, or mics that are designed for a particular musical instrument.
- *How much do you want to spend?* The eternal question. You may not have to spend an incredible amount to get what you need, but skimping will come back to haunt you. A run-of-the-mill, solid microphone

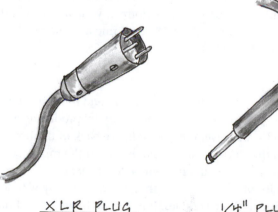

XLR PLUG   1/4" PLUG

Fig. 32. Different kinds of audio plugs

will cost you at least a hundred dollars, and unless you want to be climbing the walls later, you should put the money out. A dime-store mic can be had for five dollars, but it won't be worth the aggravation. I heavily recommend, if at all possible, that you spend the money for a low-impedance mic.

- *Does it need to be wireless?* Sometimes the mic cord will get in the way of something. Sometimes you just want the performer to have more mobility. In situations like these, you may want to get a **wireless mic**. Wireless mics have their own set of problems, though, so read the section on them before you decide.
- *What do you like?* You probably won't be able to answer this one right off, but spend some time listening to mics. Some will pick up sound more accurately than others. Some will produce more low end, or bass sound. Some will produce more high end, or treble sound. If you find a favorite mic, ask for it by name.
- *What are other people using?* I steal other people's secrets whenever possible, and I suggest you do the same. Ask people what they use. Get the benefit of their experience.

Once you know the answer to these questions, you can look at specific types of microphones. When in doubt, however, go for...

The Regular Old Mic

If you don't ask for a specific mic by name, people will assume you want a mic shaped like an ice cream cone. It will not be wireless and it will be designed to stick into a holder or be carried around with the cord trailing behind. The most common R.O.M. is the Shure SM-58. If you are ordering a mic for a podium, an emcee, or a vocal performer, you can just tell the rental company that you want an "SM-58 style" mic and they will know what you mean. A Regular Old Mic.

Wireless Mics

Wireless microphone systems continue to improve and more theaters can now afford to rent or buy them. Wireless mics work by producing a radio signal that is picked up by a receiver offstage or in the back of the house. The receiver then creates the electrical signal that is sent to the mixer. Each microphone requires its own receiver and its own radio frequency. This can get pricey if you have a lot of mics, so many theaters try to get by with just a few.

Wireless mics come in three varieties, **hand-held, headset,** and **body**. Hand-held mics are the ones you see on MTV all the time being carried around by rock-and-roll singers. They are now so accepted by audiences that it is surprising to see a performer with a mic cord anymore. This is especially helpful in situations when the performer is lip-syncing, or in less polite terms, faking it. It's gotten so you don't even have to run a cord to a lip-syncing performer anymore. You just put something approximately mic-shaped in his hand and the audience will believe it is a wireless mic. Some people don't even realize that a mic cord actually has a purpose. I had a student recently who was singing into a regular wired mic mounted on a podium. Once he got rolling, however, he decided that he needed some freedom to move, so he whipped the mic out of the stand, pulled the cord out of the mic, and dropped it on the floor. Of course, the mic quit working, a fact that confused him mightily.

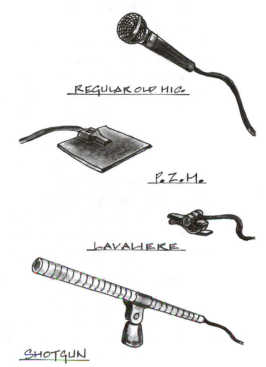

Fig. 33. Different kinds of microphones

Even with all the advances in technology, sound designers still lose a lot of sleep over wireless mics. They are battery-operated, so the batteries must be constantly checked and changed. The radio frequencies they use can pick up interference, and it is not uncommon for police and fire department radio transmissions to slip through from time to time. On Broadway, where the use of wireless mics has reached epic proportions, there are now specific frequencies assigned to each show. New show openings can be delayed until another show closes and frees up enough radio channels.

Headset Mics

For a while, these mics were known around the business as the "Madonna" mic, because she was one of the first major performers to use them. The great advantage of a headset mic is, not surprisingly, you don't have to sing into your hand. Consequently, these have become the mics of choice for performers who dance, play an instrument, work a ventriloquism dummy, or any other activity where it would be really nice to have your hands free. Headset mics are also much easier to rig than hair or body mics and the element is usually larger and farther away from the actor's face, which protects it from perspiration.

The first couple of generations of headset mics were big, black, and bulky. They weren't really intended to be hidden. Part of the whole "Madonna" effect was that she was wearing a mic that was high-tech and cool, so no one cared if it was visible. Most rock singers still don't care if the mic is visible, 'cause, let's face it, the people in the crowd know that Garth Brooks is wearin' a mic.

There are other performers, however, who are now benefiting from a new generation of near-invisible headset mics. These slender, pinky-peach or black* marvels are so tiny that any audience member more than fifty feet away might miss them altogether. They are still not invisible enough to work for "realistic" theatrical shows, but they are very popular in trade shows, conventions, or themeparks, where hair mics are too much trouble and we really don't mind if a few people notice that Cinderella has something on her cheek.

Body Mics

The human voice is an incredible instrument, and it is capable of astounding depth and volume when properly trained. Unfortunately, the trend in the modern theater is toward amplifying actors artificially, particularly in musicals. The demands on a modern musical theater performer are huge. Modern pit orchestras are louder than ever before and actors must be able to perform up to eight times a week. Furthermore, as I said in the opening chapter, the modern, film-oriented audience is more demanding about being able to hear the performers clearly. Small wonder that today's theatrical actors depend on small, nearly invisible mics mounted on their bodies in order to be heard.

Still, I would like to encourage theater artists everywhere to approach body mics with caution and reluctance. No sound system in the world is a match for the nuance and persuasion of the human voice. Actors should make vocal training a high priority for their careers, and they should seek to develop a voice that will fill a large house without amplification. Though the task is difficult, the rewards are immense.

Having said that, we can begin exploring this rather touchy technology. Wireless body mics were developed to be hidden on actors in musicals. They consist of two pieces: a pencil eraser–sized microphone and a cigarette pack–sized belt pack. The two pieces are connected by a cord that runs underneath the costume. The mics are generally concealed in the actor's hair or over the ear. The over-the-ear placement is used if the actor is balding or if a hat is put

*Yes, okay, they are called "flesh-colored" in the catalog, but I refuse to continue this trend. I know too many people whose flesh isn't pinky-peach.

on or taken off during the show. In a pinch, the mic can be put on the collar of the costume, although designers tend to avoid that one because it may pick up too much of the low frequencies and lead to a sound that is unnatural. They can also sound hollow if two actors are close together. Plus, a good hug will produce an earth-shaking thump, as the mic gets banged around.

Other circumstances might influence mic placement as well. If you are doing *South Pacific*, for instance, you've got to deal with the "I'm Gonna Wash That Man Right Out of My Hair" scene when the character actually washes her hair on stage, precluding any kind of a mic placement above the neck.

Besides the mic itself, you also have to hide the **belt pack**, which contains the batteries and the **transceiver**, the part that actually sends out the radio signal. Despite its name, the belt pack rarely goes on the belt. In a perfect world, the mic is clipped in the hair, the cord runs down the back of the neck, and the belt pack rides in a pocket in the costume in the small of the actor's back. This isn't always possible, however, since a close-fitting or revealing costume may not cover the pack. In fact, belt pack placement may take some ingenuity. Sometimes a costume modification is necessary. Shoulder holsters, which place the pack underneath the arm, are fairly common, as are hip, butt, breast, and, I kid you not, codpiece packs. "Find the Mic" and "Find the Pack" are two games you can play the next time you go see a show with body mics.

Even if you find good places for the mic and the belt pack, you're only halfway home. Heavy physical action, such as a fight or dancing, can work the mic loose. Perhaps the biggest killer of body mics, though, is sweat. The mic itself is quite tiny, and a single bead of sweat will cover it. If this happens, the mic will begin to sound like someone has his hand over it and soon after, it will go out altogether. This is called **sweating out a mic** and there isn't much to be done except get the actor offstage and dry it out or change it.

If you are wearing a body mic and you think your mic is out, you aren't lost. If you can't get offstage, try standing right next to another actor and say your lines into *her* mic. It's not perfect, and it may make for some interesting blocking, but it will get you through a scene.

PZM Mics

PZM stands for "pressure zone modulation," but who cares? Not me. The **PZM microphone** is specifically designed to sit on the floor, where it picks up not only the sound coming directly from the source, but also the sound that bounces off the floor right in front of it, making the microphone more sensitive. You can grasp this by standing in front of the apron during rehearsal and leaning down within an inch or two of the stage. When you get within an inch of the stage floor, you should hear the actor's voices get louder. While you may have to put up with Indian guide jokes, you will understand why PZMs are so efficient. You often see PZMs lined up across the front of the stage, looking like little black cigar boxes. Sound people sometimes refer to them as "mice." Careful, don't kick them. That's a bad thing.

Lavaliere Mics

Lavaliere, or lav, mics are those black, marble-sized mics you see clipped to people's lapels on talk shows. Lav mics pick up voices quite well, and they are useful in situations where you don't want to see a mic in front of someone, or when you don't want the speaker to be tied to a microphone mounted on a podium. If you are doing video interviews, this is your boy. Meeting planners, take note. Lav mics are great for speakers because they can walk around the stage and gesture up at overheads and so on. For true mobility, get a wireless lav. They still have all of the radio frequency problems, but at least they don't sweat out like the tiny body mics. Of course, they are harder to hide than body mics, but you usually use them in situations where you don't care about concealment anyway.

Shotgun Mics

In placing a mic on the stage, proximity is everything. The best way to pick up any sound is to get close to whatever is making it. If you are not using hand-held or body mics, then you may have to get creative about where you put mics onstage. Sometimes you just can't get a mic close to the source and it must be mounted farther away. In this case, you want a mic that will only pick up what is directly in front of it, rejecting the sounds to either side, even if the target sound is far away. Enter the **shotgun mic.** It's often used by television camera crews when they can't get close to something they need to record. In the theater, they are used when the only good mic placement is far away: for example, when you have to put a mic high above the stage on an electric pipe. A shotgun mic will tend to reject sounds to the side even if they are closer than the target sound, minimizing unwanted noise.

Even with a shotgun, you may not have the solution. Depending on the quality of the mic, it may only work ten to thirty feet away, and the sound quality may be questionable. At best, this can be a real problem solver. At worst, it's a low-quality stop-gap.

The Backstage Survival Guide to Keeping Microphones Happy

- *Turn the mic on.* Many mics have switches, so if your mic isn't working, look for one. Wired mics have them on the side, wireless are usually on the bottom.

- *Use low-impedance mics on balanced lines.* It will help you to eliminate noise.
- *Do not run mic lines next to power cords, video cables, or lighting equipment.* Ditto.
- *Don't blow into a microphone.* Hey, we don't blow into each other's ears to see if we're listening, do we? If you want to keep sound people happy, don't blow into the mic. It may damage the diaphragm. If you need to check if a mic is on, tap it gently.
- *When speaking into a mic, put your mouth about a hand's width away from the mic and keep it at a constant distance.* The mic's ability to pick up your voice drops radically when you move away, even a few inches. Likewise, don't "eat" the mic. The low frequencies in your voice will be unnaturally amplified and your voice will be distorted. Plus, you'll slobber on it.
- *Don't point the mic at a speaker.* This will create **feedback**. Want to become the least popular person in your theater? Take a live microphone, and stick it right in front of a speaker. If everything is on, you will be rewarded with a deafening squeal that the Brits call "howlround," the Americans call "feedback," and everybody else calls annoying.

Feedback is the audio version of a short circuit. It happens when a sound comes out of a speaker and immediately reenters the sound system through a microphone. These nearly instantaneous round trips cause the sound pressure level to build rapidly on itself until it reaches the crisis point and wango! Feedback.

Besides being painful to listen to, feedback is also not a good thing for equipment. It can fry electronics and blow speakers. When feedback starts, you should deal with it immediately, like *right now*. If you are holding or speaking into a mic, turn the mic away from whatever speaker is closest to you. If there are several speakers, or you do not know which way to turn the mic, then just leave it. There is nothing you can do. The person on the mixer will have to solve it. There is a common myth that, if feedback starts, you should put your hand over the mic. *Do not do this.* It will actually make it worse. If you are running the sound system when feedback starts, turn the volume down. Try to figure out which mic is the culprit. If the feedback has just started, you may be able to drop the volume just a little bit and no one will be the wiser. If a feedback cycle really gets going, though, you may have to turn the volume all the way down to break it up.

The most important thing is to listen for it. Except in extreme cases, feedback starts softly, either as a high-pitched whine or as a little ringing sound at the ends of people's words. Listen for it, and back the volume off before

Fig. 34. Where feedback comes from

the crisis begins. The best way to fight feedback is to have a good *equalizer* in your sound system, as well as somebody who knows how to run it. More about that when we get to signal processing.

Other Sources: Tape Decks, CDs, DAT

Microphones are fine for amplifying voices or other "live" sounds but, at some point, everyone wants to play back prerecorded sound. These days, there is one familiar format (compact discs), one older format that is still around (cassette), two exotic formats that still show up in professional applications (DAT and MiniDisc™) and three new formats that are rapidly growing in usage (MP3, samplers, and WAV file playback). We'll deal with the familiar first.

Compact Discs

Tape is dead. While there are theaters out there that are still running **reel-to-reel tape decks** or cassettes, it is time for those poor souls to enter the twenty-first century. The compact disc has become the format of choice for small and medium-sized theaters. It is cheap, high-quality, relatively tough, and, as long as you know how to run the CD burner on your computer, easy to produce. It's hard to believe that the CD format is twenty years old and nothing has replaced it yet, but, because the format was well-designed in the first place, it has wiped out analog tape and withstood challenges from **digital audiotape (DAT)** and **MiniDisc**. Furthermore, CD players have now developed to the point where they are as reliable as my old reel-to-reel tape deck, and I can safely recommend them for almost any type of theatrical playback.

CD versus CD-R versus CD-RW

Commercial CDs, like the ones that you buy in the record store (a store, that, interestingly enough, no longer sells records) are pressed from a mold in a factory. The CD-R is produced in a home CD burner or personal computer with a laser beam. In practice, the CD-R works just like a commercial CD, although the CD-R is a little more susceptible to physical damage and heat. You can put them both in the same players, however, and you cannot re-record either one of them. What is there is there and that's that, so forget about using those AOL CDs to burn copies of your music collection. A CD or a CD-R is a one-time-only deal.

CD-RWs can be re-recorded hundreds, if not thousands of times, if you take care of them. The downside is that they don't always play in all CD players, which can cause a lot of frustration. For most people, the CD-R is a better choice, especially with the cost of blank CDs dropping so low. If you want to make a new program, you just toss the old CD and record a new one. This is called "making coasters."

If you don't know how to run the CD burner on your computer, now is the time to learn. If you are using a "consumer," stand-alone CD burner, make sure that you get blank CDs that are labeled "music" CDs. They are formatted differently from computer CDs. If you are burning a CD on your computer, get the "data" CDs, even if you are recording music.

A standard CD holds about 650 megabytes of information, which is about seventy-four minutes of music. There are some blank CDs that hold 700 megabytes, or about eighty minutes.

When you make the CD, make sure that you do not put any dead air before the sound begins. Some CD burners will allow you to put in a "countdown" before each track. You don't want that. You want the sound to start instantly.

Digital audio quality is described by two terms: **resolution** and **sample rate**. Resolution is the amount of fine detail that the recording contains, and "16 bit" is the standard for CDs. A bit is a piece of data. Specifically, it's a "1" or a "0." Sixteen-bit numbers use sixteen ones or zeros to describe something. An "8 bit" number only uses eight ones or zeros, so it is less exact. Think of it like a mosaic. Let's say that you have a ten-by-ten foot square in which to make a picture of your friend, using only stones. If those stones were the size of softballs, you could make a pretty good picture, although it would be a little rough. If the stones were the size of marbles, you would be able to depict your friend more accurately, with smoother curves and better shapes. A higher bit number means smaller stones, which means a more accurate rendition of the sound.

In order to understand sample rate, we need to understand **sampling**. The world is not **digital**, no matter what Bill Gates thinks. The world is **analog**. Analog information is formed by values that are continually and smoothly changing, like trees moving back and forth in the wind. The trees do not click from one position to the next. They flow back and forth continuously. They are analog.

If, however, we want to film the position of those trees, we have to shoot a picture of them in a series of positions. Every time the shutter opens, the tree is in a slightly different position, so we end up with a string of pictures, each one with the tree in a slightly different place. When we play back the frames of film in order, however, we run them so fast that we cannot see the individual pictures; we only see the trees waving back and forth in the wind. What we have done is to take a series of "samples" of the trees, then played them all back so fast that we think we are watching a continuous image.

The same process happens with sound. A digital recording device listens to an incoming analog sound, snaps a "picture" of it and stores that picture as a number. Then, after a fraction of a second, it snaps another picture and stores that one as well. Then another and another and before you know it, the device has recorded a long string of samples which, when played back quickly, produce the sound that was recorded.

The "sampling rate" describes how many of those samples are taken per second. The standard for CDs is 44,100 times per second, or 44.1kHz* Some forms of professional recording go higher (some as high as 96,000 times per second), but "forty-four point one" is pretty much the standard for CDs.

Therefore, if you are recording any kind of digital sound and you want to put it out on a CD, you should make sure that it is at least 16 bit and 44.1kHz.

Sampling eats up a fair amount of disk space. As an example, a sound approximately twelve seconds long, when sampled at 44.1 kHz uses about a megabyte of memory space. This entire book that you are reading takes up

---

*KHz is short for "kilohertz," which means, "cycles per second." Therefore, 44.1kHz means "forty-four thousand, one hundred times per second."

about a megabyte on my computer. Think about that for a moment. You are holding the same amount of information as twelve seconds of high-quality sampled sound. Gives you new respect for your ears, doesn't it?

Cassette Tapes

I said that tape was dead and I meant it. I only mention cassettes because you may be running a show where you don't have access to a personal computer or a CD burner. In this case, your next best option may be a cassette. Make a separate cassette tape for each cue, unless you have a huge number of them. That way, you can flip back and forth between them in rehearsal. Remember to rewind them at the end of every night. Cassettes, however, will never touch the sound quality and ease of use of a CD.

MiniDisc™

Sony's **MiniDisc**™ format didn't catch on at the consumer level, but it continues to survive in professional theater and audiophile usage. The MiniDisc is a recordable compact disc that offers the same **fidelity** as regular CDs, but allows you to record (and re-record) your own. The MiniDisc is smaller than a CD and requires a different kind of player. The actual disk is encased in a plastic cover, which makes it more resistant to damage. You can insert marker points to run cues more precisely and even change the order of cues on the disk. While they have been prohibitively expensive until recently, the prices are dropping to reasonable levels: As of this writing, a good player/recorder can be had for around $300 and a reusable, seventy-four-minute blank disk for around $6. (The manufacturer claims that they can be re-recorded up to one million times.) They also have a write-protect tab like a computer disk to prevent accidental erasures. If you use MiniDiscs and your show is traveling, you will have to carry the player with you, since most theaters won't have them. If you can handle owning the player, though, MiniDiscs are a high-fidelity option.

One note about MiniDiscs: They are only made by Sony, so the long-term availability of equipment, disks, and service depends on Sony's commitment to the format. If you want to archive material for your biographer, you may want to pick a format that is widely supported.

DAT

Digital audiotape, more commonly known by its acronym **DAT**, was on a quick road upwards as a professional format of choice until the advent of personal computer playback systems. DAT tape looks like a smaller version of a cassette tape and operates the same way, except that it stores sound in a high-fidelity digital format.

DAT is as easy to use as a cassette, too. Simply load the tape, push "play," and you're on. Tape is available at stereo stores and pro audio dealers for about twice the price of an analog cassette. Precise start points can be marked electronically on the tape so exact cueing is possible. The DAT also accesses cues much faster than any other kind of tape, so you can keep an entire show on one tape and still skip around during rehearsal. It also starts up faster then a reel-to-reel when you hit the "play" button so it's easier to start the cue at exactly the right moment. The tape is still enclosed so you can't cut and paste it like a reel-to-reel, but, all in all, DAT offers the easiest use of any tape medium.

Being a tape-based medium, however, the DAT is losing ground to the next generation of theatrical playback machines: the PC-based playback system.

The **PC-based playback system** is changing the entire face of theatrical sound. It's like e-mail: Once you realize what you can do with it, you will never go back to writing letters.

Basically, all the various PC-based systems allow you to store a group of audio files (**WAV** files, generally) and play them on command. After that, the similarities disappear. PC-based systems basically fall into two categories: stand-alone and software-based.

Stand-alone audio playback systems do not require a computer. Actually, that isn't quite true because they have a computer inside them; it just isn't one that you can use to play backgammon and read your e-mail. These machines generally allow you to load up a whole bunch of files and then play them back at the touch of a button. You can alter the volume of the file, the start and stop points, and sometimes the playback speed. These machines were created for broadcast applications, like radio stations, to replace the tape-based cartridge machines that were used to play commercials, station IDs, sound effects, and other audio bits. As such, they sometimes have features like timers and playlists, which theatrical folks may or may not find useful. The big benefits of PC-based playback systems are that they hold a LOT of material and they are easy to use.

One particular kind of stand-alone system is called a **sampler**, and it has actually been around since the late eighties, which in computer terms, makes it fairly ancient. Samplers are designed to record, or "sample" analog audio and turn it into a digital file. That digital file is played back, either from a front panel button or from a piano-style keyboard.

Samplers are most commonly used these days by DJs and keyboard players. DJs use them to sample little bits of music and sound to sprinkle in with their phat mixes in a club atmosphere. Keyboard players attach samplers to their keyboards and load them up with samples of all kinds of different instruments. That way, they can change from a grand piano to a saxophone to a string orchestra with the flip of a switch.

Samplers, however, are also very useful to people in the theater, for two reasons. One, they are great when you want to create sound effects, although not nearly so flexible as a good ProTools system. Second, they can play back a show that is very heavy on very specific sound effects.

Let's say you are doing a show like Lily Tomlin's *Search for Signs of Intelligent Life in the Universe*. In the show, which is played on a virtually empty stage, the sound operator must follow Tomlin's every move and provide the appropriate sound. If she pretends to open a door, he must play the sound of the door. If she moves her hand as if she is pushing a shopping cart, he must play the sound of the cart. This sort of thing is difficult, no, impossible to do with a CD or a tape deck. The operator needs to be able to push a single button and get the right sound instantly. A sampler can do that.

PC-based systems have a steeper learning curve, but many more possibilities. After loading up all the sound files that you want to use, these programs allow you to manipulate how these files are played back in the theater. Most of the time, a PC-based system has multiple outputs. You may have one output going to the main speakers over the stage, one going to backstage, and several more going to speakers throughout the house. If you want a helicopter to fly over the audience, you can tell the PC to start the sound in one speaker to the audience's left, then fade it smoothly over the top of the auditorium, down to the right speaker and then fade away in the distance. *Très automatique*, and, once you get it programmed, it will happen the exact same way every time.

PC-based systems can also do more than one thing at a time. While that helicopter is flying over, there might be gunshots coming from upstage, shouts coming from the balcony and a bed of jungle noises behind it all. Any audio file you have can be assigned to play in any speaker, anywhere, at any time. This sort of thing can take a little programming work, but none of it requires a degree in engineering.

Another area where PC-based systems are very useful is connecting to other systems throughout the theater. Using a show-control protocol, you can make your audio system talk to your lighting system if, for example, you need a sound effect and a lighting effect to happen at the same instant. This kind of thing is covered in more detail in chapter 10, "Show Control." As it stands right now, PC-based systems are the WAV of the future and I am really, really sorry that I couldn't stop myself from writing that. Oh well, with or without the geek humor, the fact remains that PC-based systems are taking over the theater world. If you are not dealing with one yet, it is only a matter of time.

Software for Preparing Audio

If you are burning your CD on a computer, it makes sense to use the computer to come up with the sounds as well. This is one reason why I am not a big fan of stand-alone CD burners—you really want to be able to mix the audio on your computer. There are a wide variety of programs out there for creating and mixing audio for playback, and it can be a challenge to figure out which one is best for you. Programs like Cool Edit and Sound Forge can help you cut-and-paste audio and create new sound cues. MusicMatch and iTunes allow you to catalog songs and burn them to a CD. Programs like Jam and Toast exist just to burn CDs, so they give you the most options for that specific task. The professional standard for manipulating audio is ProTools, manufactured by Digidesign in Palo Alto.

All these programs allow you to put chunks of audio into the computer, mix them around, recombine them in new ways and then spit them back out again. Where they differ is in the features they offer and the specific task they are really designed for. When choosing software, be aware of the following choices:

- *Mac or PC?* While many programs are available on both platforms, make sure that the one you want matches the computer you have. Most professional sound designers are die-hard Mac users, so almost all the pro or semipro software run great on Macs.
- *Jukebox or audio mixing program?* Jukebox programs, like iTunes and MusicMatch, are designed to collect large numbers of songs and then re-combine them on CDs. Audio mixing programs actually let you mess with the sounds themselves.
- *Number of tracks?* Having more tracks means that you can overlay sounds on top of one another. If you want to have the sound of crickets chirping, plus the sound of a rooster, all the while playing the morning theme from *The William Tell Overture,* you will need at least three different tracks. Note that you need twice as many tracks when creating a cue in stereo.
- *Can you burn the CD from the program?* Some programs allow you to actually burn the CD from within the program. ProTools will not, for example, so you will need another application to actually manufacture the disk.
- *What can you do to the sound?* Can you change volumes? Cut and paste sections onto each other? Change equalization (EQ), compression, reverb and other effects, tempo, speed, and so on? The more features you have, the more you can do. ProTools rules supreme in this area.

As you experiment, you will find a set of software choices that work for you. For example, I use iTunes to import music and sound effects from CDs, Apple's Safari Web browser to download sounds and music from the Internet, ProTools to mix audio and create cues, and Jam to burn those cues to CDs.

Audio File Formats

If you want to use a computer to handle sound, you will quickly discover a bewildering array of file formats, each of which is good for one thing and terrible for another. Here is the rundown:

- **AIFF** (Audio Interchange File Format): Because this format was developed for Macs, it is sometimes called "Apple Interchange File Format." This is the format of choice for handling audio on the Mac. It can be mono or stereo and the resolution and bit rate can be changed to whatever you like. AIFF files can be imported into sound editing programs.
- **WAV** (pronounced "wave"): This format was created by Microsoft for handling sound on a Windows PC and that is really what it is good for, although you can send it to a Mac as well. Like AIFF, the resolution and bit rate are not fixed, the file can be stereo or mono, and WAV files can be brought into sound editing programs.
- **MP3**: This highly compressed file format is primarily used for songs. The high compression rate degrades the audio a little, but it allows hundreds, if not thousands of songs to be packed into portable **MP3** players, like Apple's iPod. MP3 files can be recorded onto audio CDs, if you have software that is compatible with this format. These days, most computers come with an MP3 player preinstalled. The world of MP3 downloading and trading is vast, uncharted, and a major pain to record companies. MP3s, however, cannot be edited unless they are converted to AIFF or WAV.
- **SDII** (Sound Designer II): files are what drives ProTools and a good bit of the Mac operating system. They are high-quality files and can be burned onto CDs, but you won't find them very often outside of the Mac.

MIDI

The Musical Instrument Digital Interface (**MIDI**) was developed in the early eighties by a consortium of music equipment companies to help electronic music equipment, like keyboards, talk to each other and to computers. When a musician plays a note on a MIDI-equipped keyboard, that keyboard sends out a message to another device to play the same note. The other device, however, might play the note with a completely different kind of sound. MIDI messages are not notes; they are *commands* to play notes. A musician could, in this way, use one device to play many devices simultaneously. Besides the name of the note, MIDI can also send a value at the same time. This value is most often used for the volume (or "velocity" as MIDI calls it*) of the note.

MIDI information is sent out on sixteen different "channels." This is a bit like having a sixteen-channel television set. (That is, if you are old enough to remember when television had only sixteen channels.) The computer can send out sixteen different strings of commands to sixteen different machines at the same time. You set each device to listen to a particular channel of information, just as you change the channel on your television. Each machine will only listen to the commands coming in on the channel to which it is assigned. In some cases, a machine might be set to "omni" mode, which means that it listens to all the channels at once.

Soon after MIDI appeared, composers began using **sequencer** programs to record thousands of notes of music on separate tracks and play them back on stacks of different keyboards and sound modules. A great deal of film and TV scoring is done this way today, as well as most of what you hear on pop music radio stations. If you are hiring a composer to score your show, chances are good that he will be working on a MIDI setup.

MIDI is very convenient for theater, because it is easily changed to match changes in the show. For example, it is easy to change what key a song is played in. Should your star show up with a cold one day, a click of the mouse can set the entire song three notes lower.

One of the most common uses of MIDI in live performances is with electronic drum sets. Each drum pad is a separate MIDI trigger and, when struck, it sends out the command to play a sound. That command goes to a sound module, which has been prerecorded with some large number of sounds, each of which is assigned to a particular MIDI note. When the command arrives from the drum trigger to play the note, the sound module obligingly sends out the sound that is assigned to that note. With the magic of computer programming, that sound could be any sort of noise, from a snare drum, to a saxophone, to a bleating sheep. Some creative performance art groups use MIDI triggers placed around the stage to trigger all sorts of strange and wonderful sounds.

_____

*MIDI uses the term *velocity* because it actually refers to how fast a key travels from its top position to its bottom position. A key that is struck harder will travel faster and, presumably, make a louder sound.

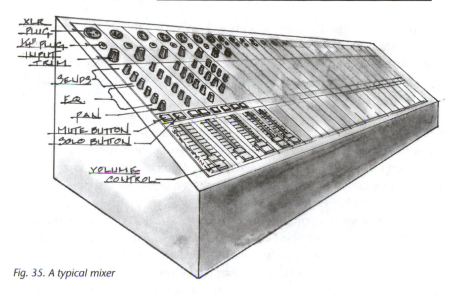

Fig. 35. A typical mixer

One major limitation in MIDI is distance. A MIDI signal is only designed to run about twenty-five feet or so, making it impractical for any use that involves longer distances.

Mixers: Telling the Sound Where to Go

Mixers are among the most visually daunting objects in technical theater. Their considerable width, carpeted with buttons and knobs, gives them a menacingly complicated appearance. I think technicians get into the fact that the mixer looks so, well, "technical." But let's face it: A mixer is just a big freeway interchange where sound enters from all different directions, gets shunted around, and gets spit out in new directions. Whatever else you forget about mixers, remember this, a mixer just takes in sound, reorganizes it, and sends it out somewhere else. That's all.

Most mixers are made up of four parts: **input modules**, **equalization**, **auxiliary sends** and **returns**, and **output channels**. Big words for simple things. Actually, equalization and auxiliary sends are contained within the input module, so let's do that first. Then we'll do the returns and the outputs. This section is best enjoyed if you are sitting in front of a mixer, so go sit in the sound booth, if you have one.

Input Modules

Any source of sound that we have mentioned so far can be fed into a mixer. A mixer has a number of places to plug things in—inputs. In fact, the first way in which we usually describe a mixer is by saying how many inputs it has. A "sixteen-channel" mixer has sixteen places to plug things in. A microphone would take up one of those places. A tape deck or CD player would take up two places, since these items put out a stereo signal. Stereo signals need two inputs, a left and a right.

Looking at a mixer, we see that the input modules are laid out in columns, each column containing a set of identical controls. One of the reasons that mixers have so many knobs is that each of its functions is duplicated for each input module. Each input module may, for example, only have six knobs, but multiply that by sixteen inputs, and suddenly you have a forest of ninety-six knobs.

The controls for each module are laid out in a vertical column. You can think about the sound entering the module at the top and flowing downward. There are exceptions to this idea, but let's not muddy the pool.

An input module begins with an input where you plug in the incoming signal. This input may be on the top, front, or back of the mixer. This input may be a quarter-inch plug or an RCA plug (for unbalanced input) or, for a microphone input, it may be an XLR plug (balanced input).

After the sound enters the module, the first thing it meets is an input level control, also known as the **input trim**. Remember when I said that there were different levels of signal—mic level and line level? The input trim (sometimes called "input gain") allows you to boost a mic signal up to where the mixer can use it. This control may just be a switch between "line" or "mic," or it may be a rotating level control that you adjust. If you are feeding the mixer a mic-level signal, you turn the input level up. Turn it down for a line-level signal.

After going through the input control, the signal hits the **equalization**, or **EQ** controls, if there are any. EQ is just like the treble and bass controls on your stereo. Mixers may have two controls, one for the high end (treble) and one for the low end (bass), or they may have three or four, all to shape the color of a sound, boosting it or cutting it wherever necessary.

After EQ, it's time for the **sends**. Remember how I said that a mixer is a traffic interchange? Well, these are the first exits. A sound engineer will often want to send some sound somewhere else, like into an effects processor to mess with it, or to a monitor system, so people backstage can hear the sound. For these purposes (and many more), the engineer opens up an "exit" (a **send**). It's important to understand that turning on a send does not mean all the sound goes out that way and none of it continues down the input module. In that sense, it isn't like traffic at all. Making some of the sound turn off the freeway doesn't reduce the amount that continues onward. Then again, traffic seems like that sometimes, too.

The next thing the signal usually encounters is some sort of routing that tells it which **output** it is destined for, that is, which way it is going to exit the mixer. Depending on how many outputs you have, there may be several switches and knobs here, or only one. There might be buttons for various master or submaster outputs, but no matter what it says, it's basically just telling the sound which way is out. One control that is common in this area is a **pan** control. A mixer is usually sending out a stereo signal, and a pan control tells the sound which side of that stereo signal the sound is going to. The pan knob might be turned all the way to the right (known as "hard right"), which means that the sound is only going out the right channel, or it might be set all the way the other way ("hard left") which means that it is going entirely to the left. Or, it may be set anywhere in between, including right in the center. In this last case ("panned center"), the sound would go equally to the left and right sides.

Two other controls that may be found in this area are **mute** and **solo**. Mute simply turns this channel off. Solo turns every channel off *except* this one. Solo is often used during setup to hear a channel by itself in order to set volume, to set EQ, or to search out a problem. In most cases, the solo switch doesn't affect the main output—only a monitor signal that the engineer is listening to.

Way down at the bottom of the module is the volume control. This is usually a long slider.

Auxiliary Returns

Let's go back to that signal that took the exit marked "send." As I said, one use of a send is to feed sound to an **effects processor** (see "Effects Processing" below).

By plugging a cable into the opening marked "send" on the back of the mixer, we can connect that signal to the sound processor. Then, we take another cable out of the processor and back to the mixer where we plug it into the socket marked "return." We have now created an **effects loop**. The sound travels from the input module, out the send, through the processor, and back to the mixer through the return.

When the signal gets back, however, it does not go back to the input module. Rather, it goes into the main outputs along with the other sounds that are coming directly from the input modules. A signal coming from a send does not necessarily have to go to an effects processor, or return to the mixer. It may go to a tape player or a monitor, for instance, and never return at all. Every sound setup is unique, and mixers are designed to be flexible. Remember: The mixer is just a big audio cloverleaf.

Effects Processing: Sound Sculpting

Besides simply amplifying sound, or recording it, sound equipment is capable of performing a dizzying variety of tricks on the sound itself before it spits it out.

Ever record yourself talking, singing, or playing an instrument and then wonder why it doesn't sound as good as a recording on the radio or an album? Of course, the pros record on higher-quality microphones and tape decks, but another big reason is that professionally recorded sounds are being *processed*. If you want to experience a quick example of processing, try listening to your local public radio station for a while, preferably an NPR newscast or something like that. Once you have gotten used to the quality of the voices, switch the dial over to your local rock-and-roll station and listen to the DJ. Sound different? It should. The rock-and-roll DJ's voice is being processed to make it more dynamic, richer, and more in line with the voices on the records he is playing. NPR processes announcers' voices as well, but in more subtle ways.

Processing comes in various forms, discussed below.

Reverb

If you've sat in a large church or a well-designed concert hall recently, than you've experienced reverb in its natural state. **Reverb** is just sound bouncing around in a space—caroming off hard surfaces and coming at your ears from all directions. The more places it has to go, and the fewer absorbent places that exist in the room, the longer the sound bounces around. We refer to the span of time that the sound bounces around as the **reverberation time**. The reverb time is the time that it takes a sound to completely die out in a particular space. A good theater, where the clarity of the spoken word is all-important, will have a relatively short reverb time—from one to two seconds. A concert hall, where we are more concerned about the richness of the sound than the intelligibility of speech, should have a longer reverb time, two and a half seconds or more. Large churches will have reverberation times of four, five, even ten seconds.

In the early days of recording, it was common to have a "reverb room" in the studio. This was a room with a speaker at one end and a microphone at the other. Sound was played into the room through the speaker and re-recorded through the other microphone. In this way, sound engineers added the natural reverberations of a space to the voices. These days, this effect can be recreated electronically by an **effects processor**. The sound is fed into the processor from the mixer and the circuitry inside the box processes it, adding reverb to it. When the sound comes out, it sounds as though the original sound were created in another kind of space. Most processors let you choose what kind of space you would like to imitate, both in size and quality. It might have options like "small room," "ensemble hall," or "concert stage," as well as "warm," "dark," or "rich." By adjusting the processor, you can choose what kind of reverb you want. Want more reverb time? Dial up a larger room. Want to make a voice sound cold and distant? Try the "dark" setting. Some boxes provide literally hundreds of options like "Wood Concert Hall," and "Empty Gymnasium." It can get pretty fun. By altering the balance between the "dry," unprocessed sound and the "wet," processed sound, the engineer can decide how heavy to make the effect. Too dry, and the effect may go unnoticed. Too wet, and the performer will be singing in Carlsbad Caverns.

An effects processor is something every medium-size-and-up theater should own. It will help you produce better sound effects tapes as well as make offstage voices sound more interesting. Other organizations may also choose to own them in order to make their sound systems more flexible. Rock-and-roll bands can't live without them.

Of course, no processor can approach the acoustics of a large concert hall or, best of all, an old-style cathedral. Many classical artists take advantage of these spaces and record their albums there. Please attend these concerts so that you can bask in the best thing the Laws of Physics ever did for music—rich, natural reverb. For some reason, modern church designers always put in carpets. From a musical perspective, that's a sin.

Equalization

Anyone who has ever made a tape at home and then played it back in the theater will understand the need for **equalization** (EQ). The tape sounds different in different spaces. Acoustically speaking, every room in the world is different, depending on the textures it has (carpets, furniture, paneling, and so on) as well as the shape of the room itself. Every room will kill certain frequencies and accentuate others.

But wasn't there EQ in the mixer? Yes, there was, but only a few controls. A true equalizer is a separate unit that lives outside the mixer. It has a long row of sliders or knobs that increase or decrease the amount of sound at each frequency. It takes time and experience to set up, not to mention a certain amount of trial-and-error. It also takes a sharp-eared technician. Once the sound is optimized for a space, you should put a lock on that EQ and leave it forever, or at least until you get different carpets.

Besides this kind of colorization, EQ also provides an important function in getting rid of feedback. The shape of the room will cause some frequencies to feed back more than others. Because EQ allows you to decrease those specific frequencies, it can allow you to push the overall volume up higher. Live music depends heavily on EQ for this reason.

Compression, Limiting, and Gates

Ever go to an amateur night and listen to a bunch of people who don't really know how to use a microphone? As they sing or speak, their voices may get louder or softer. They may pull the mic away from their mouth, or get it too close, causing the sound to die away or boom out like Moses. An overexcited performer might yell into the mic, causing the sound system to overload and distort. Compression and limiting help audio people to deal with these problems.

A **compressor** and a **limiter** are two different versions of the same thing. Both devices follow the sound level and, when it climbs above a certain volume, pull it down. Compressors use a ratio to determine how much to reduce the sound. If they are set at 4:1, then they drop the volume one decibel for every four decibels it is over the limit. A limiter is less subtle: You give it a volume level and it prevents the sound from ever getting louder than that level—an audio "line in the sand." Because they reduce the really high sound levels, compressors and limiters help guard against overloads. This means you can bring the overall volume up without worrying about distortion ruining your speakers. The softer voices will be more audible and the louder voices won't be so annoying.

A gate is at the other end of the volume scale. This device turns the circuit off when the volume drops *below* a certain level. This is useful if, for example, you have a mic on an electric guitar amp and you only want the channel to be "hot" when the guitar is actually being played. Putting a gate on the guitar channel prevents the audience from hearing low-level hum and hiss of the amp during the tender choral intro to "Rock Me with a Big Stick." Once the guitar starts playing, the audio level from the amp will rise above the threshold of the gate and the cannel will open allowing the thrashing lead guitar to be heard. If you like that sort of thing.

Because they are so similar in function, compressors, limiters, and gates are often built into the same unit.

Amplification: We're Going to Pump You Up

Having been pre-amplified, routed, and processed, our heroic sound wave now exits the mixer and heads for the gym to build some real muscle.

Remember: Up to this point, the sound has only existed at **mic** or **line level**. While these levels are good enough for the electronics in your system, they are not strong enough to really create audible sound. Therefore, the sound has to go through some kind of **amplifier** before the audience can hear it.

Amplifiers come in lots of different sizes but only two common types: **mono** and **stereo**. A mono amp has one input and one output. A stereo amp has two separate inputs and two separate outputs. In fact, it's really like having two separate amplifiers. The manufacturers just package them in one box for convenience.

When you play an album on your home stereo, the sound going to the left and right speakers is slightly different because studio engineers go to great lengths to make it that way. After all, you have two ears, and by giving those ears slightly different sound, the engineers can give the illusion that all the instruments you are hearing are located at different places in space. Therefore, every home stereo is . . . um, stereo.

In the theater, however, this does not work and here's why: In order for stereo imaging (the $2 name for this effect) to work, the output from the two speakers has to reach your ears at approximately the same time and volume. This is not too hard in your living room: Your speakers are about the same distance from you most of the time. In the theater, however, the vast majority of the audience is not sitting dead center in the middle of the auditorium where both speakers would be the same distance away. Most of them will hear one speaker much more strongly than the other, and the stereo imaging will be lost. For this reason, *most sound in the theater is mono, not stereo.* This means that you will not have to have two separate audio signals, even if you have speakers on both sides of the stage.

You might still need a stereo amp, however. Since theater speakers are quite large, each speaker needs its own amplifier. You can use one side of a stereo amp for one speaker and the other side for the other speaker. Just make sure that they are both getting the same signal.

A stereo setup is also useful for sound effects. Directors often want an effect to appear to be coming from one side of the stage or the other. Having a stereo setup allows you to send part of the audio signal (a car starting, a barking dog, gunshots, whatever) to one speaker and not the other.

One final note about keeping your system happy: When turning your system on, always turn the amp on *last*. When turning your system off, always turn the amp off *first*. Other kinds of electronic equipment, such as mixers, decks, and processors, can send dangerous "pops" through the system when they turn on or off. Making sure the amp is off when this happens will prevent damage to your speakers. So, remember:

Amplifiers are last on, first off.

You can remember this by thinking of your amp as the most dangerous element in the system. Because it is the most dangerous (at least to the other equipment), it should be on the least amount of time.

Speakers: The Bottom Line

If you are buying a new sound system, my advice is to be economical everywhere *except* the speakers. The quality of your sound system is more dependent on your speakers than on anything else.

Here's how speakers work: In your speakers there is a curved piece of cardboard-like material, called the **speaker cone**. This cone has a magnet attached to it. Remember the magnet in the microphone—the one that moved and created an electrical signal? This one works the same way, only backwards. Instead of the magnet moving the electricity, here the electricity moves the magnet. This magnet has to be a lot bigger than the one in the microphone since it has to move the cone enough to create large waves of pressure in the air: sound waves.

The core and the magnet together make up a **speaker element**. Most speakers have two of these elements, one for the high frequencies—the **tweeter**—and one for the low frequencies—the **woofer**.

Speakers have one statistic that you should be aware of: **resistance**. Resistance describes what kind of opposition the signal is going to run into when it gets to the speaker, and it is measured in **ohms**. There are two common kinds of speaker: 8 ohms and 4 ohms (occasionally you might find a 2-ohm speaker). All you need to know is that the resistance of the speaker should match the amp. Your amp will probably say on the back which kind of speaker it is calibrated for. Look for something that says: "100 watts into 8 ohms" or something like that. If the resistance is mismatched, it can cause a variety of problems, some of them potentially damaging.

If you are plugging in speakers, make sure they are "in phase." The positive terminal on the amp must be attached to the positive terminal on the speaker; same with the negative terminal. Plus sign to plus sign and minus sign to minus sign. If you are not sure which is which, try it one way or the other. Hooking up speakers out of phase will not damage them—they will just sound bad. The most common symptom is a lack of bass. If your system uses quarter-inch plugs for the speakers, you're in luck. They only go together one way.

One final thing about speakers: Proper speaker placement within the space is critical. Speakers are "directional": They are made to throw sound in a particular direction. High-end signals, like flutes, cymbals, and violins, are more directional than low-end ones. The high-end signals will go in whatever direction the speaker is pointed and they will stop when they hit a wall. The low-end signals will go in all directions, regardless of which way the speakers are pointed, and they tend to seep through walls. That is why, when the guy in the apartment upstairs turns on his stereo, you only hear the bass. Bass notes are less directional. Take a moment to notice the effect before you ask him to turn it down. You might get peace and quiet by just asking him to turn down the bass a little. Worth a try, anyway.

Some lucky theaters have speakers specifically designed for very low-end sounds. These are called **subwoofers** and they are wonderful for creating rich, full sound. Because low-end sounds are nondirectional, you can put a sub-woofer anywhere in the theater and everyone will hear it. Dance clubs almost always have subwoofers—it sends the beat right into your bloodstream.

Proper speaker placement is also critical to avoid feedback. Try not to put speakers where they will pump sound into microphones. It is not always that simple, however. If you have lots of speakers and/or lots of microphones, you may get stuck with some feedback-prone positions. For another thing, singers in bands want to be able to hear themselves, so it is necessary to install speakers, or **monitors**, pointing directly at them, which means directly at the microphones. Sound engineers use equalization to deal with these problems. If you have consistent feedback, try adjusting your speaker placements.

Since theater sound is generally mono, you do not have to worry about getting a good stereo setup, but you do want the sound to appear to come from the direction of the stage. It usually isn't practical to put the speakers right in front of the performers, however, so there is some trickery involved.

The most common trick is to put the speakers directly over the stage. We determine the location of a sound by hearing it arrive at our two ears at different times. (Our brain is capable of distinguishing differences as little as three-thousandths of a second, which is the time it takes for a sound to travel from one side of our head to the other.) Since our ears are on the sides of our head, not the top or the bottom, we distinguish left and right much better than up and down. If you have ever stood on a balcony over someone's head and tried to get his attention, you know what I mean. You keep shouting his name and he keeps looking around, trying to figure out where you are. "No, you ninny, look *up!*" you shout, and round and round he goes, trying to figure out where you are. It's not his fault. Our ears have evolved to find things that are on the same level as we are. I guess saber-tooth tigers didn't drop down from above very often.

By putting the speakers directly over the stage, then, we fool the audience a little. It's difficult to distinguish between sounds coming from straight in front and those coming from a higher position.

From the microphone to the mixer, through the processors, the returns, the outputs, the amps, and the speakers, all in thousandths of a second. It is a strange and wonderful journey.

CHAPTER 10

Show Control: Why Can't We All Just Get Along?

More toys for grown-up boys (and girls). As theater moves further down the technological road, more and more elements of the theatrical experience are being computerized, automated, and digitized. Lighting controllers, digital audio, computerized scenery—seems like every time I turn around, another part of the technical world gets assigned to a silicon brain.

What happens, though, when you want those brains to talk to each other? Let's say you want the lighting cues to happen on particular notes of music. Or you want a metal bucket to fall over at the same moment as the ricochet sound from the bullet that "hit" it. Or you want to tie audio samples together with the movements of a dancer. Or you want three platforms to roll out together with a light cue, a musical intro, and a laser drawing letters in the air to spell "Hello Cleveland!"

You could depend on several different operators, of course, following the commands of a talented stage manager. Hey, back in the dark ages (ten years ago), that was pretty much how it was done. But some people can't leave well enough alone, so they design shows with absurd levels of technology, expect ridiculous degrees of coordination, and then want it to happen (and here is the heart of the matter) the *exact same way every time*. If there is one thing a computer is good at, it is doing the same damn thing over and over, without getting distracted, creative, or bored. Show control adds consistency and reliability.

For this reason, a lot of "show control" appears in theme parks. Most of the theater in places like Disneyland, Universal Studios, and Busch Gardens is highly computerized. They ain't doin' Arthur Miller over at the

Fantasyland Theater. They are doing short, fast-paced, visually impressive extravaganzas that play well across language barriers and generation gaps. With all this visual spectacle, twelve times a day, designers tend to use a lot of show control.

Show control is silently slipping into all theaters, however, from Broadway to Bellingham High School. Companies that produce more experimental or abstract shows are particularly interested, because it creates new ways of tying technology together with live performance.

But what is it exactly? Show control is the process of electrically connecting together two or more separate entertainment control systems. In some cases, a dedicated show control computer serves as a central brain, telling all the other machines what to do. In other cases, one of the devices, such as the lighting control board, audio system, or scenery computer will boss the other machines around. Show control programmers refer to the device in charge as the "master" and the others as "slaves."

Show control set-ups differ widely depending on what they are designed to do, so it is most useful to look at some general concepts.

Synchronous versus Asynchronous

Sometimes the events of a show run in order, with all elements following a pre-arranged script. This situation is most familiar to theater people, who generally live in an environment where this scene follows that scene and this light cue goes with that sound cue. Technical events always happen in a particular order. This is known as synchronous show control. In a synchronous situation, there is usually some sort of "clock" that keeps all the events in order. That clock might be a human being, like a stage manager, who follows the script and calls all the cues in order. It might also be a show control program that is preprogrammed to run all the cues in order, with the operator giving the system a "GO" when it is time to do the next thing.

An asynchronous show allows events to happen in any order. A show control system running a haunted house is asynchronous. If a guest walks in front of an infrared sensor, the computer switches on a light, plays a spooky sound effect, and shakes a model of a mummy. It doesn't matter if that event happens before or after the exploding witches brew effect. It happens whenever it needs to happen.

Real-world Example

The Me-now-You dance company performs a live piece where the soundtrack is created by the dancers' movements through the use of an asynchronous control system. The dancers' costumes are covered with sensors, each of which is triggered by a particular movement. The sensor sends a message to a computer, telling it to play a sound effect or snippet of music. As the dancers move, they trigger these sensors, which in turn trigger the sounds. It doesn't matter when they make a particular gesture. Whenever they do, the sound is heard. In this way, the soundtrack literally accompanies their every move.

Event-based versus Time-based

When setting up a show-control system, one of the most critical decisions the designers make is how to deal with time, and I don't mean the fact that there is never enough. How do you tell the different machines in your system that it is time for them to do their thing? This question basically has two answers.

First, you set it up so that nothing happens unless you specifically tell it to. This is called an "event-based" system. When an event happens on stage, such as an actor saying a line, the operator pushes a button and the lights change, the sound plays, the platform moves, etc. Nothing happens until a human being says "GO." Nice and simple.

But what if there are too many things happening in a short amount of time for an operator to keep up? Or what if the "show" continues all day long, like a museum display or an automated fountain? In this case, it might be better to set up a clock and tell all the machines to do their thing at a particular moment in time. This is known as a "time-based" system.

Some time-based systems actually use the time of day as their clock. In other words, the machines are told to do their thing at a particular time of day, say 3 P.M., or every hour on the hour. This works well for museum displays and fountains, but not for theaters. Theatrical time-based systems generally make use of time code a very precise timer that ticks along during the show, providing a time reference for all the control devices.

Time code comes in two common flavors: a **MIDI time code** (known as "MTC") or a **SMPTE time code** (pronounced "SIM-tee"). MTC is an extension of the MIDI standard (see chapter 9) and is often used with musical or audio devices. SMPTE time code, originally developed for video, is much more common. SMPTE time code counts off in hours, minutes, seconds, and frames, with either twenty-four or thirty frames per second. Film runs at twenty-four frames per second, while video runs at thirty frames per second,* so system designers tend to use one or the other depending on what the

---

*This is only true in the United States, where we use the NTSC video standard. In Europe, where the PAL standard is used, both film and video run at twenty-five frames per second, a nit-picking difference that causes no end of confusion.

overall system is controlling. There is also a variation of time code called "drop-frame" which, for reasons that some people write doctoral dissertations about, skips a number every now and then.* What you need to know is that every device in the system must use the same kind of time code, whether twenty-four or thirty, drop-frame or nondrop-frame. Otherwise, things will start happening at different times, rather like a team of bank robbers who forgot to synchronize their watches before leaving the hideout.

Of course, when trying to decide between basing your show on event- or time-based, the most common answer is "Yes." Most systems use some of each. For example, when you hit the "GO" button on the light board, it runs a cue for a certain amount of time, thereby combining an event (you push the button) with a time (the preprogrammed length of the cue). A complicated stage show might be set to follow time code, but have several events where live operators push buttons to start sequences or confirm that it is safe to move scenery or explode pyrotechnics.

Any time you have time code, you have a device that is generating it and one or more devices that are **chasing** it. Chasing time code means that the device is watching a clock that is being run by another device. A show control computer, for example, might be generating time code. A lighting console might have a series of cues, each of which is programmed to happen at a particular time code number. The lighting console chases the time code, and, when the time-code number equals the console's preprogrammed "cue," the console runs the proper cue. When time code is in use, it is generated by one machine and chased by all the rest. Note that this is a different usage of the word *chase* than we talked about in the section on lighting effects.

Real-world Example

The music and special effects extravaganza *The Voyage of Harold,* follows the swashbuckling exploits of Harold the Cluefree, a wayward explorer who fights dragons and evil queens while trying to rescue an old college girlfriend and capture a treasure of old lottery tickets. The show has extensive lighting, sound effects, and pyrotechnics, all of which have to be tightly integrated with a prerecorded musical soundtrack. The audio playback system generates SMPTE time code, which the lighting console, audio sound effect system, and pyrotechnic controller chase, running light cues and sound cues at the preprogrammed times. The twenty-minute show is divided into four blocks

_____

*If you must know, NTSC video actually runs at 29.97 frames per second, a discrepancy that causes it to be out of sync with thirty frame-per-second time code by a grand total of 3.6 seconds per hour. Drop-frame time code, therefore, skips about two frames every minute, to keep the time code in sync with the video.

of cues, each of which has to be started manually. The opening sequence of cues starts at the top of the show. Then there is a pause while the actors talk. At the appropriate moment in the dialogue, the operator starts the audio playback, the time code comes spitting out, and the second sequence begins. This continues throughout the show, with each series of cues separated by a show stop, where the time code stops running and the crew waits until the actors get to the next section.

Interfaces

The interface is the place where the computer and the human communicate with each other. It may be the screen and mouse of a personal computer or it may be a custom-designed panel full of buttons. Besides the main interface where the system operator sits, there may also be other switches around the set where cast and crew can communicate with the system.

Contact Closures

When an operator or a guest pushes a button, it creates a **contact closure**. Contact closure just means that two pieces of wire have been brought together and are in contact with one another, thereby completing an electrical circuit. If the computer "sees" that the circuit is closed, it does whatever it is supposed to do. For example, a carnival fun house may have a contact closure wired to a particular section of floor. When the guest steps on it, the floor moves down, closes the circuit, and tells the computer to play the sound of a werewolf howl.

Enable Buttons

One type of contact closure is an **enable button**. An enable button is used to tell the computer that it is okay to do something. They are most common in time-based systems where the computer is just rolling merrily along, running cues and sending out commands, but needs to know if it is safe to do something. For example, if the computer is going to move a platform on stage, there may be an enable button placed next to the platform. A stage manager must be holding this button down for the platform to move. If the computer doesn't "see" that button being pushed, it aborts the platform move. Likewise, if the stage manager sees that it is not safe to move the platform, she does not push the enable button and thereby prevents an accident. This is often called a **dead man's switch**. If the stage manager is dead (or distracted by a costume change gone wrong) and no one is watching the effect, no one gets hurt.

Limit Switch

A limit switch is another type of contact closure. When a piece of scenery is designed to move, the system designer always wants to control how far it goes. The technicians may place a small switch on the platform that will hit some-thing and close when the platform reaches its destination, or as techies say, "the end of its travel." This switch can be moved to adjust the final rest-ing place of the platform. **Limit switches** are used to keep the stagecoach from crashing into the saloon full of dancers. A "de-cel" limit switch tells the system that the platform is approaching the end of its travel and should start decelerating.

Emergency Stop

Also referred to as an **E-stop** switch, this is a big red button that tells the system to stop what it is doing, and I mean *right now.* This shuts down the entire system to prevent injury to people, equipment, and the corporate lawyer's stomach lining.

Dedicated Show Control Computers

In many show control systems, one of the controllers is acting as the master, while another controller is acting as a slave. For example, an audio playback system might be sending commands to a lighting console. In larger, more complex systems, however, it is advantageous to give all the master duties to a computer that does nothing but control other controllers—a dedicated show control computer. Show control types sometimes refer to this as "serial control," which is a bit of a misnomer. In fact, almost every kind of show control interface is a serial interface. *Serial* means that the bits of data are sent one after another, just as serial killers put an end to their victims one at a time. The opposite of serial is *parallel,* an interface that sends data over a number of different cables all at the same time. A "parallel" killer would mean that a lot of people were killing a lot of people simultaneously. I guess war is a parallel killer.

Nevertheless, the term *serial control* is often used to describe a setup where a show control computer uses a serial computer cable to talk to other machines. These serial interfaces go by names like RS-232, RS-422, and Ethernet.

This type of dedicated show control computer is useful when the informa-tion you want to send is rather complex. Sometimes, one computer will have to take control of a device and give it all sorts of different information and commands, like "Turn 30 degrees left and stop" or "Turn on jets twenty-three and forty-seven at 50 percent for three minutes, but not until the enable button down right has been pushed."

Fig. 36. A typical show control setup

Dedicated show control computers require dedicated show control programmers. This is not something that you want to set up yourself with no experience.

Real-world Example

The live Broadway show *Les Depressed* follows a group of modern revolutionaries as they set up barricades outside the studios of a major television network. The show uses live video, moving scenery, lighting, audio, and special effects to dazzle the audience and spread righteousness throughout the airwaves. A dedicated show control computer with a custom-designed interface, operated by the stage manager, sends serial commands to a motion-control system that drives the scenery, a pyrotechnic controller that makes things go boom, a video server that puts the pictures on the screens, a hard drive–based audio system that provides music and sound effects, a computerized lighting console, and a network of lights and switches that allows the cast and crew to interact with the system. Sprinkled throughout the theater are enable buttons that allow the crew to tell the computer that an effect can be run safely, while each moving effect is equipped with limit and safety switches that protect the human beings.

MIDI Show Control

Up until 1989, there had never been a protocol specifically designed for show control—all of the devices and protocols had been borrowed from other industries, like manufacturing. That year, a working group of theater pros dove into the problem and eventually spawned **MIDI show control,** a protocol designed to do exactly what we are talking about here. MSC provides commands for many common show control applications, like "STOP," "GO," and "NEXT." MSC is gaining acceptance through the industry, although it is worth noting that it is an "open loop" interface, meaning that it sends out commands without checking to see if any machines are listening, and it doesn't wait for feedback from those machines before moving on. This makes it an unpopular choice for any application where dangerous machines, moving scenery, pyrotechnics, and stunt rigging are involved. With lighting, audio, and video, however, this isn't so important, and MSC is now the most popular choice for sending remote commands to lighting control consoles.

MIDI show control has become quite popular around amateur, academic, and semipro theaters because it is the easiest to work with of all the show control protocols. If you are willing to put in a few evenings with a manual, you can actually put MSC to use without a degree from M.I.T.

Note that MTC (MIDI time code) and MSC (MIDI show control) are two different things, although they often work together.

Real-world Example

Bob and Lucy's Animal Show is a production that features animal performers and a big video screen upstage. Because the video clips are part of the show, the programmers have designed a computer interface that serves up various video clips when the stage manager pushes a button. The director has requested that, when the video clips play, the lights go down onstage. The programmers use the MSC protocol to allow the video computer to talk to the lighting controller. Each video clip is paired with an MSC command that instructs the lighting controller to run a lighting cue. The particular combination of lights that come on in each cue is programmed into the lighting console. MIDI show control is only used to tell the lighting board to "GO."

PC versus PLC

In many cases, show control programs run on garden-variety personal computers, or PCs. This is fine when you are tying together lighting consoles, audio systems, motion control, pyrotechnics, and other devices. When it comes to the devices themselves, however, you don't want a machine that is designed for e-mail, word processing, and digital jukeboxes. You want a device that is dedicated to that task alone. You want a **PLC.**

A **Programmable Logic Controller** is a computer that controls something, generally something that moves. This type of device used to be called a programmable controller, but that term had to be expanded when the growth of the personal computer made the acronym situation confusing. A PLC is a dedicated piece of hardware that is designed solely to control machines (and is far less likely to crash than that computer sitting on your desk). It is a requirement for any type of system that involves **life safety.** In other words, if your system is the kind of thing that could hurt someone, like a rigging system or moving platforms, it must be controlled by a machine that doesn't do anything else. As my grandmother would say, "Stick to your knitting." Do what you do best and don't get complicated.

PLC programming should be done by a trained programmer, especially when moving scenery is involved. A trained person will know best how to maintain a safe and sane stage.

Real-world Example

The *Monster Marketplace* show is a comedic romp through the classic monsters of Halloween, like Frankenstein and Dracula. Dracula makes his entrance through a revolving bookcase that turns while a puff of smoke hides the effect. Because the movement of the bookcase could injure the actor, the effect is equipped with a number of safety devices, including footswitch enable buttons, a dead man's switch for the stage manager, and various indicator lights so both crew and actor can see what is happening. All of these switches and lights are connected to a PLC, which has no other job than to rotate that bookcase safely, protect the actor, and scare the bejeezus out of everybody else.

Entertainment Protocols

Two other protocols deserve mention here, even though they are treated more completely in other parts of this book. Both DMX and MIDI sometimes become part of show control systems, even though they are more typically used in the world of audio (MIDI) and lighting (DMX).

MIDI is sometimes used as the language of "triggers," which is a fancy word for a button. Any time that you want a trigger to initiate a sound, you might want to use MIDI. It's a good way to turn a physical action (like striking a piano key or a button) into an audible sound. The leotard covered with sensors in the Me-now-You dance company example cited earlier in this chapter could very easily be rigged with MIDI.

DMX is sometimes used to talk to smoke machines, snow machines, and strobe lights, among other things. It's a good solution when the thing that you are controlling is somehow related to the lighting system. If you want the fog machines to come on with a particular light cue, DMX is what you need.

Remember: show control takes some of the backstage jobs away from humans and gives them to machines. In my experience, it never reduces the number of people necessary to run a show—it only makes that show more reliable and consistent, allowing a greater level of complication and new ways of linking machines and actors. The best show control in the world—that is, the best way to keep any show under control—is still a human being.

CHAPTER 11

Properties: Research, Detail, and Crafts

Unlike most things in the theater, prop work is most often done by individuals. Carpenters, electricians, riggers—all these people tend to work in crews, but props are most often created by people working solo. **Props** are chosen (or invented) by the **scenic designer** or **prop designer**, working alone; realized by a craftsperson or located by a researcher, working alone; placed by a single prop person backstage; and, if they are handled during the show, tend to be handled by a single actor.

Prop work is composed of three distinct types of work, and as such, is populated by three fairly distinct types of people. It's worth taking the time to recognize which type your prop person is. Of course, many prop people are a combination of more than one type and every now and then, you meet someone who embodies all three (*hire 'em!*), so take these definitions loosely. They are offered here because of the intimate, one-on-one nature of prop work, as well as the necessity of getting to know the people in this department on a personal basis. The following are not individual job titles, just some general personality types that you will likely encounter.

The Artisan

Some people have a gift for creation and imitation. These people take great joy in mastering long lists of materials and techniques while devising new and previously unheard-of ways to construct anything the designer can invent. This process is not so much mental struggle as mental exercise to them, and they generally have flexible minds: able to see peas as pearls, pop tops as chain mail, and washing machine agitators as royal crowns. They are problem-solvers, more often discouraged by bureaucratic obstacles than overwhelmed by an unsolved design problem. They can make anything of the free junk most folks throw in a dumpster. And the best ones can do it by Thursday. These people are often called "crafts" people and they are best called in to construct particular pieces, such as fantasy props or furniture.

The Detailer

Look in the dictionary under the words "mind-numbing detail" and you will find the reference: "see also: props." There are shows in the world without a lot of props, but don't hold your breath waiting for one to come along. Someone has to coordinate the sheer numbers of props, particularly in shows with complicating factors such as real food, animals, multiple scene changes, or trick props that have to light up, explode, break, or fire on cue. Fortunately, there are people in the world who take joy in making sense of this kind of detail. These people live with lists on legal pads and ballpoint pens hung around their necks. They will not rest until their clipboard has a long list of check marks and completed quests. The telephone is a shrine to them. They know how to combine errands to save time. They can read a map. These people are invaluable in heavy prop shows and low-budget theaters that must do a lot of borrowing and begging.

The Researcher

All propmasters inevitably collect a long list of antiques stores, junk shops, and bargain stores where they find many of the pieces that they need for shows. A true researcher goes even further, mentally (or physically) cataloging thousands of pieces all over town, taking joy in searching out the perfectly odd prop. For her, prop work is a quest—a journey into a wilderness of goofy, unexpected, hidden treasures. She is inventive with her sources, and will call places you and I would never think of. I once watched Jolene Obertin, the prop coordinator at Seattle Rep and a true researcher, find a ten-inch-high scale model of the Statue of Liberty in two minutes flat without leaving her desk. She got it on her second phone call—to the gift shop at (where else?) the Statue of Liberty in New York City. (They ship, for a small fee.)

So, now that we've met the prop staff, let's get down to business.

Making the Prop List: When to Buy, Borrow, or Build

Prop Genesis, v. 1

In the beginning, there was the Script. And the Script listed all the props that were necessary for the action to take place, as well as a few more that were mentioned because they were used in the original New York production.

Prop Genesis, v. 2

And the Director said, "Let there be a Concept," and he saw that many props were needed to realize his Vision, so he turned to the Stage Manager and said, "Can we get a stuffed alligator to hang up there?"

Prop Genesis, v. 3

And the Producer said, "Let there be a Design," and the Designer called for many more props, either by sketching them in great detail or by writing little notes in the margins like "Fill shelves with books and other stuff."

Prop Genesis, v. 4

And the Producer hired the Actors, who realized as rehearsal progressed that they needed notebooks and pens, funny hats and noses, and cigarettes with long, elegant filters or they, too, would not realize their Vision.

Prop Genesis, v. 5

And the Propmaster saw that order needed to be put upon the land, and so she made the **prop list**, which contained every prop that she had heard of in her travels. And she was sore afraid—for the list was long and complicated. Yet she took heart, for Opening Night was six weeks away and she had no time to Freak Out.

And so was born the Prop List. And it was Long.

Setting Up the Prop List

Everything begins with The List. The prop list should contain every prop that will finally end up on stage, and it should be compiled as early in the production process as possible. Like everybody else, prop people like to know what is expected of them early in the game.

The list should identify a prop as one of three categories: **set props**, **personal props**, and **set dressing**.

Set props are preset on the stage and generally left there. They are handled, sat on, picked up, dialed, or passed around by actors, as opposed to set dressings, which are considered purely decorative. Set props include furniture, lamps, appliances, rugs, phones, and so on. They are the most important props since (a) they are large enough to be clearly seen by the audience and (b) they are used by actors.

Personal props, since they are also employed by the actors, are also high on the list of priorities. They rank second only because they are smaller,

For Our Eyes Only *Prop List*

TYPE	ITEM	PRE-SET POSITION	USED BY
Set	Seltzer Bottle	Drink table	
Set	Dictionary	Side table	
Set	Table Lamp	Side table	
Set	Candlestick	Hearth	
Set	Coffee Table	Down center	
Set	Sofa	Center	
Set	Rocking chair	Left	
Set	Drink Table	Wall stage left	
Set	Side Table	By sofa	
Personal	Giant Key	SL prop table	Andre
Personal	Cigarettes	SL prop table	Rick
Personal	Matches	SR prop table	Rick
Personal	Walking Stick	SR prop table	Mrs. Doddyworth
Personal	Letter from Paul	SL prop table	Susan
Personal	Dead Chicken	SR prop table	Paulina
Personal	Journal	SL prop table	Kitty
Dressing	Painting of Grandpa	SR wall	
Dressing	Bowling Trophy	UC shelf	
Dressing	Sailing Calendar	Kitchen wall	
Dressing	Bulletin Board	Kitchen wall	
Dressing	Newspaper Clippings	SL wall	
Dressing	Feathered Headdress	SL wall	

Fig. 37. A prop list

and, relatively speaking, they require a little less effort since their appearance is less noticeable to the audience. Personal props are preset on the prop table and carried onstage by actors. They include things like pens, cigarettes, documents, money, and anything else handheld that is assigned to a particular actor.

Set dressing is the lowest priority since it doesn't affect the action. Set dressing includes things like pictures on the wall, knick-knacks to fill up shelves, draperies, and anything else that fills up empty space and helps to communicate the nature of the space to the audience. In some situations, set dressing doesn't even appear on the prop list since it consists of whatever the designer and prop master can find in the prop room. Nevertheless, efforts should be made to get these props on the list, since it will make it easier for the prop people to pull things from storage. Furthermore, if those people know what you are looking for, they can keep an eye out during their shopping trips.

Once the list is under way, the next step is to divide the props into four other categories: build, buy, pull, and borrow. This is where the detailers come in. The decision about where to get the prop depends on several factors:

- *Money* is, of course, the basis of all such decisions. A propmaster balances the money available in his budget against the money needed to buy a prop. If the budget will support it, buying a prop is the least labor-intensive way to get a prop.
- *Available labor,* which is another way of talking about money, will determine what can be built. This is where the artisans come in. Prop building requires a number of different skills, including carpentry, sewing, foam carving, plastic molding, and more. Prop artisans are unusual craftspeople, and prop-building technique is unlike anything else. A household furniture builder, for example, will be surprised at how his creations are treated on stage and will hold his head in dismay as the joints come loose.
- *Time,* the third leg of the logistics stool, determines what you have time to make.
- *Availability* means "Can I find it?" With period shows, this is a major factor. Sixteenth-century furniture doesn't grow on street corners. Nor do specialty props, that is, props that sprang from the mind of a sadistic playwright. The show *Ten Little Indians,* for example, requires ten porcelain Indians, seven of which get destroyed every night. No, no, thank *you,* Dame Agatha Christie.

So . . .

- Buying a prop saves time and labor, but you are dependent on availability and budget.
- Building a prop is usually cheaper then buying and solves the availability problem, but you need the necessary talent.
- Borrowing saves time and money, but it is completely dependent on availability (and the goodwill of the lender).
- Pulling a prop from stock is always the best option but, if you don't have it, you can't pull it.

Furniture: Why the Stage Isn't Like Real Life

There is one really unfortunate thing about stage props. Many of them bear a striking resemblance to things we have in our own homes, like tables, chairs, and sofas. It isn't unusual, therefore, particularly in low-budget theater, for people to raid their own homes and the homes of others to find furniture for their shows. On the contrary, go visit the home of any community theater luminary and he will probably have a story for every piece in his living room: "Oh, yes, that's the sofa from *The Boy Friend,* and that chest was used in *Man of La Mancha,* and the desk is from *Harvey . . .*" and on and on.

Most theaters can't afford to buy furniture for every production and it is simply impossible to have every kind of furniture that you need in stock. Hence, theaters borrow all the time. This is not a bad thing, but you should proceed with caution. Let me illustrate with two stories.

Some years ago, I did a production of *The Music Man,* the musical comedy about everybody's favorite con man, Harold Hill. In the second act, while trying to seduce the town librarian, Hill sings "Marian, the Librarian" to her in the middle of the town library, which is full of chairs and tables. The song becomes a raucous dance number, all the more fun because it is going on in the normally sedate library, with Marian frantically trying to shush everyone back into silence. Fun stuff. At least it was fun until the choreographer decided to introduce a little Donald O'Connor choreography with the chairs. You may be familiar with O'Connor's very physical dance routines, particularly the ones involving furniture. Our choreographer created a very exciting sequence that had all the dancers leaping onto a chair, stepping up onto the back of the chair and then riding it down backwards until the chair landed on its back on the floor. Really fun.

And really dangerous. The chairs and tables had been borrowed from a local high school and they were built entirely of wood. There was no way that they were going to put up with that kind of strain and, sure enough, after a couple of weeks of rehearsal, most of them were broken. We were very fortunate to escape without a broken dancer as well.

Household furniture is made to be sat on, slept on, eaten on, even made love on, but it is *not* made to be jumped on, danced on, stomped on, or marched on. It is also not made to be thrown, dropped, kicked, or used as a weapon in a fight. This doesn't mean that you *can't* do all these things (and more) with household furniture; it just means that it wasn't *designed* for it.

Even if your play is devoid of violence or dancing, you will find that stage furniture goes through more punishment than the furniture in your home. For one thing, it gets moved around all the time. If you're anything like me, your living room furniture hasn't moved since you vacuumed under it the last time your mother came to visit. Theatrical furniture gets moved all the time, sometimes several times a day, if you have scene changes. It gets thrown up onto storage shelves, dropped in the wings, and loaded into pickup trucks. All this moving is very hard on the joints that hold furniture together, and they will weaken and come apart much more rapidly than furniture at home. Furthermore, actors are much more concerned with portraying a character on stage than they are with sitting down properly. They will collapse harder into a stage chair than the one at home and, no matter what their stage mother tells them, they will invariably lean back. Bottom line? The stage is not like life and prop furniture feels the pain.

What to do? Well, sometimes you have to build furniture especially for this kind of punishment. Those chairs that Donald O'Connor is flinging around in his dance routines were specially built out of steel to stand up to his needs. Sometimes, rather than building a piece from scratch, you need only fortify regular furniture with extra steel or wire. One common trick is to add an "X" of tightly wound wire between the four legs of a chair.

Fig. 38. A chair strengthened with wire

Step one: Talk to your propmaster. Tell her which pieces of furniture will receive special abuse and how often. Then, *listen* to the propmaster. If she tells you that a chair is not strong enough for what you have in mind, don't dismiss her input as alarmist. It might save you a broken chair (or a broken arm) later on.

Besides keeping your performers healthy, it is also important to keep relationships with lenders healthy. When I did *The Miracle Worker* a few years back, I brought in my own dining room table for the famous breakfast scene. In this scene, the young Helen Keller falls into a rage because her teacher, Annie Sullivan, forces her to eat her breakfast with a spoon instead of with her customary fingers. In response, she hurls her spoon violently down on the table. Annie puts it back, Helen throws it down. They repeat this pattern over and over until Helen finally gives in.

I delivered the table to rehearsal and didn't check back with the stage manager for a week or so. When we went to pick up the table for the first tech rehearsal, I was amazed to find the top of the table deeply gouged from the repeated spoon attacks. One-quarter of the table (the quarter that the actress could reach from where she sat) was completely stripped of its finish. After just a few rehearsals, the action of the scene had laid waste to the table. Because it was my own table, the only person I had to worry about was me, but if the table had come from another source, I would have had a real problem. Instead, I had another one of those "Look, there are the gouges that Helen Keller put on my table" stories that abound at theater people's dinner parties. Had the table been borrowed from a member of the theater's board of directors, it might have been a source of anguish, especially since a felt pad would have prevented the entire thing.

The moral? Be aware that theatrical action takes a higher toll on furniture, and, whenever possible, take steps to prevent the damage.

Weapons: Safety and Proper Handling

As with doors and windows, the first question to ask about a gun is: Does it need to be practical? In other words, does it need to fire? If not, then by all means, don't use a real gun on stage. The only exception to this is in an *extremely* intimate theater where the audience can clearly see that a prop gun is being used. Other than that, there is no compelling reason to use a real gun on stage if the gun isn't fired. Even if it is fired, a starter pistol that can fire only blanks should be used, if possible.

The first problem with guns and, in fact, with any weapon at all, is theft. I tell my students over and over, "*Weapons walk.*" This has been demonstrated over and over. There is a fascination with weapons, among both actors and technicians. Somehow, when you put a weapon in someone's hands, it brings out a primal hunter-killer personality, and he won't want to give that violent talisman back. Lured by television and movie images of weapons, people get a charge out of carrying and using them. Hence, when there are weapons around backstage, if you don't go to absurd lengths to protect them, they will walk away. They will, they will, they will. Trust me.

If you have weapons in a show, whether they are practical or not, there should be one person (usually a prop person or a stage manager) who looks after them personally. If possible, the location of their storage place should not be common knowledge and they should be kept under lock and key. If a gun must fire, have the person responsible load it at the last possible moment and hand it to the actor just before the actor goes on stage. When the actor comes off, the same person should be there to receive and unload the gun. If you are using a real gun, be aware that, in some states, the person handling the gun may need a firearm license.

Safety Alert! All guns, even blank guns, are dangerous. An unfortunate example is the untimely death of Brandon Lee, a young actor tragically killed on a movie set by a gun that was firing blanks. This accident was highly unusual, but it still reminds us of the extreme care that must be taken with all firearms.

Even though blank pistols do not have a bullet in them, they still emit a blast that can be harmful or even deadly. They often throw out wadding or other materials with deadly force. Never fire a blank gun when it is pressed against a person's head or body. Never fire a gun when it is pointed at a person's face. Back off. Aim lower, or to the side. The audience will be startled by the gun going off anyway, and they will never know the difference.

———————

One other note about guns: It is not unusual for a blank cartridge to misfire or not fire at all. Therefore, when you load a blank gun, load all the chambers, just in case. Actors, take note. If you pull the trigger and the gun doesn't fire, pull the trigger again, and again. Nine times out of ten, you will get the bang on the second or third try. Also, if you are handling a gun on stage, learn the location and operation of any safety switch. Otherwise, you may unwittingly flip that switch and be left with an inoperative gun, and there aren't many ad-libs that will get you out of that one.

There is one legendary story about an actor whose gun wouldn't fire, even after repeatedly pulling the trigger. After looking around helplessly for a knife, a rope, *anything* lethal he could use to cover the moment, he finally cried out, "Aha! I will kill you with my *poison ring!*"

Of course, any blades you use should be blunted. If the blade is being handled so close to the audience that they can see that it is blunt, then you are handling the blade too close to the audience. Any blocking that requires a blade to be thrown or kicked across the stage should be rehearsed fanatically. If you do have a weapon being thrown or kicked, you should block the moment in such a way so that, if the actor misses, the weapon will fall harmlessly against the scenery or backstage. Never stage a fight with weapons out in the audience. All stage fights should be rehearsed before every performance.

During a production of *Henry IV, Part One,* at Brown University, the actor playing Hotspur caught the tip of a sword across his forehead and began to bleed profusely. He finished the fight, died dramatically, and was dragged offstage. As it happened, there was a critic in the audience who gave us this review: "The fights were admirably staged, although the bloody death of Hotspur felt overdone."

Handling Props During the Show: Prop Tables

It is essential to have good prop tables. Find a big table to put by each entrance to the set. Cover the table with a large sheet of white paper (usually called "butcher paper" and available from an art store), and, using the real

Fig. 39. A prop table

props, draw their outlines on the table with magic marker. That way, you can tell at a glance whether you have everything. Props should be preset on the table by whichever entrance they come in, and actors should be trained to pick them up just before they enter the scene and drop them off as they leave. Props should never be taken to the dressing room, with the exception of costume props, like watches and jewelry (they're usually handled by the costume people anyway). Actors get attached to props and they sometimes want to keep those props with them, but this practice inevitably results in the actor suddenly realizing, seconds before his entrance, that the critical walking stick is hanging on the back of his dressing room chair. I have seen enough mad dashes to the dressing room by frantic stage managers to state this without reservation: Leave the props on the prop table. I've said it before, and I'll say it again: Actors aren't stupid, they just have a lot to think about.

CHAPTER 12

Stage Management: The Best Port in a Storm

Theater is complicated. Theater is stressful. Theater is a lot of hard work by a lot of people all trying to work on the same project at different times and in different places. Sometimes these places are in different cities, states, or countries. All of these people have different ideas, different methods, and different definitions of the word *deadline*. What to do? Hire a **stage manager**.

Stage managers are helpful people. They have to be. Their job description includes words like "Eye of the Hurricane" and "Safe Port in a Storm." They are at the center of everything. They are the communication link between everybody and everybody. This puts them in a position of uniquely intense stress. As the joke goes: How many stage managers does it take to change a light bulb? Answer: "One. And it's on my list."

Still, even with all this access and ability, many stage managers are not given the tasks that they should be given. Furthermore, since stage management does not necessarily require a lot of technical skills, it is a job often taken over by nontechnical people. For these reasons, all nontechnical people should know what a stage manager does.

Before beginning this discussion, I should mention that *stage manager* is a term with several variations. One of the primary variations is **production manager**. In a large theater company, there is often one person who oversees the entire production process. This is particularly true when one theater is producing more than one show at a time. This person is responsible for overall scheduling and logistics for the entire operation, while each individual show is run by a stage manager.

Communication: The Central Issue

Throughout the show, from concept to close, the stage manager must be in communication with the cast, the shops, the producers, and the director. One of the SM's primary responsibilities is to relay the director's thoughts to everybody else. If the director suddenly decides that an actor should be reading a book during a particular scene, it is up to the SM to ask him all the questions that the prop people will ask: What kind of a book? Hardcover or soft? What color? Any particular title? How big? How thick? Where does the actor get it from? Does that mean we need a bookshelf? and so on. Some of these questions may be initially dismissed as unnecessary, but it is surprising how much details begin to matter once it is too late to change them. It's up to the stage manager to find out these details ahead of time, *before* the propmaster shows up with a small red paperback and finds out that the director really wanted a thick, black, scholarly text. If the propmaster is making a second (or third) trip to storage, muttering under her breath, then the stage manager hasn't done his job.

An experienced stage manager knows that any change that happens during a rehearsal affects somebody who is not there, and it is up to the SM to let that person know. The most important examples are the times when scenery, props, or costumes will be stressed or abused by some kind of action. These include (but are not limited to) fights breaking out, liquids being spilled or thrown, objects being broken, pies in the face, actors having to crawl, run, climb, grab, hide, fall, collapse, or die. If someone stands up in the house during a final dress rehearsal and says, "What do you mean she's going to bleed on that dress?" then the SM hasn't done his job. *It is the stage manager's job to eliminate surprises.*

Besides personal one-on-one communication, the SM should create and maintain several other avenues of communication.

The Contact Sheet

The **contact sheet** is a list of everyone related to the show: cast, designers, crew, and anyone else who may need to be contacted about the show. It should include work and home phone numbers, cell phone numbers, fax numbers, and any other way to contact that person, including e-mail addresses, if they exist. It should also include pertinent phone numbers at the theater, such as backstage, the production office, or the box office. It does not hurt to list the numbers of pizza take-out places and local drinking establishments, particularly if large contingents of show personnel hang out there. Don't forget cab companies and public transportation information lines. Dance companies will generally include a physical therapist's name and number on the contact list. Musicals may list a music store. The stage manager's number should be in bold. Cast and crew should know that, if they have a crisis, they should call 911, and immediately thereafter, the stage manager.

Everyone involved with the show should get one. Update them as things change.

The Callboard

The second major communication thing that the SM should take care of is the **callboard**. This is a centrally located bulletin board that contains information that the cast and crew should know. This might include (but is not limited to):

- *Contact Sheet:* Of course, you should also give a copy to everyone in the show, but, hey, people lose 'em.
- *Sign-in Sheet:* This is a checklist with each person's name on it with a space for each night of technical rehearsal or performance. The cast and crew should be trained to sign in as soon as they get to the theater.
- *Rehearsal Schedule:* From the prompt book (see later in chapter).
- *Today's Calls:* This is a list showing what is happening today, where it is happening, and who should be there.
- *Next Day's Calls:* Same thing, but for tomorrow.
- *Reviews*: Some people put up all of them, but I only like to see the good ones.
- *Scene Breakdown:* From the prompt book (see later in chapter).
- *Directions:* To the rehearsal space, to the theater, to the shops (for costume fittings, for example), to company parties, etc. Anywhere that people might have to go. Remember to include information on public transportation.
- *Telegrams, Postcards, Congratulatory Notes:* Anything that keeps people's spirits up.
- *Rules and Regulations:* Find out what the appropriate rules and regs are in your theater. Professional shows are required to post union regulations as well, so make sure you are in compliance.

Basically, anything that the cast and crew needs to know should be on the callboard. This does not preclude spoken announcements. In fact, it is always best to give people information more than once. Announce it, then post it.

If you are a performer, make a habit of checking the callboard every day. And, of course, sign in as soon as you arrive at rehearsal.

From Coffee Shop to Load-Out: Schedules

The creation of a show can begin anywhere from three weeks (or less) to three years (or more) before opening night. The production cycle breaks down into four major blocks: **preproduction**, **production**, the **run**, and **closing**; and there are different schedule needs for each.

Preproduction

This is the time before the show is cast, before the shop has started building a set, before anybody other than the major players—the director, the designers, and whoever is putting up the money—has started working. This is a time for major decisions to be made: Which play are we doing? What time period are we setting it in? When do we open? How much money will we spend on each area? Because these decisions are so important to the process, they need to be made up front. It's up to the stage manager to see that they get made and that everybody else knows what the answers are. Consequently, the first events the stage manager should schedule are **concept meetings**. Concept meetings are "pie-in-the-sky" brainstorming sessions between the director and the designers. The stage manager need not (and should not) attend. These meetings are for drinking amaretto and philosophizing about Shakespeare's mother. It is here that the general concepts for the show should be decided (or, in the case of a strong-willed director, shared).

Once those concepts are agreed upon, the scenery and costume designers go off to their monk's quarters and come up with **renderings** and floorplans. After the designers have had some time to create (at least a few weeks), it is time to hold the **design conference**. Here the designers present their work and field questions from the director and other staff members. Lighting and sound designers, without the ability to show renderings, may give vivid descriptions.

Once things are moving along, it's time for the first of several **production meetings**, to which the heads of all departments should be invited. Production meetings are for sharing logistical information and for solving problems involving time, space, and money.

It is essential to recognize the differences between these meetings and not allow one to become another. As soon as a production meeting descends into conversations about whether to put the heroine in a red dress, you have slipped into a design conference. If you begin to debate the artistic integrity of red-coated heroines, you have landed in a concept meeting. In either case, you are wasting the time of the other people at the table, and the stage manager should gently but firmly call a halt to it.

This does not mean that you can't go back and have a design conference once you have started production meetings. On the contrary, if you discover a design problem in a production meeting, you should table the issue and sequester the relevant people at a nearby coffee shop to work it out. Likewise, if the design meetings are not going well because of inconsistencies in the concept, it will be necessary to backtrack there as well.

The stage manager should run the design conferences and production meetings. The head of each area (scenery, costumes, lighting, props, audio) should speak in turn, relaying progress reports and potential problems to the group. The stage manager should facilitate the discussion and move things along swiftly, not allowing lengthy discussions to erupt. These longer discussions must, I repeat, *must* be carried out in smaller one-on-one (-on-one) meetings and not in the larger meetings. If a design conference or production meeting takes longer than an hour, you have a problem.

Production

Once the design is complete and actors have been chosen, the show moves into production. Suddenly, a lot more people are involved, and these people are a lot more spread out. You will probably never get all these people into the same room until you tap the keg on opening night.

Much of the scheduling during the production period is handled by the individual shops. The SM should not worry about scheduling when each piece of scenery gets built or when the propmaster makes her run to the antiques store. Once you are in production, the SM should concentrate on scheduling rehearsals.

Production meetings still continue during this period, of course, and the stage manager should continue to schedule and run them. Most theater staffs find that a weekly one-hour production meeting does the job. The SM must also assume the position of attendance cop. As people get busy, priorities tend to shift, and members of the production staff will begin to find excuses not to attend. The SM must be unrelenting in reminding these people to show up. One way to improve attendance is to make the production meeting a regularly scheduled event, say, every Tuesday at 3 P.M.

The other important schedule that the SM should oversee during the rehearsal period is **costume fittings**. The costume shop should provide a list of which actors they need to see and the stage manager should build a schedule that ensures that these fittings happen.

Tech Week

The final countdown to opening night is hellish for everyone, but especially so for the stage manager. Every theater and staff approaches tech week differently, but it is usually a step-by-step process that slowly grows in complication each night. First the actors get on stage with the scenery, then come the

lights, then the costumes, then the makeup and hair. Each night more elements should be thrown into the mix.

The center of this hurricane should be the stage manager. Again, many
directors do not use the SM to the fullest extent, choosing to run these
rehearsals themselves. Rest assured, this is counterproductive. A director
should be concerned with what the audience will see and hear and how they
will react. If he takes on the job of making sure that all the details get taken
care of, then he will not have the kind of mental space necessary to create
the show. Of course, many directors in smaller community or school shows
habitually operate without stage managers, but these directors lose a lot of
stomach lining as well. If you do not have stage managers available, then it
is time to start developing them, for the sake of everybody in the show.

The Run

In many professional theaters, the director leaves the show in the hands of
the stage manager after opening night. These SMs make a report to the producer every night about the quality of the show and sometimes schedule
"brush-up" rehearsals to maintain the quality of the show.

In smaller theaters, the director maintains contact with the show after
opening night, but he should still let the stage manager handle the moment-
to-moment management of the show. This management does not include
artistic decisions, however, just logistical ones.

Closing

When the show is closing, the stage manager should, with the technical
director, compose a plan of attack for **striking** the show.

The mood at strike will differ widely depending on the production, and
may even differ among people working on the same show. Younger, less
experienced performers are usually sentimental and a little sad. Older performers, who know that the next show is waiting in the wings, may be more
philosophical. Staff that has been working on a long-running show may be
downright relieved. I myself have always enjoyed strike. To me, it seems like
a way of restoring order to the world, of decreasing entropy. In any case,
strike may be quick and efficient, or it may be interminably painful. Most of
that difference comes from how it is planned.

First, determine what jobs can be done by unskilled labor and which jobs
require skilled technicians and special tools. The first category includes
cleaning, transporting, and general destruction. The second includes removing machinery, disassembling complicated scenery (especially when it is
being saved), and anything involving rigging. Divide your forces into teams,

with each team having a crew head. Write out their jobs on a separate sheet of paper and give it to them. Make sure that all the spaces in the theater are covered, especially dressing rooms and storage places.

Most important, have a checkout sheet that people have to sign out on. Give that sheet to one person and have her enforce attendance. It's a funny thing, but no matter what you do, there always seem to be fewer people around at the end of strike than there were at the beginning. Go figure.

In addition to the strike after the final performance, the stage manager should confirm that all borrowed props and costumes are returned to their rightful owners and that the theater itself is left clean.

Lists and Lists and Lists of Lists

A stage manager should be the repository of all information about a show, with the exception of some specific technical information that the shops require for construction. If you are not sure if the SM needs to know something, then she needs to know it. SMs are the enemies of trees. Paper is their life. Of course, computers are important, and much information is kept on them, but no SM worth her stopwatch would forgo having a hard copy on a real piece of paper somewhere.

Here is a list of some of the lists that the stage manager should have. This is *not* a complete list:

- *Contact Sheet:* This is a complete list of names, addresses, and phone numbers for everyone working on the show. Be sure to update it as people move around. Unfortunately, the SM needs to be a bit of a gossip (always collecting info, never giving it out), because it may be necessary to contact someone in the evening, which means knowing where his romantic interests lie.
- *Costume Plot:* This is a complete list of every costume that a character wears, and when they wear it. The plot should also show where quick changes happen. A quick change is defined as any costume change where the actor does not have time to get back to the dressing room and has to change clothes in the wings.
- *Prop List:* This is a complete list of all props, showing what they are and where they start on the set. See chapter 11 for more info.
- *Scene Breakdown:* This is a list of all the scenes in the show, showing the name of the scene ("Act Two, Scene Four," "Brazilian Samba," or whatever name scheme you are using), who is in each one, and page numbers where they begin and end.

- *Lighting Cue Sheet:* This is a list of all the lighting cues showing when they happen and what they do ("All lights go out except special on Agnes"). See chapter 6 for more info.
- *Sound Cue Sheet:* This is a list of all the sound cues showing when they happen and what they do ("Pounding Surf"). See chapter 9 for more info.

Biblical Scholarship: Keeping the Prompt Book

By now it should be clear that one of the stage manager's primary jobs is to collect information. All that information needs to be kept in one, easily accessible place. That place is the **prompt book**, or prompt script. (I prefer the first term since the book holds a lot of things besides the script.)

The prompt book should be a large, three-ring binder with the stage manager's name, address, and phone number on the front and back. In that binder resides every piece of information needed to produce the show. Often, it is the only thing kept when a show ends. If a show is later revived, the staff will depend on it.

In most production situations, the prompt book should never leave the theater. Do not take it home. Do not risk forgetting it, losing it, or leaving it in the trunk when your car gets stolen. Often, companies will keep two identical prompt books, one for the SM and a backup for the ASM. This is especially important if you have several different rehearsal locations and the books get carried all over town.

Besides all the lists and schedules above, the prompt book should contain the authoritative copy of the script, showing all cuts and revisions, as well as all **blocking** (the actors' movements) and sound and lighting cues.

Before you start the rehearsal period, make a photocopy of every page in your script onto 8½-by-11-inch paper. Since most scripts are smaller than that, you will end up with a large border of white space around the text.

When a particular movement is determined in rehearsal, make a small, vertical mark next to the word in the script where the actor starts to move. Then draw a long horizontal line all the way out to the *left* side of the page. Write the movement on the line, out in the white margin.

Abbreviate everything. It's the only way you will fit all the information on the page. Write in all caps to ensure legibility. All characters and objects on the stage should be reduced to as few letters as possible (try for three), and all movements should be referred to as *crossing*, abbreviated as "X." It doesn't matter if they are walking, running, stumbling, skipping, fleeing, or crawling. If they are moving, they are crossing. Use "NTR" and "XIT" for comings and goings.

If Hamlet, rapidly dying from the touch of a poison dagger, staggers to the throne and falls, you write: HAM X THRN, FALL.

If Lenny, caught up in George's vision of a beatific future on the rabbit farm, runs to the top of the platform downstage left, you write: LEN X PLAT DL.

If Mame enters from the central door upstage (doesn't she always?), sweeps to a café table downstage right, and sits, you write: MAM NTR UC, X DR, SIT.

For shows with large casts, it will not always be practical to notate blocking in this way. For crowd scenes, get a floorplan on 8½-by-11-inch paper and make a bunch of copies. Insert a floorplan into the script when you need one and draw out the blocking on it with names and arrows. For a show with lots of crowd scenes (like a musical), take your script to a copy shop and have them photocopy the floorplan on the back of every page.

When it comes time to write the lighting and sound cues in the script, use the margin to the *right* of the text. Draw a small vertical line next to the word where the cue happens, then draw the line out to the edge of the paper. Write the cue on this line, once again abbreviating everything. Lighting cues are "LQ." Sound cues are "SQ." Cues should be numbered to help you keep them straight.

In some cases, a cue might be a **visual**. This means that the cue doesn't happen on a line; it happens on something that the actor *does,* like turning on a light switch.

(While we're on the subject, every now and then someone gets the idea that the stage lights should actually be tied to the light switch on the set so that, when the actor hits the switch, the lights come on. I do not recommend it. Sure enough, some night the actor will miss the switch, or forget, or the lead will be sick and the understudy will go on and nobody will have told him about it. As I have been saying throughout this book, actors are not stupid, just preoccupied. I say, protect the actor and let the technician take up the slack. Make the light switch a fake one and bring the lights up when the actor gestures in the general direction of the switch.)

Lastly, each cue should have a **warning** about a minute before it happens, so the operators will be ready when the time comes. All warnings should be notated in the script just like cues. There is no need in the prompt book to write what a lighting or sound cue really does, just that it happens.

So, if the lights come up on Peter's bedroom in the early morning (light cue one) and the alarm clock rings (sound cue one), Peter shuts it off, gets out of bed and turns on the light switch, you write:

LQ 1
SQ 1
SQ 1 END ON VISUAL (PET TRN OFF)
LQ 2 ON VISUAL (PET HIT LIGHT SWCH)

ACT 2, SCENE 5

AT LIGHTS UP, CHA, MAU | *Charley and Maude come out of the house and sit in the porch swing.*
NTR UC, X SWING, SIT

CHARLEY
That was a wonderful dinner, my sweet. What ominous looking clouds.
Looks like rain.

MAUDE
Charley, be a dear and turn on that porch light, won't you?

CHARLEY
CHA X SWITCH | Why sure, I'd love to. |

Charley goes to the light switch and turns it on. | _____ VISUAL   LQ 43

MAUDE
Thanks ever so much.

CHARLEY
CHA X SWING, SIT | Maude, darling, there's | something that I've been wanting to tell you.   SQ 18

A car is heard offstage.

MAUDE
MAU STAND | Is that a car coming up the driveway? Whoever could it be?

CHARLEY
I don't know, but they had better hurry up and get inside. The rain is
starting. | _____ LQ 44, SQ 19

*There is a flash of lightning, followed by a clap of thunder. A torrent of
rain begins to fall.*

CHARLEY
What did I tell you?

ABBY (offstage)
Hello! Anybody home?

MAUDE
Why, it's Abby and Ricky! Come on up out of the rain.

ABBY, RICK, NTR DR | *Abby and Ricky dash in, running from the rain. They have newspapers
X PORCH | over their heads.*

ABBY
Well, then, what a sudden downpour!

Fig. 40. A typical prompt book page

Of course, remember that all things change, so mark all blocking and cues in *pencil.*

The prompt book should be maintained with the goal that the stage manager could be removed at any moment and the assistant would still know everything necessary to run the show. Other things that should be in a prompt book:

- *Program Copy:* This includes a list of every person working on the show with their proper title. Circulate a copy of this list around rehearsals and shops so that each person can initial their name, confirming that it is spelled correctly. Program copy may also include acknowledgments of individuals or businesses that have provided support to the show, biographies of people in the production, as well as comments or quotes that the director would like to include.
- *Publicity Information:* This varies widely depending on your situation, but it might include press releases, schedules of interviews, reviews, or biographies of people in the production.
- *Any other piece of information that relates to the show in any way:* Remember, if it is a piece of paper, the prompt book should contain a copy.

I witnessed an event at Seattle Rep that proved the validity of this statement. We were doing an absurdly complicated production of *Caucasian Chalk Circle.* There were hundreds of light and sound cues, dozens of costume and set changes, and thirty-six computer-controlled projectors. Running the show was a nightmare job: The stage manager was calling cues continuously for over two hours. As it happened, the SM had become pregnant prior to the start of production, and by the time tech week arrived, she was quite far along. The pregnancy never interfered with her duties until, one night, right in the middle of a performance, she suddenly fainted. As the wardrobe staff (the only free hands at that moment) rushed to the light booth to care for her, the ASM sprinted from backstage, slid breathlessly into her chair and headset, and began to read the cues from the book. The show continued seamlessly and neither the audience nor the actors were aware of the problem. That kind of save can only happen when the prompt book is accurate and up-to-date. Mother and baby are doing fine, by the way.

Preparing the Rehearsal Space and Running Rehearsals

Another of the stage manager's missions is to run rehearsals and call the show. A stage manager should make sure that the rehearsal starts on time (never delayed by tardy actors) and ends on time (never held over by a suddenly inspired director). Of course, once the rehearsal has started, the director is in charge until the SM gently tells him that time has expired. Diplomatically, of course.

To prepare the space for rehearsal, the first thing to do is **tape the stage**. Get hold of several rolls of **spike tape**, a cloth-backed, colored tape sold by theatrical supply stores. Spike tape will not harm floors, tears easily, and comes in a rainbow of colors. You can get away with colored vinyl tape from the hardware store, but spike tape is a lot easier to work with.

Get a copy of the floorplan from the set designer. Using the spike tape, mark out the shape of the set on the floor of the rehearsal space. Make a complete outline of each platform, showing all doors and windows. For a staircase, outline each step and make an arrow that shows which way is up. Use different colors as necessary. Show the edge of the apron and any other feature of the set that may impede movement.

There are lots of different kinds of rehearsals in the production process and the SM's duties will vary with each one.

First Read-through

This is the first time that the entire cast will be in the same room together and is generally a jolly affair. The material is fresh, the energy is high, and no one has any grudges yet. Make the most of it. Designers will sometimes show up to say hello and meet the cast.

There will be a lot of bookkeeping and logistics at this rehearsal and you should do it all before you start reading. Once the scripts come out, you will have lost everyone's attention to the material. The cast should get a copy of the rehearsal schedule and the contact sheet. Ask them to notify you of conflicts immediately, if not sooner.

A representative of the costume shop (the designer, more often than not) should be at first rehearsal to take measurements. As some people are not comfortable having a measuring tape wrapped around their bodies in public, it is best to set this process up in an adjoining room. The designer can quietly pull people out of the main room while the script is being read. Actors with major roles may have to be measured during a break.

Once the bookkeeping is over, the cast should read the script from beginning to end, stopping only for intermissions. The SM or an assistant should read the stage directions.

One more tip for this rehearsal: You should time the read-through. More often than not, the production will run about as long on opening night as it runs in first read-through. You'll impress the heck out of the box office if you give them an accurate running time two months before the show opens, especially if you're right.

- People Needed for First Read-Through: *Director, Cast, SM and ASM, Representative from Costume Shop (Costume Designer), Other Designers (Optional)*

Table Work

Most directors will want to spend some time tearing the script apart while sitting around a table with the actors. Sometimes, the stage manager can skip these rehearsals, since they are mostly discussion, but you should still make sure they start and stop on time. Go make phone calls or something while they do all that artistic stuff.

- People Needed for Table Work: *Director, Cast, SM (only at beginning and end)*

Blocking rehearsals, Scenework, Polishing, Dance rehearsals, Music rehearsals, Partial run-throughs, etc.: Every director is different. Every production is different. Every director will construct a rehearsal period his own way. You may have any or all of these rehearsals in your schedule. Make sure that the appropriate performers are called for each one, along with the SM or ASM.

Another important job for the SM in these rehearsals is to be **on book** once the actors are **off book**. In other words, once the actors have put their scripts down and are reciting the lines from memory, someone else in the room should be following the script. If an actor has a memory failure, he should call out "Line" and the SM should immediately read the next sentence that the actor is supposed to say. Don't try to act it, just read it. Read one sentence and stop. If the actor needs more, he will ask for it. One note to actors: There is no need to break character or look at the SM when you need a line. Stay where you are, stay in the moment, and ask for the line. A good SM will provide it quickly and cleanly.

First Run-through

First run-through is also known as "stumble-through." This is the first time that the cast attempts to run the show from top to bottom without stopping. Besides its obvious value to the cast and the director, first run-through is also very important to another member of the production: the lighting designer. She cannot design the lighting until she knows where the actors are at each moment of the play. First run-through must be scheduled well before lighting load-in (see below).

- People Needed for First Run-through: *Director, Cast, SM and ASM, Lighting Designer*

Paper Tech

Tech week, the time when we add the scenery, lighting, and costumes to the production, is approaching. Before it ever starts, the designers (minus the costume designer) should gather with the director to talk through scene shifts, light cues, sound cues, and special effects. If design meetings have been used wisely and the director and designers have done their homework, then most of the decisions about what these cues will look like will have already been made. The paper tech should consist of communicating this information to the stage manager so it can be written into the prompt book.

By the end of this meeting, the stage manager should know where all the lighting, sound, and scene-change cues occur during the show.

- People Needed for Paper Tech: *Director, SM, Lighting Designer, Scenic Designer (if there are scene changes), Sound Designer, Any Special Effects People*

Load-in

If your set is not constructed in the theater itself, then you will need to schedule a time to deliver it and set it up. Talk to the technical director and determine how much time will be needed. Props should also arrive during load-in, but not until the first rush of scenery is over. Costumes should *not* be brought into the theater at this point.

- People Needed for Load-in: *Technical Director, Stage Crew, Propmaster, Prop Crew*

Lighting Load-in

Lighting and scenery crews can work side-by-side sometimes, but for the most part, it is best to assign them separate hours onstage. Once these hours are determined, the heads of the two crews can negotiate with each other. Often, the lighting crew can start hanging lights in the "front-of-house" positions (out over the audience) while the scenery crew works on stage. Once the lighting crew begins working over the stage, the scenery crew will have to curtail its operations. Focusing sessions, with their need for quiet and darkness, should be done with only the lighting crew present.

- People Needed for Lighting Load-in: *Lighting Designer, Lighting Crew, Dimmerboard Operator*

Lighting Rehearsal

Once the lights are hung and **focused**, the director and the lighting designer should sit in the dark theater and set all the light cues. Someone (an ASM, for example) should be recruited to walk around on stage so that the designer and the director can see what the lights will look like on a person. If light cues are designed with only the scenery onstage, the actors' faces will almost always look too dark during the show. The stage manager (or her assistant) should be present to make sure that all the cues in the prompt book are accounted for. All necessary operators should attend as well, although, if follow spots are being used, you can usually get by with just one person to operate them. The cast should *not* attend.

- People Needed for Lighting Rehearsal: *Director, SM (or ASM), Lighting Designer, Dimmerboard Operator, Follow Spot Operators (if appropriate), Stage Walker*

Sound Rehearsal

Basically the same thing as the lighting rehearsal above, except with sound cues. The director should set volumes for all the cues, remembering that the cues will sound softer when the theater is full of people. If microphones are being used, someone should be onstage to talk into them. If "live" sound effects are being used (offstage noises, thunder claps, etc.), they should be tested during this rehearsal.

- People Needed for Sound Rehearsal: *Director, SM (or ASM), Sound Designer, Sound Board Operator, Anyone Needed to Produce "Live" Effects, Microphone Talker*

Special Rehearsals

Occasionally, a show will have a complicated or potentially dangerous effect that will require a special rehearsal. This includes magic tricks, animal tricks, firearms, explosions, trick doors, traps, stage violence, and any other effect that requires some extra tweaking that could best be done when everyone else is not standing around watching. This rehearsal should happen before first tech and may take anywhere from five minutes to several hours. You should consider having one any time a particular effect is beginning to look complicated. They are obligatory for shows where people are flown or engaging in stage combat.

- People Needed for Special Rehearsals: *Director, SM, Any Crew or Cast Who Perform the Effect*

Dry Tech

The dry tech is a chance to run through all the cues on stage without the actors. Having actors onstage while the tech crew is going through their cues for the first time is wasteful for everybody. It is hard for the actors to remain patient and involved during the long silences while the crew is tweaking their equipment, and the crew does not need all those bodies in the way. So, have the first tech rehearsal "dry," that is, without the performers.

- People Needed for Dry Tech Rehearsal: *Director, SM and ASM, Lighting Designer, Scenic Designer, Sound Designer, All Running Crews (except costume and makeup)*

Cue to Cue (frequently abbreviated "Q2Q")

Now, and only now, should the actors take the stage again. They will not go through the entire show, however. A Q2Q rehearsal jumps through the show, only performing the lines right before and after a technical cue. The process works like this: Start at the beginning of the show. Run the opening sequence of cues, including house lights going out, curtain (if you have one) going up, and so on. Then, the stage manager should find a line in the script that is thirty seconds or so before the next cue and tell the actors to skip to there and wait. Actors should hold until the SM says "Go ahead, please." When the SM gives the word, the actors begin speaking and, at the appropriate moment in the script, the cue is run. The SM calls out "Hold, please," and checks with the director to see if the cue was satisfactory. If not, then corrections are made and the cue is run again. Once the director is happy, the stage manager calls out a new starting place for the actors and the process begins again with the next cue. This kind of work is hard on actors, to be sure, but it is necessary to get through the show in one pass, and it helps ensure that the run-throughs coming later will go more smoothly, at least from the technical standpoint. If the show is fairly simple technically, the staff may forgo this rehearsal and go straight to the first tech run-through, stopping only for disasters.

- People needed for Cue-to-Cue rehearsal: *Everyone from the Dry Tech Plus the Cast*

Since this is the first time that the crew and the actors are really working together, it is a good time for a survival guide.

The Actors' Backstage Survival Guide to Tech Rehearsal

- *Prepare to be bored.* Tech rehearsal takes longer than you think it will and *a lot* longer than you think it should. Keep in mind that while you—the actors—have been rehearsing for weeks, this is the first time the crew has been able to run the show. Remember *your* first run-through? Bring a book, a deck of cards, your cell phone, whatever you need to occupy yourself when you are not needed on stage. When you *are* needed, be prepared to stand on stage doing nothing for substantial periods. There is actually a great deal of activity going on around you. Lists are being altered, computers are being programmed, a thousand details are being attended to. It just *feels* like nothing is happening.
- *Find your light.* See that stressed-out person sitting in the audience, hunched over a desk full of mind-numbing drawings, squinting at the stage and mumbling cabalistic strings of numbers into a headset? That's the lighting designer, and she is trying to make you look good. Help her out by paying attention to the pools of light you are standing in. Become sensitive to what it feels like to have strong light on you and what it feels like to stand in shadow. When you are standing in a pool of light, be aware of where the edge of it is so that you don't deliver your most impassioned monologue with half your face in shadow. Sometimes moving six inches will make the difference between good and bad light. Mark your spots during tech rehearsal and you will never have to think about them during performance. This doesn't

mean that you have to tell the lighting designer that you are poorly lit. Believe me, she knows when something isn't working. Just be aware of where the light is so that you can use it to best effect.

- *Be consistent in your timing and your blocking.* The lighting designer is also using this time to program light cues. A good lighting designer will track your movements around the stage so that the right amount of light is in the right place at the right time. If you have already read the lighting chapter, you know that lighting works like the camera in film—it focuses attention in the proper place and lets the director "zoom in" on the action. The more consistent you are in your movements, the more attention can be focused on you. If your movements change from night to night, the designer will be forced to light the stage more generally, robbing you of the visual focus that you so richly deserve. I encourage actors to use a tech rehearsal as an opportunity to train themselves. Learn to use your tools—your body and your voice—consistently and the tech people will be able to help you.
- *Do not wear white.* Creating a balance of light onstage is a delicate operation. An actor in white will upset the balance of light, making one side of the stage appear brighter than the other. When the actor comes on in the real costume during dress rehearsal, one side of the stage will be too dark. Of course, if your real costume is white, then you *should* wear white to tech rehearsal.
- *Maintain quiet in the theater.* Tech rehearsal requires a number of people to communicate with each other in a clear manner. This becomes insanely difficult if there is extraneous noise in the theater, even just a little. Help the process move quickly by being silent.
- *Do not disappear.* If the tech staff can build up a good rhythm, they can fly through the rehearsal on eagle's wings. The fastest way to break that rhythm is to have to stop and send somebody to find an actor. If you are the actor who had to be hunted down, do not be surprised at the cold wind of resentment that hits you when you finally make it to the stage. Stay aware of what is happening onstage and when you will be needed.

First Tech

If you have already done a Q2Q, then this rehearsal should be a run-through with no stops. Any work left to do should be fairly minor and definitely should not interfere with the action. If there are major pieces of scenery, lighting effects, or sound cues that are missing at this point, you should seriously consider cutting them and doing without.

- People Needed for First Tech Rehearsal: *Same as Cue-to-Cue*

Second Tech

A repeat of first tech, but with slightly higher stakes. If a technical effect that has any bearing on the actors is still not done, cut it. Then do not dwell on it. These things happen, and part of the experience of live theater is the opening night deadline. If this were film, we could just shoot it later and it would only cost us money. This is not film, however, and the box office is not about to postpone the show because the tree swing effect had too many problems to make it onstage. Let it go. Use what you have.

Actors should not wear costumes for this rehearsal unless they are difficult to move in (period clothing, masks, soap bubble costumes), must be changed or altered as part of the action (like an actor who gets dressed or undressed onstage), or require insanely fast changes. The only other reason to wear a real costume at tech rehearsal is if it does tricks, like the exploding hat in *Annie Get Your Gun*.

- People Needed for Second Tech Rehearsal: *Same as First Tech*

First Dress

Time for the costumes! By this point, the show should only stop if someone's dress is falling off. Actors should keep going, no matter what, unless they hear "hold" from the stage manager. First Dress is sometimes preceded by a **costume parade**, where the director and costume designer sit in the audience while each of the actors is brought onstage to show how their costumes, hair, and makeup look under the lighting. Costume parades can be a time-consuming pill to swallow, but they are almost always beneficial, giving the director and designer valuable time to focus on the costumes without distractions.

- People Needed for First Dress Rehearsal (and Costume Parade): *Same as Tech Rehearsals Plus Costume Designer, Makeup Designer (if there is one), Wig Designer (if there is one), Costume and Makeup Running Crews*

Second Dress

The costume shop will still be working at this point, so no one should freak out if a few chorus members are still in their blue jeans. If a costume *effect* (breakaways, magic tricks, etc.) or a fast change is not working, alter it or cut it. The decision to cut a costume is often harder than cutting a prop or scenery because almost every change in costume, makeup, or hair will affect an actor. Remember, though: The audience is not going to walk out saying, "I would have loved the show, but that wig spoiled everything!"

- People Needed for Second Dress Rehearsal: *Same as First Dress*

Final Dress

If there is any aspect of the Final Dress that differs from the real performance (other than the lack of an audience), you have a problem. Final Dress should be a performance. If possible, it should start at the same time as a real performance and should follow performance protocol. The actors should not stroll through the house in their costumes and the show should never stop for any reason other than an unsafe situation (when a real performance should stop as well). If anything is missing, do not even think about whether to cut it. It's gone, by definition.

- People Needed for Final Dress Rehearsal: *Everyone Who Will Be in the Theater for a Performance (except ushers and front-of-house staff)*

And so ends Tech Week.
Still breathing? Good! Time for the fun part.

Opening Night and the Run

Because you had a successful dress rehearsal (you did, didn't you?), you have already experienced a real performance, right? So you don't have anything to worry about, right? Because everything is going to happen just like it did in rehearsal, right?

Well . . . maybe.

There is a kind of electrical force that flows through the backstage area when the audience—a real audience, not just the house staff and invited friends who slip in at dress rehearsal—starts flowing in the auditorium doors. The force is exciting. It is the reason we do this insanity, after all. It is also dangerous. The best rehearsed, most reliable parts of a sure-fire production will suddenly turn difficult and unpredictable in front of a paying audience, so it is up to the stage manager to maintain consistency and calm throughout the production.

Because of this phenomenon, many theaters perform "previews." These are real performances for real audiences (usually paying cut-rate ticket prices), but everybody in the house knows that the show is still considered imperfect and changes are still being made. In this case, critics agree not to review the show until it "opens."

Once opening night is over, things calm down for the SM. The nightly schedule should be the same as Final Dress, with the possible additions of post-show parties, brush-up and understudy rehearsals, photo calls, and strike. Parties are up to you, but let's talk about the other three.

Photo Calls

We all love photos of our shows. We all hate photo calls. There. I've said it. Now we can get past it.

There is no good time to take photos of the show. If you do it during a rehearsal, that insane clicking of the shutter can drive actors mad. Plus, the photo quality is lower since people are moving and there never seems to be enough light.

If you get people together before a performance to pose, then everyone is thinking about the show and feeling pressured, knowing that every minute they are out here on the stage is a minute when they could be backstage getting ready. The time pressure can be crippling and the end result may reflect people's nervousness. On the other hand, getting people together after the show is sometimes impossible, what with post-show euphoria setting in and friends trying to pull them out the door to a party. Schedule a photo call after a show and you are likely to suffer a constant whine of "Can we go yet?"

Still, there is less tension after a show than before, so in most cases the best time is after, but try to find time after a dress rehearsal rather than a performance. At least you are not competing with the party.

Before the photo call begins, the SM should ask the director and designers which moments in the show they would like to photograph. Each moment should be identified with a scene number, a page number, and a light cue. Then, type this list up in reverse—from the latest moment in the show to the earliest. That's because, after a rehearsal, the costumes and set are set up for the end of the show. As you progress through the shoot, the costumes and sets get changed in reverse. When you are done, the stage should be preset for the next night's show (a little selling point you can use to convince unwilling technicians to participate). Give the list to the set, lighting, and costume designers (the sound people get to go home early, for once) so they know what you need and when. Keep things moving and you can get a very complete set of pictures in a minimal amount of time.

- People Needed at Photo Call: *Director, SM and ASM, Cast, Lighting Staff, Stage Crew, Costume Crew*

Brush-up and Understudy Rehearsals

If your show runs for more than one weekend, it is normal to schedule a brush-up rehearsal before the second weekend, particularly with a nonprofessional cast. Brush-ups are notorious for getting giggly and out-of-hand, so it is up to the SM to maintain discipline, supported by the director. One smirk from either one of you, and that will be the end of it. It is important that neither of these people put themselves in the position of "I would be joking around with you guys, but old Mr. Serious there wouldn't like it." The director and SM must present a united front at brush-up; otherwise discipline will fly out the window.

If possible, brush-up should happen on the set, but generally a full tech rehearsal is not necessary. Technicians have the luxury of being able to consult lists and notes during the show, and brush-up exists mostly to jog the actors' memories.

- People Needed at Brush-up: *Director, SM and ASM, Cast*

If your show has **understudies** (actors who have agreed to take over another actor's role in case of illness), then the stage manager should schedule rehearsals after opening night to allow these actors to be trained. In the professional theater, the director leaves after opening night, so understudy rehearsals are run by the stage manager, who is responsible for maintaining the director's intentions.

- People Needed at Understudy Rehearsals: *Director (if possible), SM, Cast Members Who Appear in the Scenes with the Understudies.*

The Payoff: Calling the Show

Once again, the stage manager is not responsible for deciding if the lightning flash goes before or after the thunder roll; she just tells everyone when to do it. Every person backstage should have a nerve wired up to the stage manager's voice, and that nerve should fire when the SM says the magic word: "GO."

Go

"GO" means "Do it *now*." It should always be said at the end of a sentence, as in: "Lighting cue 49. GO," and it should never be ignored unless there is a question of safety. This means that, even if you think the stage manager is calling the cue in the wrong place, you should run it when the SM says so. (Likewise, the SM should never say the "G-word" unless he means it.) If it is in the wrong place, the SM will be so informed by the designer or director and will adjust the timing. If operators start taking cues on their own initiative, it will be much harder to track down who got it wrong.

Half-Hour

In some companies, the stage manager will announce that one hour remains until the show, but in most cases, the first call comes thirty minutes before the show, at a time traditionally referred to as **half-hour**. At half-hour, the SM should confirm that everybody is in the theater for that evening's rehearsal or performance. If someone has not arrived by half-hour, it is time to make alternative plans: Prepare the understudy, find someone else to run the lightboard, etc. If you are not in the theater by half-hour, you have created a problem for somebody.

Personally, I have always found the **call** of half-hour to be reassuring and exciting. It means: "Heads up, everybody. We're doing a show."

Pre-show Calls

The proper form for all pre-show calls is: "Half-hour, ladies and gentlemen. The call is half-hour. Half-hour, please" or something very similar. A trifle formal perhaps, but why not? Theater is an honorable profession with deep traditions and half-hour calls are a well-worn comfort to us all.

All pre-show calls should be answered (unless the SM is announcing over an intercom and cannot hear you). The proper answer to a pre-show call is a cheerful "Thank you." This tells the SM that you appreciate her dearly and, more importantly, that you heard her.

Pre-show calls should also be made at fifteen minutes, ten minutes (usually accompanied by the "crew to places" call), and five minutes, using the same format and getting the same response.

If the show is not going up at the proper time, then the SM should announce backstage: "Ladies and Gentlemen, we are holding for [how many] minutes due to [whatever the reason]." Usually, holds are because the audience is late getting in, but occasionally, some other kind of problem will crop up.

About two minutes before the show, after being told by the front-of-house staff that the audience is almost seated, the stage manager should make the stomach-tightening announcement of "Places, ladies and gentlemen. The call is places. Places, please." The ASM should confirm that those actors who are on at the top of the show are in place.

Once *places* has been called, the show may start at any time, so heads up!

Once the show has started, it is up to the individual actors to be in the right place at the right time. They must not depend on the stage manager for calls once the curtain has gone up.

Headset Etiquette

Generally, the stage manager, her assistants, and the operators will be connected by a headset system during the show.

Nonessential conversation must be kept to an absolute minimum on the headset. It produces distraction that *will* cause mistakes.

This is an extremely hard policy for a stage manager to enforce, but it is essential. The stage manager is concentrating on a great many things, and chatter on the headset is one more thing that must be filtered out in order to keep a clear head. Make it easy. Keep it down.

It is a *huge* temptation to indulge in gossip and meanness on the headset. If you allow this kind of thing to go on unchecked, rest assured that, sooner or later, these comments will find their way to their subject and feelings will be hurt. On several occasions, I have heard comments made over a headset about someone who was actually listening in at the time. Not good. The moral is: Be professional over the headset. In fact, there is no reason for people to have their microphones turned on, unless they are responding to something the SM says.

One other piece of headset etiquette: If you are going to take your headset off, make sure that the mic switch is turned off. Having an open, untended microphone backstage makes it hard to hear on the line. Besides, the "CLUNK" of a mic being laid down on a table is painful to hear. Get in the habit of checking the mic before you take your headset off.

Calling Cues

The stage manager's prompt book should be marked before the show with all the cues, so calling the show is basically a process of reading from the book. About a minute before each cue, the SM should warn the operators over the headset, like this: "WARNING, Lights 49." If there are cues happening close together (or simultaneously), the format is: "WARNING, Lights 49 and Sound 7." If you warn too early, people will relax between the warn and the cue. Too late, and they will not be ready in time.

When the cue comes, your goal is to say "GO" at the exact moment that you want the cue to happen. The format is: "Lights 49 . . . GO" so you have to anticipate a little bit and start talking before the actual moment happens. It takes practice to get WARNs and GOs in the right place, but that is why we have rehearsal.

If more than one cue is happening simultaneously, then the format is: "Lights 49 and Sound 7 *together* . . . GO."

When the SM gives a warning, operators should respond so the SM knows they are ready, saying, for example: "Lights WARNED." Responding to a "GO" is usually not necessary since the SM can see whether or not a cue happened.

Note that, when calling a warning, you say "WARNING" and then the cue number. When calling a cue, it is the other way around: the cue number and then the "GO." Just one more way of avoiding confusion.

After the Show

After the last cue, when the stage lights are down, the house lights are up, and the show is really over, the stage manager should thank everybody on the headset and then get off it. If corrections or notes need to be given, they are best done in person.

CHAPTER 13

Corporate Theater: How to Do a Show in a Hotel

Shareholder meetings, conferences, corporate parties, product rollouts, news conferences, kickoff meetings. You might not think of these as "theater," but think again. What is theater? Someone stands on a stage and speaks, emotes, demonstrates, sings, pleads, presents, listens, and, in some way, performs for an audience of people who may or may not be interested. I call it theater. Even with all the theaters in the world, from community to Broadway, there is probably more theater done in hotels than anywhere else.

Doing a show in a hotel, however, has an entirely different set of problems to attend to. While you have the same general areas to worry about—lighting, scenery, sound, and so forth—hotels present a different set of solutions.

Lighting: Trees, Trusses, and the Demon Track Light

The first question you will need to ask about lighting is "How many lighting instruments do I need?" Like so many things in lighting, the answer may come down to "How many can you afford?" but I'll try to give you a rough guide to use.

If you are hiring a lighting company, here are the questions they will ask:

- *How big is the stage?* Obviously, the bigger the stage, the more lights you will need.
- *Are you shooting video or image mag?* **Image mag** means that the image

of the speaker is, quite literally, "magnified" by pointing a video camera at him/her and projecting the picture on a large screen so that people sitting far away can see. You will need bright light, or the face on the screen will look shadowy and dark.

- *Are the performers staying in one place, or moving around?* You can save money if you are principally lighting a podium. If you have dancers, though, or a big awards ceremony, then you will need bright light all over the stage.
- *Do you need follow spots?* Do you have runway models? Lounge singers? A roving emcee who likes to go into the audience? Consider (strongly) a follow spot. If you have talking heads at a podium, forget it. If you have a band, it's a nice touch.
- *How "professional" do you want it to look?* Brighter lighting with more colors and more "looks" will help your show look more professional and slick. There is no point in spending a lot of money on a flashy set and then lighting it poorly. For that matter, there's no point in renting an expensive ballroom and then making the whole thing look cheap by underlighting the stage that everyone is looking at.
- *How "theatrical" do you want it to look?* "Theatrical" means lots of colors. Remember, you can't change the color in each individual instrument during the show. If you want the stage to be blue for one number and red for the next one, then you need a set of blue lights and a set of red ones.
- *How "flashy" do you want it to look?* "Flashy" means theatrical but more so. This is where you spend the big money on moving spotlights, mirror balls, and lots and lots of colored back light.

If you are doing it yourself, however, you will still want to have the answers to these questions when you meet with representatives of the rental company. They can help you come up with the lighting package that you need. Read through the following section to get a general idea, then talk to them about what you want to do.

Think about how big your stage is. Mentally divide the stage into eight-by-eight-foot squares. For each square, you will need two lights from the front. This is a good rule of thumb since hotel stages are generally made from four-foot-wide platforms, so the stage size is almost always a multiple of four. So, for example, a sixteen-by-twenty-four-foot stage divides nicely into six eight-foot squares so you will need twelve lights. If you are having a band or some other kind of entertainment, you may wish to add trees upstage as well, to provide colored lights and back light. For back light, figure on one instrument for every six-by-six-foot square. Our sixteen-by-twenty-four-foot stage, then, has eight areas, so figure another eight lights for back light.

If all you have is speakers at a podium, you can get away without the back light, *unless* (are you tired of hearing this exception yet?) you want good videotape of the event. Video loves back light.

Track Lights

Any event in a hotel begins with a meeting with hotel personnel. During the course of the meeting, the subject of lighting will invariably come up and, two times out of three, they will try to tell you that they have lighting already installed in the room and don't worry about it.

What they are talking about is **track lights** and they are almost always inadequate for what you are trying to do. Track lights are wonderful for chic living rooms, restaurants, and art galleries, but lousy, lousy, lousy for theater. Generally, they do not put out enough light to illuminate a stage, plus it is very difficult to aim them in the right direction. They are generally at least twenty feet in the air and I have never been successful at getting the maintenance guy to show up before the performance and turn them the right direction.

The only time that track lighting really works is for a small meeting where you don't particularly care about shifting the focus up to a stage or a podium. If you could do your meeting in an ordinary office conference room, then you can do your meeting in a hotel without adding any lighting.

In most cases, however, you will want to bring in your own lighting equipment, especially if you want to videotape the event. If you have any kind of artistic performance—like a band, dancers, a magician, a guy in a bunny suit, or anything else—you will want to bring in lighting.

Besides making it possible for the audience to see the performers clearly, additional lighting adds an air of pizzazz to the occasion. People will listen more closely to a speaker who is well lit. Focusing attention on the stage and turning the lights down in the audience turns the event into a "show," making whatever is happening on stage more special. It also adds variety to what might otherwise be a long day of meetings.

So, now that you've decided that you need real theatrical lighting for your event, how do you get what you need?

There are two levels of lighting for hotel shows: trees (or booms) and trusses.

Trees

A **lighting tree** is a pretty simple thing: a vertical pole with a horizontal crossbar, held up by a flat or folding, triangular base. There are variations, of course. Some of them come in three separate pieces: pole, crossbar, and base. Some of them come as a folding unit that unfolds like a camera tripod. They vary in height from six to twelve feet.

Lighting instruments attach to trees the same way they attach to any other pipe in a regular theater. Put the C-clamp on the lighting instrument over the pipe and tighten the bolt. If you are going to set it up yourself, make sure you have a ladder at least as tall as the crossbar on the tree and that ubiquitous lighting tool, the eight-inch Crescent wrench.

When using trees, you do want to get the lights as far up as you can, since you are still trying to get that same 45-degree angle that you used in the regular theater. You don't often get it with trees, but you should try. Many trees use a telescoping action to push the crossbar higher, but beware. Don't push the crossbar up too high, or the tree will become top-heavy and might fall over. Most trees have a mark showing the upper limit. Find it and pay attention to it. If you are renting the trees, ask the rental company where the mark is.

Each tree can usually hold four lighting instruments—six if they are small. Larger instruments include PAR 64s (the automobile headlight instrument) and all ellipsoidals. Smaller instruments include six-inch fresnels and any PAR smaller than a 64. I do *not* recommend overloading them. Again, they will be top-heavy and unstable.

Here are three sample arrangements of trees for three sizes of show:

- *Small show* (a speaker or small musical group): Two lighting trees, each tree contains four six-inch fresnels
- *Medium show* (five-piece dance band or awards ceremony): Four lighting trees, two trees in front of the stage with four PAR 64s each; two trees in back of the stage with four six-inch fresnels each
- *Large show* (large chorus, "big band," or beauty pageant): six lighting trees, two trees at downstage corners of stage with four PAR 64s each; two trees directly in front of the stage have four six-by-nine ellipsoidals; two trees in back of the stage have four six-inch fresnels each; portable follow spot in the back of the audience

Trusses

If you are doing a larger-scale show, you will want a **truss** or two. A truss is a horizontal gridwork of pipes that hangs across the front of a stage. Because it runs the full width of the stage and is higher in the air, it provides a far better lighting angle than trees do. Because it is much longer and stronger than a tree, it can hold many more lighting instruments. The downside? A truss requires professional riggers and much more time and money to install. Two lighting trees can be set up by two people in a hour or two. A full-size truss might take a professional crew of four riggers twelve hours to rig, including the time necessary to hang and focus the lights. Hanging a truss is not something to do yourself, but for medium- and high-budget shows, it is a far better option for lighting a stage. To really look good, a large stage should have at least two trusses, one in front of the stage and one in back to provide back light.

Trees versus Trusses

Trying to decide between them? Here's the rule of thumb. If you can afford a truss, get one. If your stage is thirty feet across or less and you don't have a lot of money, use trees; either two, four, or six of them, depending on your budget and the size of the show. If your stage is wider than thirty feet, you need a truss. If you are really determined to make the show look great, get two trusses, one in front and one in back.

Power

Now that you have made your decision about trees and trusses, let's talk about where you are going to get enough power for all these lights.

If you haven't already, this would be a good time to go read the "The Birds and the Bees: Where Does Power Come From?" section in chapter 6.

There are three levels of power available to you:

- If you are working with a small lighting setup, you may be able to plug into the wall and be done with it. A normal wall circuit is 15 amps, so you must make sure that you are not trying to use more than 1,500 watts of lighting instruments (100 volts × 15 amps = 1,500 watts). For example, PAR lamps often come in 350-watt sizes, so you could hang four of them (1,400 watts) and still plug the whole mess into a 15-amp wall circuit. If you have two separate circuits (ask the hotel which outlets to use), you could plug one set of four into one outlet, one set into another outlet, and have eight 350-watt PARs to light your stage—perfectly adequate for a small platform with a podium and a chalkboard.
- If you need more than two circuits, but you don't need more than 15 amps at a time, the hotel can provide a group of circuits all in one place. In this scheme, the hotel electrician opens up a special circuit in the wall and plugs in a suitcase-sized **breakout box**. A breakout box is simply a box that plugs into a high amperage (usually 30- or 50-amp) outlet and has a whole mess of plugs on it. You can plug lots of different things into this box, including your slide projector and laptop charger, but make sure that you ask the electrician what the *total capacity* of the box is. It may have four outlets, for example, each of which can take fifteen amps individually, but the total capacity of the

box may be only 50 amps, instead of 60. Ask, and ye shall not blow the circuit breaker.

- If your lighting setup is too big for wall circuits, then you must ask the hotel to provide more power. A large lighting setup may require hundreds of amps, far more than a wall circuit can provide. In this case, the hotel can provide a **power drop**, which is a fancy name for hooking your dimmer pack directly into the hotel's power system, bypassing the regular plugs and circuit breakers. I am not going to bother you with a lot of detail here because this job must be handled by qualified personnel. What you should know is, if you need more power than normal wall circuits, you must ask the hotel management for it. Some hotels are easier to work with than others. Smaller, older hotels with antiquated power systems (not to mention antiquated staffs) will be more likely to give you a hassle. Large, modern hotels do this kind of thing all the time and shouldn't give you any trouble. In any case, you will want a trained crew person to be handling the setup because it involves sticking bare wires into a big metal box full of power. No place for an amateur.

Portable Dimmers and Control Consoles

Your rental company should provide you with a list of available dimmer packs and control consoles, depending on how many lighting instruments you are hanging. The rental house will probably have pre-assembled lighting packages with instruments and dimmers already picked out. Once you know what is available, call the hotel staff to see what kind of power they can give you. If your system can be plugged into wall circuits, you should be able to handle it yourself. If you need a power drop, then you will need to hire someone who can do it for you.

Don't know where to start? First of all, decide whether you are using trees or trusses. If trusses, then sit back and let the experts make the decisions. If trees, then determine what size show you have. Call the rental company and find out what your options are for dimmers and control consoles. Then call the hotel to make arrangements to get enough power.

House Lights

This is one area (the only one, really) where hotels have made it easy to do theater. Most conference and ballrooms have a variety of different house lights that can be mixed and matched for different looks. Turn the chandelier off and leave the wall washers at a glow for the slide show. Put the chandelier at half strength for the ballroom dancing. Point the track lights at the decorations and turn everything else off for a dramatic moment.

As soon as you get into the space, get someone from the hotel staff to show you all the different "looks" that the house lights can create. Sometimes the hotel management will insist on having their own person run it, but many places will show you how the lights are programmed and then let you handle it. In any case, try very hard to get them to leave that little door that hides the switches *unlocked*. Nothing is worse than waiting around to set up a slide projector while someone is paging a maintenance guy with a key.

Sound: Plug and Play, or Truck It In

Sound in hotels is almost always provided by the hotel itself, unless you have a band or a very large event. Many hotel ballrooms and conference rooms, particularly modern ones, are set up to "plug and play." In other words, you take a microphone, stick it in the wall, turn up a volume knob, and you are ready to go. No further setup is required because the amplifier is built into the walls and the speakers are already in the ceiling. Note that plug-and-play systems are rarely set up to accept cables from a CD player or a tape player so, if you want to play relaxing music before your presentation, you'd better bring your daughter's boom box (a thoroughly acceptable low-tech solution, in my book).

Here are the questions that the hotel audiovisual staff will want answered when you are requesting a sound system:

- *How many microphones do you need?* If you have a panel discussion, do you want a microphone for each person or will they be amenable to passing one microphone among them? Don't forget to have a microphone placed in the audience if you want audience members to ask questions.
- *What kind of stands do you want?* Here are the options: **podium stand** (also known as a **gooseneck**), for a speaker who is addressing the audience in a formal way; **straight stand**, for a speaker who is standing up, but does not require a podium; **boom stand**, for a speaker (or singer) who is playing a musical instrument or sitting in a wheelchair; **table stand**, for a person seated at a table, such as a panel discussion; or none, for speakers who are walking around with the microphone or have it mounted on their bodies, like a lavaliere microphone. Speaking of which . . .
- *Do you need a lavaliere microphone?* **Lavaliere**, or lav mikes, are small, pencil eraser–sized microphones that attach to a lapel or a collar and allow the speaker to operate "hands-free." Very useful when the speaker likes to use a pointer *and* carry notes. Some speakers like to carry

hand-held wireless mics so they look like rock stars. Speaking of rock stars, Tony Robbins prefers a headset mic, as do aerobics instructors.

- *Do you need wireless microphones?* Do you want your speakers to be able to walk around unencumbered by a cable dragging along behind them? It's generally more expensive, but it's often worth it, particularly for more animated speakers. Absolutely essential for speakers who want to walk around the audience, Donahue-style.
- *What else do you need?* Do you need to play tapes or CDs? How about videotapes? DVDs? Does your PowerPoint presentation have a sound-track? Make sure that the hotel staff knows about any other kind of sound that you might want to put through their system.

Scenery: Four Feet by Whatever

Scenery in the hotel ballroom is generally limited to what you bring in your-self, with two exceptions. Bare, no-nonsense platforming, and drapery to dress it up.

Platforms

Hotel platforms are usually folding platform sections in multiples of four feet. Common sizes include four by four, four by six, and four by eight. Basically, you can have any size and shape of stage that you want, as long as it can be built out of four-foot squares. The sections have little levers underneath them that allow them to lock together in various configurations. Because they don't require nailing or bolting, they are also quick and easy to change, even at the last minute. When you discover that the four-piece band you hired is actually a ten-piece ensemble, call in the hotel staff and have them throw on a few more platforms. Assuming that the *room* is big enough, of course.

As for heights, portable platforms usually come in a variety of heights at eight-inch increments (eight, sixteen, twenty-four, etc.), but many hotels have made a somewhat arbitrary decision to buy platforms of one specific height. Find out what is available, but be ready to compromise on this one. Some hotels have simply decided that twenty-four inches (or thirty-six, or thirty . . .) is the right height for everybody. Whatever height you order, make sure that you specify steps. I always order a set for every side, on principle.

Drapery

The drapes will come in two varieties: borders, and pipe-and-drape.

- *Borders.* Borders are all those pre-fab little curtains that hotels slap (gen-erally with Velcro) on all sides of the portable platforms to make them look like they really aren't so portable. I have seen some hotel impresarios hire scenery shops to make borders to match the rest of the show but, trust me, it usually isn't worth it. Only the first row can really see them, and if everyone is looking down there, your show has a problem and it isn't the scenery. Concentrate your time and money on making scenery for the stage itself. You are going to need it to hide the...

- *Pipe-and-drape.* Pipe-and-drape is the hotel world's answer to the question: "How can we hide these peach-colored walls for the least amount of money?" Pipe-and-drape is a very common system where drapes with pockets sewn into the top are slid over pipes that are then hung atop slender stands. The drapes are very lightweight, which means that they are easy to put up, but completely transparent to sound. Any sound that is made backstage will be heard out front. Since the drapes aren't very thick, they also will not hide all the light from backstage. Turn off all lights backstage or they will be seen through the drapes.

Projectors and Projection Systems

Convention technology has undergone a revolution in the last few years. Slides are gone. Computer and video projection are in. The standard slide show has been replaced by the PowerPoint presentation and the video. Fortunately, projector design has also moved forward at the speed of light. The five-year-old projector that was the size of a heifer has been replaced by one that will fit in your briefcase. The only downside to all of this is that you must know a little bit more about the technology in order to make it work.

The first thing to consider is what kind of media you are projecting:

- *Are you projecting a computer image?* If so, then you are projecting a computer video image, which is different from a standard video signal. Your projector must have a computer video input. You will also need to know what resolution image you are projecting. The rental house can help you to determine this, but you can help them out by looking in the "monitor" control panel on your computer and seeing what size image your monitor is set to. It will be somewhere between 680 × 480 and 1280 × 1024.
- *If you are projecting a video image, what kind of an image is it?* This breaks down to three common possibilities and one exotic one. Your regular old VCR or DVD player has a single video **port** coming out the back, usually colored yellow. This is called a **composite signal** because all the video information is squished together and shoved down the same cable. More sophisticated players will have an **S-video** port, which is

round and has four pins. In an S-video setup, the **chroma**, or color information, is separated from the **luminance**, or brightness information. This produces a higher-quality image. The next step up is **component video**, which requires three separate plugs, often colored red, blue, and green. Component video comes in two types—RGB and YUV—and the only thing you need to know is that they are, as you might expect, not compatible. Make sure that the DVD or tape deck is set to the same type of component video as the projector.

- *How big is the screen?* Projectors are rated in lumens, which is a measurement of brightness. Higher is better. A good rental house can help you figure it out, but they will want to know the size of the screen. A conference room will need nothing more than the briefcase-sized unit I mentioned above. When you start talking about ballrooms, however, you leap into an entirely different class of projector; one that is much bigger and muuuuuch more expensive. Try to use rear projection if you can. It looks a lot cleaner and your audience won't have to listen to the fan in the projector. You can only do it, though, if you have enough space behind the screen. The amount of space you need depends on the size of the screen and the size of the lens on the projector.
- *Can you turn the rest of the lights off?* The answer is *yes,* because that is the only way that you are going to get a good image on the screen unless you have a LED screen. If you have a speaker onstage, try to tie him down to the podium and put a little bit of light on him. Try not to give him a wireless mic in this situation. You'll never be able to keep him in the light.
- *What kind of screen do you need?* Get the biggest one you can for the room. Will you be using front or rear projection? Rear-projection screens can be used for front projection, but not vice versa. The sharpest rear-projection screens are the black ones, followed by gray, then white. The black screens, however, are less visible if you are not directly in front, so if your seating area is wider than it is deep, get a white or gray screen.

One of the emerging technologies in the projection world is the LED (light-emitting diode) screen. LED screens are covered with thousands of tiny LEDs that combine to create a coherent video image. They are far brighter than video projection, but with a lower resolution. They actually don't look that great up close, but step back a few feet and prepare to be impressed. When I say brighter, I'm not talking about a subtle difference. LED screens are putting out light, not reflecting it, so they actually glow. LED screens can be used *outside,* for Pete's sake, where any type of video projection will simply disappear. You can actually shine direct sun on an LED screen, which is why they are used for those huge screens at football stadiums. As you might expect, they are much more expensive, but, as I say, when you need the brightness, only LED will do.

Playing Twenty (or More) Questions: Things to Ask and to Know

In order to smoothly stage a hotel show, you will want to know the answers to a lot of questions. Hotel staffs seem to come in two varieties, very helpful and very not. I have a lot of compassion for them, however. A convention staff in a busy hotel helps stage dozens of shows every month. Every one of those shows are the "only show we do all year" to some group of people. To a convention staffer, though, your show is number twenty-four out of fifty-one shows that they are doing this month alone. My advice: Be prepared with a list of questions and get them all answered at your initial meeting with the hotel staff. This is when the staff will be at their most helpful and least stressed.

- *Is there an in-house convention services office?* Since you might be having your meeting *in* the convention services office, this may be an irrelevant question. Even at a small, out-of-the-way hotel, however, there is someone who can help you. These are the people who can answer your questions about almost anything, from lighting to platforming to dressing rooms.
- *Where is the loading dock? What is the access like to the room?* Everyone who is bringing in equipment will want to know how far the loading dock is from the space, the number of steps (hopefully none) that must be descended or climbed, the width of the doors into the space, and where the freight elevator is. Audiovisual companies or bands will often need bellman's carts to carry equipment.
- *Is there a floorplan available for the room?* Very useful for lighting and scenery companies, not to mention your own strategic planning.
- *Is there an in-house audiovisual company?* If there is, then these folks will probably handle most of your AV equipment needs. Even if you are bringing in equipment from the outside, you will want to make friends with the in-house guys. They may be your only hope when your last video projector bulb goes out.
- *Which lighting and sound company do they recommend?* This does not always give you the name of who you should use. Some hotels will advertise in-house lighting and sound companies and then simply run down to the local rental house and rent equipment for the show,

charging you an extra 50 percent for their trouble. Do some research: Find out who they recommend and then call the local rental shops and compare prices. For that matter, ask the rental houses if they have ever worked in this hotel before.

- *What kind of lighting is built into the room?* What do the house lights look like? Is there track lighting? Where are the controls? Do you need to have hotel staff to operate them?
- *What kind of power is available in the room?* As I said above in the lighting section, you may have several different options when it comes to power. Find out how many outlets are in the room and how many amps each of them can take. Some hotels have breakout boxes that can give you more outlets. If you are planning a larger lighting load-in, schedule a time when your lighting person can meet the hotel's electrician to complete the power drop (some people call it the "tie-in"). One final word about power: *Make sure you get the sound and lighting systems on different circuits.* Otherwise, the sound system will buzz when the lights turn on. If you have a video system, make sure that it gets its own power as well.
- *How high is the ceiling in the room?* This will affect the height of the scenery and the lighting trees.
- *What kind of platforming is available in the room?* How high? What sizes? Stairs? Borders? Handrails? What kind of surface is on the stage? Unless you have dancers, carpet is the way to go. If you do have dancers, they will need a slick surface, so you should arrange to have dance floor or a masonite surface put down.
- *Are there ladders available?* With modern insurance regulations, the hotel may be loath to lend out their equipment, but you can ask.
- *Do they have a map with directions already printed?* Very helpful for getting all the right people to all the right places.
- *Where are the bathrooms?* Do you need separate dressing rooms for entertainers?
- *Where is security?* Who are you going to call if there is an accident, an intruder, a theft, a lost child, a lost wallet?

Of course, the hotel management will have some questions of their own, so you will want to have answers ready to the following questions:

- *How many people are coming?* The single most critical number. It determines the size of the room, the staff required, the number of meals to be served, and more.
- *Do you need platforming?* Trust me, the answer is yes. Now, how much

platforming is another matter. I've given you a quick and easy guide for estimating below. Find the type of event you are staging, then decide if you are doing a tight show (you are on a budget and you need to squeeze), an average show (you want people to be comfortable, but you aren't here to show off), or a spacious show (you've got a generous budget, and it's the event of the year). All sizes are specified width by depth. Remember, these are only rough guesses, and you may need more or less space for any number of reasons. Just remember, platforming is cheap, and you can always take away what you don't need.

	TIGHT	AVERAGE	SPACIOUS
Speaker			
alone on stage	8 × 8	16 × 8	30 × 12
with six chairs	16 × 8	24 × 12	40 × 16
Bands			
grand piano	12 × 8	24 × 12	40 × 24
string quartet	8 × 8	12 × 12	30 × 16
five-piece dance band	24 × 12	36 × 20	44 × 40
twelve-piece band	30 × 20	40 × 20	48 × 24
"Big Band"	30 × 20	40 × 20	48 × 24
Awards Ceremony	12 × 12	20 × 12	44 × 16

- *What other kinds of space will you need at the hotel?* You may need additional space besides the main room. Here is a short list of possibilities to consider:
  - Office space
  - Storage space (essential if you have a band coming)
  - Backstage space (room to store scenery or props)
  - Dressing-room space
  - Green-room space (where performers await their entrances
  - Parking space
  - Space to feed cast and workers
  - Space to sell tickets or souvenirs

- *Do you need phones in the space?* In this era of cell phones, you may be reachable without a phone in your space, but remember, this is usually an easy one for the hotel, and you never know who's going to have a flat tire and need a last-minute lift. While we're on the subject, how about a fax? A photocopier? A computer with an Internet connection?
- *Do you need security?* Will you need to restrict access to backstage or to sensitive materials (such as unreleased products or trade secrets)? Is

there expensive equipment that will need to be stored in a safe place? Where can performers leave valuables during a performance? Do you need "backstage passes" to monitor access?

- *Are you providing food for cast and/or crew?* After years of working conventions, meetings, and parties as a crew member, musician, and speaker, I have one piece of advice for a successful event—feed your people. Hungry people are angry people. People who have to run across the street to a fast food restaurant for dinner between the load-in and the show are stressed people. People who sit down and have dinner together are friends. Feeding your crew and your performers is one of the best investments you can make in your event. And the better you feed them, the better your investment. It is demoralizing as a performer to watch your audience eating prime rib while you are choking down a dry ham sandwich. At least get the good mustard.

CHAPTER 14

The Essentials: Things You Should Know and Things You Should Own

Every theater in the world is different, but some things never change. Here is a short list of essentials that every person backstage should know or own.

Things Every Theater Person Should Know

- *Stage directions:* On stage, directions are always from the actor's perspective, not the audience's. That is, if you, the actor, are facing the audience, **stage left** is to your left and **stage right** is to your right. If you really want to talk about things from the audience's perspective (when you are talking about seating arrangements, for example), you say **house left** and **house right**. As far as the other dimension goes, **upstage** is away from the audience, **downstage** is toward the audience. (In the early days of Elizabethan theater, the audience sat on a flat surface and the stage was pitched to allow the actors to be seen. Hence, when you moved away from the audience, you really were moving "up." Nowadays, the audience is generally on a sloping surface and the stage is flat, but the term persists.)
- *"HEADS!":* No doubt about it, backstage can be a dangerous place. This is particularly true when one person is working over another person's head. Fingers get sweaty, people get careless, things get dropped. If you do drop something, don't swear, don't berate yourself for being a clumsy oaf, don't do anything except yell "HEADS!" Heads is the all-purpose, look-out-or-you'll-get-socked-in-the-head shout and if you are going to be hanging out backstage, you should begin to train yourself

to yell it whenever you see danger coming from above. Any other word might not do the trick. Of course, if you hear someone above you yell "HEADS," get away quickly. Do not look up. Do not ask questions. Run. If you are onstage, and the call comes from above, head for the wings. You are almost always safest against a wall. Besides using "HEADS" in emergencies, technicians will sometimes use it in calmer situations to alert people on stage that something is about to be lowered. In this case, they will follow it with the name of what is coming down, as in "Heads up! Ballroom drop coming in!" Pay attention to these calls. They are made for your safety.

- *Where the callboard is:* In theater, communication is everything. The primary way that technical people tell nontechnical people things (and vice versa) is by posting them on the callboard. Find it. Read it.

- *How big ten feet is:* I have been involved with a lot of conversations about how big something should be, and most people have trouble visualizing a dimension. Once, when doing a show with an extremely polite director of Kabuki theater, we translated his beautiful watercolor renderings into shop drawings by asking him repeatedly, "How tall is this one? How about this one?" and studiously writing down the heights he called out. Once the entire set was built, he came to the shop to see it all set up. He smiled graciously, looking carefully at each piece we had built. "Very nice." he said, smiling politely, "It's very nice, but it should be *much* bigger . . ." He gestured up toward the shop ceiling, three times as high as the scenery. After he left, we built him a new set that reached the roof. We grumbled, of course, but we did get a good catchphrase: "Very nice, but *much* bigger . . . " Ten feet is a good baseline dimension to begin visualizing size. If you have a feel for ten feet, then you can judge larger distances by multiplying it and smaller distances by dividing it. Find something in your life that is ten feet long, like your dining room, a hallway, your car, anything you are familiar with. Then, when someone says, "Hey, will five feet be enough?" you can think, okay, that's half the length of my dining room, and you will have a handle on it. It's also useful to find a couple of measurements on your own body. I know, for instance, that if I stand and reach up, it is exactly eight feet to the last knuckle on my middle finger. It may sound trivial, but you have no idea how many times that distance has come in handy when I needed a rough measurement and I didn't have a tape measure. Another good one is a dollar bill, which is just a shade over six inches long.

- *The difference between an ellipsoidal and a fresnel:* These two lighting instruments are the basis of almost every light plot in the theater, and you should be able to tell them apart. The ellipsoidal (often called a "Leko" after one popular brand) is the one that puts out a sharp-edged light that can be shuttered and shaped. The fresnel puts out a soft-edged light that cannot be shuttered, but blends more easily. The fresnel can be spotted by the circular ridges on the lens. Ellipsoidals have smooth lenses.

- *The difference between a flat and a platform:* Flats are walls, platforms are floors. Mixing up these two is the quickest way to show your amateur stripes.

Things Every Show Person Should Own

- *This book:* Hey, if I don't think you need it, why should you?
- *A Mini-Maglite:* The toughest, brightest, small flashlight made. Forget about all the little colored lenses—they're a pain to put in and you'll lose them anyway.
- *A Swiss Army knife:* A regular folding knife is OK, but you'd be surprised what you can do with that screw driver. The corkscrew comes in handy at a cast party, too.
- *A tape measure:* At least sixteen feet long, longer if you don't mind carrying the weight around.
- *An eight-inch Crescent adjustable wrench:* The one essential tool for doing lighting.
- *A clipboard with a pen attached:* Put your name on it, or kiss it good-bye.
- *A set of black clothes, including black tennis shoes:* Essential for fading into the background backstage.

Things Every Show Place Should Own

- *A roll of black, two-inch-wide gaffer's tape:* A cloth-based tape that has held more sets together than I can count. Don't let them sell you "duct tape." It has a gooey adhesive that stays behind when you take the tape off. Black masking tape is also insufficient—it's just not strong enough. Go to your theatrical supplier and pay the extra couple of bucks for the good stuff.
- *A Mikita cordless Driver-Drill:* There is a time for brand loyalty and this is it. The Mikita is the ultimate stage tool—strong, light, and adaptable. The Jeep of the modern theater.
- *Phillips-head drywall screws:* Drywall screws go in and out of wood quickly, and they are quite strong. Keep several sizes around, like 1¼ inches, 1⅝ inches, and 2 inches for use with the Mikita cordless.

- *A fifty-foot tape measure:* Or longer. You should be able to measure all the way across your stage diagonally.
- *A roll of one-inch-wide white gaffer's tape:* The best way to make things visible in the backstage area. Phosphorescent or "glow" tape will work on the stage itself, but behind the scenes it will not get enough light on it to "charge up." Use white tape backstage to mark pathways, obstacles, and stairs.
- *Aluminum utility lights covered with blue color filters:* For "running lights." Sprinkle them around the stage to light prop tables, walkways, and exits. Make sure you take a look from the audience during a blackout to see if the light is spilling on stage.
- *A callboard:* A bulletin board where the performers and technicians can look to see schedules, announcements, phone numbers, and maps to the opening night party. Everyone should get trained to look here for info.
- *Tie line:* A black, cotton/polyester line about the thickness of a shoelace, but stronger. Use it to tie up cables, draperies, rope, and everything else.
- *A hot-glue gun:* The props coordinator at Seattle Rep once told me, "If I can't fix it with hot glue, tie line, and gaffer's tape, it wasn't built right to begin with."

In Closing

There are a lot of folks who keep repeating this phrase: "There are no stupid questions."

This is wrong.

I know, because I have asked most of those questions. A stupid question is any question that you wouldn't need to ask if you knew something that someone in your position should know.

Ignorance is like your appendix, though: You only have to get rid of it once. Sometimes the process of learning is about asking stupid, uninformed questions. Sometimes it's about asking intelligent, informed, sophisticated questions that open up new and exciting realms of discussion, but I think it's safe to say that you will need to do the first part before you get around to the second.

Sure, the technicians that you ask are going to look at you funny, laugh into their shirts, and roll their eyes. It would be nice if they didn't, but technicians are people, and it is a fact that people with a particular kind of expertise have a tendency to look down on those who don't have it. However, with luck and tenacity, you will find many enlightened, compassionate technicians who are not afraid to be good teachers for you. Trust me, there are more of them than you think, particularly if they know you are trying to make their lives easier by becoming better informed.

So go ahead and ask your questions, no matter how stupid. Sure, the person you're talking to might think less of you, but the *next* one won't. Nor will the one after that, or after that. Once you know something, it's yours.

And every bit of knowledge will rest on the one before, building higher and higher, until you have a pile of knowledge that will let you reach that last brilliant chocolate chip cookie on the top shelf of wisdom.

Thanks for reading my book. Let me know how you do.

Glossary

a vista: in view of the audience, as in an *a vista* scene change.

ACL (aircraft landing light): a very narrow-beamed instrument, used on airplanes and rock-and-roll lighting plots.

acoustical shell: a large, half-dome-shaped shell used behind choruses and musicians to amplify the sound.

acting area: a small area of the stage that has its own set of lights. Lighting designers often divide the stage into acting areas in order to create balanced lighting.

actor trap: a slang term assigned to any technical situation that will trip up an inattentive actor, e.g., an uneven step on a staircase.

AIFF: a computer file format for audio, commonly used with Apple computers. Stands for Apple Interchange File Format.

aircraft cable: thin, steel cable used to hang scenery.

amperage: a measure of power flowing through cables, plugs, and circuit breakers.

amplifier: a electronic device that makes an audio signal strong enough to create sound.

analine dye: a type of color used on drops that need to be translucent.

analog: any electronic device that uses constantly changing electrical current to represent constantly changing sound; the opposite of digital.

arbor: in a flying system, the cage where the operators put the counterweight to balance the weight of the scenery.

ASM: *see* **assistant stage manager.**

assistant stage manager (ASM): the all-purpose technical assistant; the backstage entry-level position.

audience blinders: a bank of small PAR cans all mounted in the same fixture. Used to create a bright wash of light on the audience.

auxiliary returns (return): an input on a mixer that accepts a signal from an effects processor; part of an "effects loop."

auxiliary sends (send): an output from a mixer used to feed an audio signal to a processor or a monitor.

back light: light coming from upstage of an actor.

balanced (and **unbalanced**) **lines:** two different varieties of cable. Balanced lines require three wires and resist noise. Unbalanced lines require two wires and collect noise.

balcony rail: a lighting position on the front edge of the balcony; originally installed in most Broadway theaters.

ballast: an electronic device used by fluorescent and HMI lights. Necessary to start up these kinds of lights.

barn doors: a color frame with two or four flaps that cut off excess light.

base station: the main station in a headset system; the part that provides the power and connective ability for all the other headsets.

battens: metal pipes that hang over a stage; used for flying scenery and lighting instruments.

beadboard: a flexible, lightweight, synthetic material, commercially marketed as Styrofoam™, among other brands. Sold in sheets.

beam: a horizontal lighting position over the audience.

belt pack: part of a headset system that connects the headset to the rest of the system.

blackout: what happens when you turn all the stage lights off.

blackout drop: a black drop that lives behind a scrim drop, making it fully opaque.

blackout switch: a switch on a lighting control console that turns off all the lights. A very bad idea.

blocking: the movement of the actors onstage.

blueboard: a synthetic material, similar to beadboard but more dense. Sold in sheets.

body mic: a small, almost invisible microphone that mounts on an actor's head or body.

boom: a vertical lighting position, either backstage or in the auditorium.

boom stand: a microphone stand with a horizontal attachment that can reach over a keyboard or other musical instrument.

border: a horizontal drape that runs across the top of the stage, hiding the lighting instruments.

border light: *see* **strip light**.

bounce: stray light beams that bounce off shiny surfaces and go where they don't belong.

box booms: a lighting position in the auditorium, commonly on either side of the proscenium arch.

box sets: an interior set with three complete walls; the fourth wall is open to the audience.

breakaway: any scenery or prop that is designed to break on cue.

breakaway glass: a fake glass made of a material that can be safely broken without producing dangerously sharp pieces.

breakout box: a group of electrical plugs installed in a single box; used by hotels to provide extra outlets.

bricks: *see* **counterweights.**

bump buttons: buttons on a lighting control console that "bump" the lights up to full when pressed.

bump cue: a lighting cue (usually at the end of a musical number) that quickly pushes the level of light to a brighter level.

business: a series of actions that one or more actors do onstage. Something that takes time and pulls focus.

cable: any long, rubbery cord with plugs on each end that carries electricity. The larger ones carry power to lighting instruments; the smaller ones carry data or audio signals.

callboard: the backstage bulletin board where announcements, schedules, and other information is posted.

calling a show: the process of calling out the lighting, sound, and scene-change cues during a performance; usually done by the stage manager over a headset.

calls: the announcements made backstage (usually by the stage manager) telling cast and crew how many minutes remain before curtain time. Also means the specific time that the cast and crew must arrive at the theater.

carbon-arc spot: an older type of follow spot used in large venues that makes light by "arcing" electricity between two carbon electrodes.

casein paint: an organic type of paint, made from a soy protein binder, that creates vibrant color and remains flexible.

castors: the wheels on a platform.

C-clamp: the metal clamp that holds a lighting instrument to the bar it's hanging on. So named because of its C-like shape.

center line: an imaginary line down the center of the stage, from upstage to downstage.

chain pocket: a fabric pouch running the length of a drape along the bottom. It is designed to hold a chain that weighs down the bottom of the drape.

changing booth: a small, temporary booth in the wings where an actor can make a costume change without going to the dressing room.

channel (audio): an input on a mixer.

channel (lighting): in computer lighting control consoles, a way of controlling a group of dimmers.

charge artist: a scenic painter.

chase effects: special effects, produced by a lighting control console, that cause a series of lights to turn on and off in sequence. Used for marquee lights and fire effects, among other things.

chasing: the process by which one device monitors the time code coming out of another device.

chroma: the color information that is carried in a video signal.

circuit breaker panel: a box containing all the circuit breakers for a building or room.

circuit breakers: electronic devices designed to shut off power if it goes above a certain level. Used to protect electrical systems and prevent fires.

circuit plot: a list of all available circuits in a particular theater.

closing: the last night of a show.

coffin locks: metal brackets embedded in platforms that help lock separate platforms together. So named because they were developed to hold down coffin lids.

color filter: a piece of colored plastic used to change the color of light.

color frame: the metal frame that holds a color filter.

color scrollers: color frames that hold a roll of color. Used to change color filters in the middle of a performance.

color temperature: a scale used to describe what color a video camera will recognize as white.

company manager: the person who arranges food, lodging, and other details for the cast and crew.

component video: a video signal where each color is carried on a separate cable.

composite signal: a video signal where all three colors—red, blue, and green—plus both the chroma and the luminance, are carried on one cable.

compressor (audio): the electronic device that reduces loud signal levels, making the overall sound level more consistent.

concept meeting: one of the first meetings of the production period, where general concepts are hammered out.

condenser mics: microphones that pick up sound using a small electrical field. Disturbances in the field are detected by the circuitry and converted to an audio signal.

contact closure: The situation that occurs when two electrically-charged wires come together and compete a circuit. Also, a device that creates this situation, such as a button.

contact sheet: the list of addresses and phone numbers used to keep track of everybody's whereabouts during the production period.

control console (dimmerboard): the panel that controls the lighting instruments.

cool fogger: a fog machine that uses dry ice or frozen carbon dioxode to chill theatrical fog, making it lay close to the ground.

costume designer: the person who researches the costumes, decides which styles and fabrics to use, and then draws or paints the costumes in renderings.

costume fitting: the meeting where costume personnel measure actors and test-fit their costumes.

costume shop manager: the person who decides how to construct the costumes and gives individual workers their assignments.

costume parade: an event held in the theater where each actor walks onstage wearing his or her costumes, one at a time. Designed to show the costumes to the director under the stage lights.

counterweight flying system: a system of moving scenery up into the air using cables and counterweights.

counterweight trap: A trap door in a stage that, with the use of a counterweight, drops straight down, allowing an actor to ride it up and down.

counterweights (bricks): the slabs of iron that are loaded into a counterweight system to offset the weight of the scenery.

cove: a lighting position out in the auditorium where lighting instruments are concealed from view.

craftspeople: people working in properties shops who are proficient in carving, working with fabrics, and/or any number of other construction skills.

crossfader: the lever on a lighting control console that simultaneously fades all the channels from one cue to the next.

crossing (a **cross**): moving from one part of the stage to another, as an actor.

crossover: a passageway that leads from one side of the stage to the other, out of view of the audience.

crotch light: a position on a lighting tree, usually two to three feet off the floor. Generally used in dance.

cue (cueing): something that happens at a particular point in the show, such as a change of lighting, scenery, or other technical event. Also used to describe the verbal command to do that thing.

cutters: costume shop workers who cut the fabric for the costumes, using patterns and/or intuition.

cyclorama (cyc): a large backdrop meant to resemble the sky.

DAT: *see* **digital audiotape.**

dead-hung: scenery or lighting that is hanging in the air and not designed to be moved during the performance, as opposed to "flying" scenery or lighting that is designed to be moved up and down.

dead man's switch: *see* **enable button.**

deck: the stage floor, or a temporary floor that has been built on top of the permanent floor.

design conference: a meeting that happens early in the production process where designers present their work to the production staff.

designer fabrics (e.g., Rosco): specialty fabrics for the stage, such as slit drape, shimmer cloth, and so on.

deus ex machina: originally, a theatrical device in ancient Greek theater where a god would appear above the scenery at the end of the play and resolve all the conflicts. Now, any event happening late in the show that, somewhat miraculously, resolves everybody's problems.

diaphragm: the tiny membrane in a microphone that vibrates when sound hits it, allowing the microphone to "hear."

dichroic filter: a style of glass filter that reflects unwanted frequencies, instead of absorbing them.

diffusion filter: a specialized form of filter that spreads out the light coming from a lighting instrument. Used to get rid of hard shadows.

digital: any electronic device that represents sound as a string of numbers; the opposite of analog.

digital audiotape (DAT): a high-fidelity tape format for recording any kind of sound.

dimmer: an electronic device that reduces the amount of power that a lighting instrument receives, thereby reducing the light that it is putting out.

dimmer per circuit: a wiring scheme where every circuit in the theater has its own dimmer, thereby eliminating the patch panel.

dimmerboard operator: the person who operates the lighting control console during rehearsals and performances.

director: the person who makes the final judgments on all artistic decisions in the production, subject to the financial approval of the producer.

distressing: The process of making a costume, prop, or piece of scenery look old and weathered using paint, dye, dust, or brute force.

DMX universe: information that is intended for a single group of 512 DMX channels, carried on one cable.

DMX-512: a computerized language that is used for lighting control consoles to "talk" to dimmers, intelligent lights, and other lighting equipment. Usually referred to simply as *DMX*.

douser: the control on a follow spot that fades out the light by slowly closing a set of doors.

down light: *see* **God light.**

downstage: the part of the stage farthest from the audience.

draper: a costume shop worker who makes clothes by draping them over a dress form or tailor's dummy.

dresser: the person who assists actors with their costumes before, during, and after a performance.

dressing room: a space for performers to hang costumes, put on makeup, and otherwise prepare for the show.

drop: a flat piece of fabric, generally painted, that forms part of the scenery.

dry ice: extremely cold ice, formed by freezing carbon dioxide. Used in fog machines. Can burn you if it touches your skin.

dynamic mics: microphones that pick up sound with a tiny, movable strip of metal. The vibrations of the strip are converted to an electrical signal with a tiny magnet.

Edison plugs: the standard household plug in the U.S. Two parallel metal tabs.

effects loop: a loop formed by taking a cable out of a mixer, through an effects processor, then back to the mixer. Used to add effects to sound.

effects processor: an electronic device that adds effects, such as reverb and distortion, to audio signals.

electric: a batten specifically used for lighting instruments.

electrician: the crew member who hangs, adjusts, and operates lighting instruments.

electrics crew: the crew members who hang, adjust, and operate lighting instruments.

ellipsoidal: a type of lighting instrument that produces a sharp-edged beam using an ellipsoidal reflector and one or more lenses.

enable button: a button that must be pushed for an effect to take place. This is a common way of protecting actors and crew. Also known as a "dead man's switch."

equalization (EQ): "coloring" a sound by increasing or reducing specific frequencies.

erosion cloth: a very loosely woven cloth used to cover freshly seeded ground. Used in the theater for texture and backgrounds.

escape stair: any staircase out of the audience's view that is used to help actors get off the set.

E-stop: short for "Emergency Stop." This is the big red button that tells a machine to stop whatever it is doing right now.

extreme sightline: the seat in the auditorium that, by the nature of its location, has the best view of backstage. Used to determine masking requirements.

false perspective: a scenic effect that, by exaggerating the effects of perspective, makes a set look bigger than it really is.

false proscenium: a portal that sits in front of or inside the real proscenium, giving the set its own "picture frame."

fast change: a costume change that must be done very quickly, and is therefore done in the wings instead of in the dressing room.

feedback: an annoying noise caused by a sound leaving a speaker and immediately re-entering the sound system through the microphone. This round-trip is repeated at the speed of light and the resulting blare can be painful and dangerous to equipment.

fidelity: the "trueness" of a sound; how closely it resembles the original source.

film loops: strips of metal with shapes cut out of them. Inserted in the gobo slot of a lighting instrument to make a moving pattern.

fire curtain: the heavy, fire-resistant curtain that seals off the stage from the audience in the event of a fire.

first electric: the most downstage electric; generally contains the greatest number of lighting instruments of any electric.

first hand: the second-in-command in the costume shop, assistant to the costume shop manager.

flats: vertical walls of scenery.

flicker generator: an electronic device that causes several lights to flicker, simulating a fire.

flooding (a fresnel): the process of moving a fresnel lamp back in the instrument, thereby making the beam of lighting wider. The opposite of "spotting."

floorplan: the diagram showing the placement of the scenery as viewed from above.

flying: being raised up in the air. To "fly" a piece of scenery is to raise it up using ropes or cables. People may also be flown, but only by trained professionals using special equipment.

flyman: the person who operates the flying system.

focal length: in an ellipsoidal, the distance from the lamp to the point where all the light beams converge. The longer the focal length, the narrower the beam of light that the instrument produces.

focusing: the process of pointing the lighting instruments where the director wants them.

fog machine: a simple machine that produces a ground-hugging fog by melting dry ice.

follow spot: any spotlight that can be moved to follow the movements of an actor.

follow spot operator: the person who operates a movable spotlight during a performance.

footing: bracing a flat with your foot while it is being raised from a horizontal position to a vertical one.

front-of-house (FOH): anything in the audience. Commonly used to describe staff (such as ushers) and lighting positions.

front-of-house spots: spotlights that are placed in or above the audience in a theater or arena.

front light: any light that is coming from downstage of an actor.

front-projection screens: screens that are designed to be projected on from the front, i.e., with the projector behind the audience.

fullness: the number and depth of the folds in a drape. The greater the fullness, the more folds in the drape.

fuse box: a metal panel that contains the fuses.

fuses: small devices that "blow" when the power rises to dangerous levels, shutting off the flow of electricity and preventing fires.

gate (audio): an electronic device that shuts off an audio signal once the level of the signal has dropped to a certain point.

gate (video): the opening in a spotlight where the light passes from the reflector area to the lens assembly. This is where you insert templates or an iris.

gel: an antique name for lighting color filters, left over from the days when filters were made from animal gelatin.

gel frame: the metal frame that holds the color filter.

glare: the reflection of light from the floor of the stage; caused by lighting instruments pointed downstage over a floor that has been painted a shiny color.

go: the magic word. The universal way to tell someone to do their thing.

gobo: *see* **template.**

gobo rotator: a device that holds a gobo and rotates it. Placed in the gobo slot of a lighting instrument.

God light: A down light that illuminates the orchestra conductor so the singers can see him from the stage.

gooseneck (audio): a microphone holder that can be twisted and bent; designed to fit on a podium.

grand drape: the main curtain; a.k.a., the main rag.

green room: a common area where performers wait until it is time to go onstage.

grid: the network of steel beams or pipes over the stage that holds up the rigging.

gripping: moving scenery by picking it up manually.

grommets: small metal rings driven into a drop; designed to hold tie lines.

ground row: a low, horizontal piece of scenery designed to hide lighting instruments on the floor.

half-hour: thirty minutes before the beginning of the performance, when all actors and crew must be in the theater.

hand-held mic: as opposed to a mic on a stand or attached to a performer's body.

hard-wired electric: a hanging pipe that is permanently wired with circuits for lighting instruments.

hazer: a device that creates a thin mist of fog throughout the stage.

heads, or tops: the lighting instruments at head height or above on a lighting tree. Generally used in dance.

headset mic: a microphone designed to be worn on the head, like a telephone headset.

headsets (headset system): phone-like systems used to keep in touch during a performance.

hemp flying system: a system to fly scenery using hemp ropes and sandbags.

HMI (hydragyrum medium arc-length iodide): type of follow spot that uses a special lamp to create very bright light.

hookup chart: a list showing which circuit and channel is being used for which lighting instruments.

hot spot: the center of a beam of light; the brightest part of the beam.

house left: the left side of the auditorium, from the audience's point of view.

house right: the right side of the auditorium, from the audience's point of view.

image mag: the process of pointing a video camera at a speaker so that his/her image can be projected on a larger screen on the same stage.

impedance: the amount of resistance that an electronic device gives an incoming signal. Two varieties: high and low.

industrial felt: a specialty fabric used to make hats, props, and, sometimes, scenery. Looks like felt, but much heavier.

in-ones: the first set of legs behind the proscenium arch. Also used to describe scenes that are played in front of a drop placed just behind the first set of legs.

input module: the part of a mixer that accepts a single input and then adjusts and redirects the signal from that input.

input trim: a control that sets the level of a signal coming into a mixer. Turn down for a line-level signal, up for a microphone.

intelligent lighting: lighting instruments that, under the direction of a control console, can pan, tilt, change color, change size and perform other automated functions.

intelligent lighting instrument: a computer-controller lighting instrument that can pan and tilt, change colors, zoom and do other tricks in real time.

iris: the control on a follow spot that makes the circle of light bigger or smaller.

irising in/irising out: on a follow spot, making the circle of light smaller (in) or larger (out).

jackknife platform: a platform that pivots on one corner.

juliets: *see* **box booms.**

knife: a slender piece of metal attached to a platform and sticking down into a groove in the floor. Helps to keep the platform moving straight.

lamp: the thing inside a lighting instrument that makes the light. Often erroneously called a bulb.

lasers: very narrow beams of light produced by specially designed lighting instruments. Can be harmful to your eyes if you look straight into them.

lavaliere (lav) mics: pencil eraser–sized microphones that are mounted on a collar or lapel.

legs: drapes that hang to the side of the stage, hiding the backstage area.

Leko: a particular brand of ellipsoidal spotlight. This term is often (and erroneously) used to describe any brand of ellipsoidal spot.

life safety: any effect which could, if mishandled, endanger the life and limb of performers, audience, or crew.

light trees: freestanding metal poles with wide bases. Designed to hold lighting instruments.

lighting cues: the instructions that tell the lighting operators what to do and when to do it.

lighting designer: in the theater, the person who decides where the lighting instruments should go, how they should be colored, and which ones should be on at any particular time.

lighting director: on a television set, the person who decides where the lighting instruments should go, how they should be colored, and which ones should be on at any particular time.

lighting inventory: the list of lighting instruments in a theater, showing their size and type.

lighting positions: the various places in a theater where lighting instruments are hung.

lighting tree: a pole-and-crossbar stand used to temporarily support stage lighting equipment.

lightning box: a special effects device that produces bright, lightning-like flashes of light.

limiter: an electronic device that prevents an audio signal from rising above a certain point.

limit switch: a switch that is thrown automatically when a moving piece of scenery reaches its final position. When this switch is thrown, the platform stops moving.

line level: a particular strength of audio signal in electronic devices, such as tape decks and mixers.

line set: a set of cables that hold one batten in a system for lifting scenery and lighting.

liquid nitrogen: an extremely cold liquid that vaporizes when it comes into contact with warm air, producing a thick billowing fog. Should only be used by professionals. Also known as LN2.

load: something that uses power, like a lighting instrument or an appliance.

loading dock: a place where you can unload scenery, costumes, and other items that you are bringing to the theater.

loading rail: where you go to put weight on the arbor in a flying system.

lock rail: the place where you stand to operate a counterweight flying system. So named because it has a set of locks that prevent the scenery from moving. The locks are mounted on a metal railing.

luminance: the part of a video signal that determines how bright the image is.

masking: the draperies or flats that hide backstage from the audience's view.

master carpenter: the person in charge of all the carpenters.

master electrician: the person in charge of all the electricians.

master fader: on a lighting control console, the slider that causes all the lights to fade out.

mic level: a very soft level of audio signal. Generated by a microphone.

MIDI: a computer language that allows computers to "talk" to and control electronic musical devices. Stands for Musical Instrument Digital Interface.

MIDI show control (MSC): a computer language designed to provide show control functions for all types of backstage equipment, including lighting consoles, audio systems, scenery controllers, and pyrotechnic controllers.

MIDI time code: a type of "clock" used by show control systems to synchronize events backstage. First developed for audio systems.

mid-range: in a sound-system speaker, the part that puts out sound in the middle frequencies.

mids: on a dance lighting tree, the lighting instruments between the crotch lights and the highs. Usually five to eight feet from the floor.

MiniDisc™: a Sony product that allows you to record on a special kind of compact disc.

mixer: an audio device that takes in multiple audio signals, adjusts them, and sends them out to amplifiers and other devices.

monitor mixer: the person who controls which sounds are heard in the monitor speakers (the speakers that the performers listen to) onstage.

monitor speakers: speakers that are designed to help performers hear themselves.

monitor system: a system that allows people backstage (or onstage) to hear what is happening on the stage.

monitors (in the world of sound): wedge-shaped speakers that sit on the edge of the stage and allow singers to hear their own voices. In the world of computers or video: a screen resembling a television screen that shows information (computers) or pictures (video) to an operator.

mono: sound that only requires a single speaker to be played back correctly. As opposed to stereo.

motivational light: where the light in a scene is "supposed" to be coming from, i.e., the sun, an overhead light, etc.

motivational side: the side of the stage where the motivational light is coming from.

moving mirror: a type of intelligent lighting instrument where the body remains stationary while a small mirror directs the light around the stage. Also called moving beam.

moving yoke: a type of intelligent lighting instrument where the light is directed by moving the entire body of the instrument (also called moving head).

MP3: a computer file format used to compress music and audio into smaller file sizes.

multi-set show: a show that requires several distinct sets, such as a large Broadway musical.

muslin: a reasonably priced, commonly used fabric for drops and flats.

mute: a switch that turns off one channel on a mixer.

nap: the "fluffy" part of the fabric.

ohms: in the audio world, a measure of resistance. Used to match speakers to amplifiers.

on (or **off**) **book:** unable (or able) to perform a scene without looking at a script. The stage manager following along in the script during rehearsal is also said to be "on book."

output channels: the places where an audio signal comes out of a mixer.

paint shop: where scenery is painted and otherwise decorated.

pan: move side to side, as a lighting instrument or a camera or sound system.

PAR can: a very simple lighting instrument, basically an automobile headlight in a metal housing. Used for rock-and-roll and display.

patch panel: where electrical circuits are assigned to dimmers.

pattern: *see* **template.**

patterning: the process of building a costume through the use of patterns, either pre-existing or created for this costume.

PC-based playback system: a system that plays back audio from a personal computer.

period: a particular historical time when a play takes place.

personal props: props that are carried during a performance, such as guns, cigarettes, and letters.

perspective: the artist's trick that makes a two dimensional space look three-dimensional. The old "train tracks converging in the distance" thing.

phantom power: power that comes to a microphone over an audio wire from the mixer. Necessary for compressor mics.

phone (quarter-inch) **plug:** a long, slender plug used for headphones and many other audio devices.

pickup lines: the cables that attach to a batten and raise it up (fly it out).

pin rail: in a hemp flying system, the place where the ropes are tied off. Occasionally used as a misnomer for the lock rail.

pipe-and-drape: a system of curtains often used in hotels for temporary stage setups.

pipe-ends: lighting instruments hanging at the ends of electrics. Usually focused across the stage and used for side light.

platform: any horizontal playing surface, or a piece thereof.

playing space: the amount of room available onstage for the performance. Does not include wing space, storage, or any part of the stage that is not visible to the audience.

PLC: a programmable logic controller. This is a dedicated computer that does nothing but control moving scenery or pyrotechnics.

podium stand: *see* **gooseneck.**

port: the opening on a speaker that lets air in and out.

port (video): a plug on a video device where you can insert a cable and get a video signal.

portal: the archway formed by two legs and a border.

power conditioners: electronic devices that regulate power, removing fluctuations in voltage.

power drop: in a nontheatrical space, the device that allows you to tap into the power system and use higher amperages than single outlets would allow. Also known as "tie-in."

practical: able to be operated, like a window or a faucet; also used to describe a "real" lamp or other lighting fixture on a set.

pre-amp: the part of a mixer that amplifies mic-level signals to line level.

preproduction: the time period before actors have begun rehearsal and before the shops have begun to build the show.

preset: on a manual lighting control console, a row of sliders that controls all of the dimmers. Also used to describe the position of a prop at the beginning of a performance.

production: the period during which the actors are rehearsing and the shops are building the show.

production manager: the person in charge of the technical side of the production. Generally, the technical director and the stage manager report to this person (a.k.a. production stage manager or **PSM**).

production meeting: a meeting of production staff to discuss items of mutual interest.

production stage manager: *see* **production manager.**

Programmable Logic Controller: *see* **PLC.**

projection screens: specially designed sheets of plastic fabric used to project slides, video, or film.

prompt book (prompt script): the "Bible" compiled by the stage manager, containing all the pertinent information about the show.

prop carpenters: the shop carpenters who build furniture and other props.

prop coordinator : *see* **propmaster.**

prop designer: the person who selects, designs, and finds the props.

prop list: the master list of all items that could be considered props.

propmaster (prop coordinator): the person in charge of collecting and distributing properties.

props: any items that could be carried by an actor in the course of a show.

props crew: the people backstage who get the props in the right hands at the right times during the performance.

prop table: the table backstage where handheld props are put when they are not being used onstage.

proscenium (pron: pro-SCENE-ee-um) **arch:** the architectural wall that separates the backstage area from the audience.

PSM: *see* **production manager.**

purchase line: in a flying system, the rope that the operator uses to move the scenery or lighting unit up and down during the performance.

PZM microphone: a microphone that sits on the floor and uses the reflected sounds off the floor to pick up better sound.

rails: the top and bottom boards in a flat.

raked stage (rake): a stage that is slanted, either to increase visibility or to produce false perspective.

rear-projection screens: the process of projecting on a screen from the upstage side. Requires a specially designed screen.

reel-to-reel tape deck: a style of tape machine where the tape is passed from one open reel to another across a playback head.

rehearsal clothes: garments that the costume shop provides so that actors can acclimate themselves to unfamiliar types of clothes.

rendering: a drawing or painting that shows what the set or costumes will look like.

resistance: the amount of force that must be overcome to move a speaker and make sound. Measured in ohms.

resistance dimmer: an older style of dimmer that depended on "wasting" energy to dim a lighting instrument.

resolution: in a digital sound or video system, the amount of detail that the file contains.

restore: bringing the lights up or down to where they were before some event (like a musical number) occurred.

reverb: the "echo" effect produced by a large room with hard surfaces; often produced artificially by an effects processor.

reverberation time: the amount of time it takes for a sound to die out in a particular space.

revolve: a stage, or a portion of one, that rotates.

rolling: using wheels to move scenery.

rim light: light that comes from the back or side of a performer. Used to define the edge of the performer and make him distinct from the background.

rise and run: the ratio of stair height (the rise) to stair width (the run).

run: the depth of a stair step, usually used in conjunction with the "rise," the height of the stair. Also the number of performances for a particular show.

sampler: a device that electronically records a sound by changing that sound into millions of numbers.

sampling: the process of recording a sound by turning the analog sound wave into a string of numbers. Sampling happens in samplers and CDs.

sample rate: the rate at which a sampler makes samples of incoming sound. For example, 44.1 khz means that the sampler makes 44,100 samples per second.

saturated paint: a type of paint that is saturated with pigment. Because of this saturation, this paint can be heavily diluted.

saturation: the amount of color in a pigment or lighting filter. High saturation means deep color.

scene breakdown: a list of scenes showing which characters are in which scenes.

scene-change light: a dim light cue designed to allow a scene change crew to work without the audience feeling that a real scene is going on.

scene shop: where scenery is constructed.

scene-shop manager: the person who maintains the scene shop and, with the TD, decides how the scenery will be built.

scenic artist: a person who applies paint and other forms of decoration to scenery.

scenic designer: the person who designs the look of the scenery and then paints renderings and drafts floorplans.

scenic paint: a type of paint that is specially designed for use on stage. Generally more flexible and more saturated with pigment than normal household paint.

scoop: a simple lighting instrument composed of a standard bulb and a large reflector.

SCR dimmers: the standard form of electronic dimmer. Stands for Silicon Control Rectifier.

scrim: a drop that can be opaque or transparent, depending on how it is lit.

SDII: a type of audio file format used in Apple computers and in ProTools audio software. Stands for Sound Designer II.

send: on a mixer, the control that allows you to send the audio signal to an external device.

sequencer: a computer program that records notes and sends them out, usually through MIDI, to electronic music devices.

set dressing: decorations that have no function on a set, but are merely placed there to look good.

set props: props that are used only as set dressing and are not handled by actors.

sewn-in fullness: a technique for draperies where the fabric is gathered into folds and permanently sewn that way.

shinbuster: a low instrument on a lighting boom, generally lower than two feet. Used primarily for dance.

short circuit: an electrical fault where the wire leading to a load accidentally touches a wire going away from the load. Can cause fires. A major reason why circuit breakers and fuses are used.

shotgun mic: a microphone designed to pick up sound only directly in front of it.

show drop: a front curtain designed especially for a particular production.

shutter lines: the hard shadows caused by pushing in a shutter on an ellipsoidal.

shutters: the metal tabs on ellipsoidals used to cut off part of the light.

side coves: *see* **box booms.**

side light: light that comes from stage right or left of the performer.

signal: what sound is called while it is traveling through a sound system. An electrical force.

signal chain: the chain of electronic devices through which an audio signal travels in a sound system.

signal level: the strength of an audio signal as it travels through a sound system. Usually mic level, line level, or speaker level.

sign-in sheet: a list of performers and crew that lives on the callboard. Cast and crew should check off their name when they arrive.

silhouette: (1) a lighting effect when you light the performer only from upstage, or when you light a drop behind her. (2) the external shape of a costume, irrespective of color, texture, or type of fabric.

skin: the top of a platform, where the actor stands.

smoke machine: a machine that heats up mineral oil and blows it out into the air as smoke.

SMPTE time code: a type of "clock" used by show-control systems to synchronize events backstage. First developed for video and film.

snap-out (snap to black): an instantaneous blackout.

snow bag (snow cradle): a long bag strung between two battens and filled with artificial snow. Shake it gently and it will "snow" on stage.

snow machine: an electric machine that churns out fake snow that evaporates quickly.

solo: on a mixer, a button that turns off every other input.

sound designer: the person who chooses sounds, makes tapes, and designs the sound system.

sound engineer: the person who operates the sound system during a performance.

source: in a sound system, where the signal comes from, e.g., a microphone, a tape deck, etc.

speaker cone: the part of the speaker that makes sound by pushing the air and creating sound waves.

speaker elements: the assemblies that contain the speaker cone and the magnet that makes it move.

speaker level: the level of the audio signal after it leaves the amplifier.

special: a lighting instrument that is used to light a single, isolated person or thing.

spike protector: a device that protects electronic devices from electric "spikes" caused by lighting, electrical faults, or other dangers.

spike tape: colored tape that is used to mark (or "spike") scenery positions onstage.

split fade: a lighting effect where one cue fades down at a different rate than the one that is fading up.

spotting (a fresnel): the process of moving a fresnel lamp forward in the instrument, thereby making the beam of lighting narrower. The opposite of "flooding."

stage crew: the crew that works backstage during the show, shifting the scenery.

stage crew chief: the person who decides how the shift will be done and assigns the crew their individual jobs.

stage left: the left side of the stage, from the actor's perspective.

stage manager: the person who runs rehearsals, calls the cues during the show and, in general, organizes things backstage.

stage plug (stage pin, three pin): one of two common types of plugs on stage lighting instruments, it has three round pins and a square, black plug.

stage right: the right side of the stage, from the actor's perspective.

stereo: an audio signal that comes in two parts and must be played through two speakers. Generally designed to give the illusion that the instruments are arranged in space.

stitcher: the costume shop worker who assembles pieces into finished costumes.

stock scenery: scenery that is stored and used for many different productions, e.g., flats and platforms.

straight-run: a rolling platform that only rolls forward and back, as opposed to a swivel platform, which can go any direction you want. Also describes the castor that makes this possible.

straight-run wagon: a rolling platform that only moves forward and back, not side to side.

straight stand: a microphone stand that does not flex or bend.

strike: to take apart a show after the last performance; also, to remove any item from the stage.

strip light: a lighting instrument composed of a string of lamps in a long, metal housing; a.k.a. **border light.**

subwoofer: a speaker designed to play very low, almost inaudible frequencies. Always used in conjunction with normal speakers.

surge protector: a device used to protect electronic equipment from variations in the power supply.

s-video: a type of video signal that carries the chroma (color) and luminance (brightness) information on two separate cables.

swatches: playing-card-sized pieces of fabric that are used to demonstrate what a costume will be made of.

sweating out a mic: what happens when a drop of sweat covers a small body mic, making it unusable.

swivel: a castor that is able to roll in any direction.

tab: a vertical drape just inside the proscenium that masks performers in the wings. Also a term meaning to pull a drape aside.

table stand: a small microphone stand designed to sit on a table.

tape the stage: the process of depicting the outlines of the set on the rehearsal room floor, using colored tape. Generally done by the stage manager before the first rehearsal.

TD: *see* **technical director.**

teaser: a horizontal drape across the stage, designed to hide the first electric.

technical director (TD): the person who figures out how the set will be built and then oversees construction; sometimes in charge of lighting as well.

template (pattern, gobo): a metal pattern that, when placed inside an ellipsoidal spotlight, throws a shadow pattern on the stage.

three pin: *see* **stage plug.**

throw distance: the distance from the lighting instrument to the person or thing it is lighting.

tie lines: small cotton lines used to attach drapes and drops to battens.

top hats: round metal objects that are placed in the color frame holder of lighting instruments to cut down on stray light.

tormentor: masking drapes just inside the proscenium that mask the backstage area. Often called a torm.

track lighting: permanently installed lighting instruments on tracks in the ceiling. Rarely useful for the stage.

transceiver: the part of a wireless mic that sends out the signal. In a hand-held mic, it is inside the mic; in a body mic, it is a separate unit.

trees: *see* **lighting trees.**

trims: the heights of flying scenery and masking.

tripping: folding a piece of flying scenery as it goes out. Generally done to save space.

trombone: the lever on a follow spot that allows the operator to make the beam larger or smaller.

truss: a horizontal gridwork structure that is suspended from the ceiling or held up by towers on either end. Designed to hold lighting instruments. Standard equipment for larger industrial shows or rock-and-roll concerts.

truss spots: spotlights that are placed on trusses or gridwork above the stage.

tweeter: the speaker element that reproduces the high-end frequencies.

twist-lock plug: one of two common types of plugs on stage lighting instruments, it has three curved blades that lock when inserted and twisted.

unbalanced line: an audio cable containing only two wires. Generally recognized by the quarter-inch phone plug on the end. Vulnerable to noise, making it a poor choice for microphone cable.

understudies: actors who are trained to replace actors in lead roles if the leads are unable to perform.

unit set: a set that changes very little during a performance, but still creates many locations through changes in props and lighting.

up light: light that comes from underneath a performer, either from footlights or through a grated or Plexiglas® stage floor.

upstage: the part of the stage furthest from the audience.

valence: a small drapery that runs across the top of the grand drape, hiding the hardware that suspends it.

vinyl LP (a record): a dying medium.

visual cue: a cue that the operator runs when she sees something happen on stage. Warned, but not called by the stage manager.

voltage: a measure of the strength of electrical power.

wagon: a rolling platform.

walking up a flat: a method of getting a flat from a horizontal position to a vertical one.

warning: what the stage manager gives you about a minute before your cue.

wash light: unfocused, soft light that erases shadows and gives color to a scene.

wattage: a measure of how much power is required to operate a load.

watts per channel: a measure of how much power an amplifier can put out.

WAV: a computer audio file format mostly used on Windows computers.

webbing: the thick woven fabric at the top of a drape that holds the grommets.

weight rail (loading floor): the walkway where you load counterweights into the arbor in a counterweight flying system.

white balance: what video people do before they shoot to ensure that the colors they are shooting look accurate.

wing space: the amount of space on the stage that is not visible to the audience.

wireless mic: a microphone that does not have to be plugged in to a cord. The mic transmits the sound via radio waves.

woofer: the speaker element that reproduces the low-end frequencies.

xenon-arc spot: a type of follow spot that uses a special type of arc lamp. Very powerful, but must be installed permanently.

XLR plug: a plug with either three prongs or three holes set into a round casing. Used for microphone cables. Called "XLR" because the three pins carry the audio signals for ground ("X"), left ("L"), and right ("R").

yoke: the U-shaped piece of metal that attaches a lighting instrument to a clamp.

zoom ellipsoidal: an ellipsoidal with an adjustable focal length.

Bibliography

Here is a short and incomplete list of some very helpful books that are available if you would like to study technical theater further.

Scenery and Painting

Gillette, J. Michael. *Theatrical Design and Production*. Mountain View, Calif.: McGraw-Hill, 1997.

Parker, W. Oren, and R. Craig Wolf. *Scene Design and Stage Lighting*. New York: Harcourt Brace, 1996.

Pecktal, Lynn. *Designing and Painting for the Theater*. New York: Harcourt Brace, 1975.

Lighting and Projections

Gillette, J. Michael. *Designing with Light*. Mountain View, Calif.: McGraw-Hill, 1989.

Pilbrow, Richard. *Stage Lighting*. New York: Drama Book Publishers, 1991.

Reid, Francis. *The Stage Lighting Handbook*. London: A&C Black, 1996; New York: Theatre Arts, 1996.

Walne, Graham. *Projection for the Performing Arts*. Oxford: Focal Press, 1995.

Sound

Kaye, Deena, and James Lebrecht. *Sound and Music for the Theater*. New York: Backstage Books, 1992.

Props

James, Thurston. *The Theatre Props Handbook*. Cincinnati: Betterway Books, 1990.

Stage Management

Bond, Daniel. *Stage Management: A Gentle Art.* London: A&C Black, 1997; New York: Theatre Arts, 1997.

Ionazzi, Daniel. *The Stage Management Handbook.* Cincinnati: Betterway Books, 1992.

Kelly, Thomas A. *The Backstage Guide to Stage Management.* New York: Backstage Books, 1991.

Costumes

Ingham, Rosemary, and Liz Covey. *The Costume Designer's Handbook* (2nd ed.). Portsmouth, N.H.: Heinemann, 1992.

Show Control

Huntington, John. *Control Systems for Live Entertainment* (2nd ed.). Boston: Focal Press, 2000.

General Stagecraft and Rigging

Carter, Paul. *Backstage Forms.* Louisville: Broadway Press, 1990.

——. *Backstage Handbook.* Louisville: Broadway Press, 1994.

Glerum, Jay O. *Stage Rigging Handbook.* Carbondale: Southern Illinois University Press, 1997.

Ionazzi, Daniel. *The Stagecraft Handbook.* Cincinnati: Betterway Books, 1996.

Safety

Rossol, Monona. *Stage Fright: Health and Safety in the Theater.* New York: Allworth Press, 1991.

General Conceptualizing and Design

Ingham, Rosemary. *From Page to Stage.* Wordsmith, N.H.: Heinemann, 1998.

Directors Who Must Do It All

Rodgers, James W., and Wanda C. Rodgers. *Play Director's Survival Kit.* New York: Simon & Schuster, 1995.

Index

Books from Allworth Press

Allworth Press is an imprint of Allworth Communications, Inc. Selected titles are listed below.

Business and Legal Forms for Theater
by *Charles Grippo* (paperback, 8½ × 11, 192 pages, $29.95)

Improv for Actors
by *Dan Diggles* (paperback, 6 × 9, 224 pages, $19.95)

Mastering Shakespeare: An Acting Class in Seven Scenes
by *Scott Kaiser* (paperback, 6 × 9, 256 pages, $19.95)

The Perfect Stage Crew: The Compleat Technical Guide for High School, College, and Community Theater
by *John Kaluta* (paperback, 6 × 9, 256 pages, $19.95)

The Stage Producer's Business and Legal Guide
by *Charles Grippo* (paperback, 6 × 9, 256 pages, $19.95)

The Business of Theatrical Design
by *James L. Moody* (paperback, 6 × 9, 288 pages, $19.95)

Booking & Tour Management for the Performing Arts, Third Edition
by *Rena Shagan* (paperback, 6 × 9, 288 pages, $19.95)

Building the Successful Theater Company
by *Lisa Mulcahy* (paperback, 6 × 9, 240 pages, $19.95)

Producing Your Own Showcase
by *Paul Harris* (paperback, 6 × 9, 240 pages, $18.95)

Career Solutions for Creative People: How to Balance Artistic Goals with Career Security
by *Dr. Ronda Ormont* (paperback, 6 × 9, 320 pages, $19.95)

Casting Director's Secrects: Inside Tips for Successful Auditions
by *Ginger Howard* (paperback, 6 × 9, 208 pages, $16.95)